ULTIMATE INTERVIEW

THIRD EDITION

100s of great interview answers

LYNN WILLIAMS

KoganPage

LONDON PHILADELPHIA NEW DELHI

First published in Great Britain and the United States as *The Ultimate Interview Book* in 2005 by Kogan Page Limited
Second edition published in 2008 as *Ultimate Interview*
Third edition 2012

120 Pentonville Road	1518 Walnut Street, Suite 1100	4737/23 Ansari Road
London N1 9JN	Philadelphia PA 19102	Daryaganj
United Kingdom	USA	New Delhi 110002
www.koganpage.com		India

© Carolyn Williamson, 2005, 2008, 2012

The right of Carolyn Williamson to be identified as the author of this work has been asserted by her in accordance with the Copyright, Designs and Patents Act 1988.

ISBN   978 0 7494 6406 6
E-ISBN   978 0 7494 6443 1

British Library Cataloguing-in-Publication Data

A CIP record for this book is available from the British Library.

Library of Congress Cataloging-in-Publication Data

Williams, Lynn, 1955 Jan. 15-
    Ultimate interview : 100s of great interview answers tailored to specific jobs / Lynn Williams. – 3rd ed.
        p. cm.
    Includes index.
    ISBN 978-0-7494-6406-6 – ISBN 978-0-7494-6443-1   1. Employment interviewing.   I. Title.
    HF5549.5.I6W54 2012
    650.14′4–dc23
                                                                                            2011045184

Typeset by Graphicraft Ltd, Hong Kong
Printed and bound in India by Replika Press Pvt Ltd

CONTENTS

INTRODUCTION

Congratulations! You've got an interview. This is meant to be good news, so why do you feel as if you've just had advance notice of your execution?

Don't worry, you *should* feel nervous. It's natural. Interviews are very important; they stand between you and the job of your dreams, or at least an honest job with a reasonable salary. And it's possible that, with jobs in rather short supply recently, this interview is a long anticipated event. Feel nervous for the right reasons, though. Actors about to go on stage can feel tense because of two things. Either they don't know their lines, haven't rehearsed, don't know what to expect and are afraid of making a fool of themselves; or they're fully prepared and anxious to give their very best performance. The first sort of nerves makes you feel sick and hinders your delivery; the second sort gives you the extra pizzazz you need for a winning presentation.

Now, more than ever before, you need to do everything you can to get the winning edge. So how do you turn the first sort of nerves into the second sort? Like the good actor, you prepare thoroughly beforehand.

Preparing for an interview isn't difficult, but it does take time and effort. The two big things you need to know, and know thoroughly, are: what they want; and what you've got. Sort those out, match them up, put them across convincingly and you can't go far wrong. The rest of this book tells you how to do just that, along with some other important points to help you get ready.

Don't wait until the morning of the interview to read this book and find out how to prepare. Do it now and do it thoroughly. Not only will it take a lot of the pressure off you, but it will give you the chance to prepare really good answers and rehearse them exhaustively. When you know what to expect and how to handle it, you'll feel completely confident when you go in front of your live audience – the interviewer.

Ah, the interviewer. Let's scotch a few myths about interviewers:

They are not out to humiliate you.

They will not ask you trick questions for no reason.

They will not seek out your weak spots and exploit them.

If they didn't think you could do the job, they wouldn't have asked you to the interview.

There are no preferred candidates; everyone is on an equal footing.

They never ask people to interviews just to make up the numbers.

Interviewers try their very best to be impartial. However, every interviewer is an individual with individual preferences and biases. Different people put a different emphasis on different things. Some will be influenced by a confident delivery, some by a striking first impression, and others prefer someone who takes time to think things through.

What they have in common is that they all, believe it or not, want you to do your best and will go to great lengths to see that you do – preparing the questions, arranging the interview room, putting you at your ease. What all interviewers want is someone who can do the job. When you walk in the door, they hope it's going to be you. Your task is to convince them that they're right.

At the end of each chapter, you'll find quotes from the people who actually do the interviewing. This is advice straight from the horse's mouth – if they'll excuse the expression. This is what interviewers actually think and feel, and what they wish they could tell their interviewees before the interview. Look at what these experts have to say, take note of what they want, and there's an excellent chance that you'll soon find yourself being offered the job of your dreams.

1

Know your enemy

Understanding interviewers

Before you prepare for the interview, it's useful to understand how most organizations decide what they are looking for in a candidate, and how they use this to choose the questions they ask at the interview. It can also be helpful to know how the selection procedure works, why employers conduct interviews and what's likely to happen at the average interview.

What do they want?

Employers want:

someone who *can* do the job, ie someone who has:

- the experience;
- the knowledge;
- the skills;

someone who *will* do the job, ie someone who has:

- the personal characteristics;
- the enthusiasm and commitment.

By the time you get as far as an interview, your prospective employer already knows the specific details of what they are looking for – we'll look at how later. Having read your CV or application form, they also know how well you match their profile. If they are interviewing you, you can be sure you're a good match.

The purpose of the interview, then, is to probe more fully into those key areas. They need to:

check you have the relevant skills and experience stated in your CV;

clarify any puzzling, missing or less than favourable features;

complete the picture of you presented by your CV.

What sort of things are they looking for?

While they are sorting and grading the CVs and application forms, employers initially look for clear evidence of:

essential skills, qualifications, abilities and achievements;

desirable skills, qualifications, abilities and achievements;

industry knowledge;

career development;

consistency and stability of employment within the industry, including previous employers;

general employment stability, including average period in any one job.

At the interview they will be trying to confirm that you have all of the above and to fill in the details by probing your background and experience face to face.

What will happen at the interview?

Most interviewers these days try to ensure the interview follows the same course for each candidate, so most interviews follow the same basic structure:

The welcome. An introduction designed to put you at your ease, which often includes a general greeting and brief chat – *'Thank you for coming,'* *'Did you have a good journey?'* and so on – followed by an outline of the interview and a brief account of the job and the company.

The questions. The interviewer will often start the main part of the interview by asking you an open question such as *'Would you give me a rundown of your* current post?' or 'Would you describe your current responsibilities to me?' The purpose of this is to see how you apply your knowledge, skills and abilities in your current job. They will then go on to ask a set of standard structured questions they are asking every applicant.

If there are things on your CV they want to look at more closely – an unusual career path or gaps in your employment history – they will also ask you about these. Unlike the structured questions, these are person-specific and will be different for each interviewee.

Both sets of questions usually follow a logical structure and an orderly sequence. However, towards the end, the interviewer may find they want more information on something covered earlier, or they may want to go back and enquire into something in more depth, so don't be surprised if the interviewer appears to revert to an earlier question.

Over to you. When the interviewer is happy they've got all the information they want, they'll ask if you have any questions yourself.

The finish. The interviewer will usually conclude the interview by describing what will happen next – whether there will be any further stage in the interview process (a second interview, assessments or tests, etc), when you might expect to hear the outcome, whether they will ring or write to you with their decision. If they are offering travel expenses, they will usually explain what to do at this stage. They will usually end by thanking you for coming to the interview and wishing you well.

What sort of questions will they ask?

As we've seen above, most interviewers prepare two sets of questions: standard, structured questions; and person-specific questions.

The structured questions will be the same for all candidates and are usually compiled well in advance of the interview. They are based on a job description and a person specification – more about these later – and are designed to probe how well each applicant matches the criteria for that specific job. They include questions such as: 'What do you see as the main priorities of this particular job?' 'How would you deal with an aggressive client?' 'Tell me about an occasion when you had to motivate a team member. How did you go about it?' and 'Where do you see this industry expanding in the next five years?' They want to see if you have the abilities required to do the job.

Structured questions make the interview process fair because each applicant is matched against the requirements of the job rather than being rated against each other.

Person-specific questions are designed to explore your particular circumstances more fully and are based on your CV or application form. These questions often seek out and expose your weak spots: *'How well do you think you will settle down to a 9-to-5 job after extensive travelling?' 'Do you feel that this job might be a bit of a step down for you?' 'Unlike your current job, this job involves a great deal of contact with the public. How do you think you would handle that?'* and *'Why are you considering leaving your current job after only six months?'*

This is often seen as the 'sticky' bit of the interview, but looked at positively, it's actually your opportunity to reassure the interviewer and set their mind at rest. We'll look at how to do this in great detail later in Chapter 14, Tackling the difficult questions.

On the whole, the interviewer will want to investigate anything they pick up from your CV or application form that suggests:

an unusual career path;

frequent job changes and/or gaps in employment;

a lack of relevant qualifications or training;

a lack of relevant background or experience;

unclear personal attributes or specific aptitudes.

Both sets of questions can, to a large extent, be anticipated, and we'll look at exactly how to do that and prepare for the interview in Chapter 2.

How do they know what they're looking for?

Before advertising the job, the employer, or the human resources department in larger organizations, will have compiled two documents: the job description; and the person specification.

The job description gives an overview of the key elements of the job, including:

the job title;

grade;

location;

a summary of the tasks involved;

responsibilities;

key skills;

result criteria – for example, producing x number of item y to quality z;

essential qualifications needed;

who the job holder reports to;

level of authority.

The person specification is a more subjective document outlining the skills, abilities, characteristics and behaviour needed to carry out the job successfully, with each element rated as either essential or desirable. It often includes:

Education and training:

- level of general qualifications;
- specific professional qualifications;
- job-related training.

Knowledge and experience:

- job-related knowledge and experience;
- general experience;
- technical skills;
- special skills: languages, IT skills, etc.

Specific aptitudes:

- any special criteria for the job, such as verbal or written language aptitude;
- creativity, ability to work with numbers, manual dexterity, etc.

Disposition:

- characteristics: initiative, motivation, resilience, etc;
- working style: leadership ability, team-working skills, etc;
- competencies: problem-solving skills, ability to plan and prioritize, etc.

Interpersonal skills:

- communication skills;
- management and team-building skills;
- rapport-building skills: customer service skills, influencing skills, etc.

Special considerations:

> – any special circumstances specific to the job – ability to live in, ability to travel, being on call, shift pattern availability, etc.

These two documents will be used to draw up the job advertisement. They may also be used to compile the application form, and they will almost certainly be used to compare, rate and rank applicants. They will, ultimately, be used to decide which key areas the structured questions at the interview will cover and will form the basis for the questions you will be asked.

As CVs or application forms come in, they are given a brief initial read-through and those meeting the basic requirements go on to a more thorough screening to select people for interview.

Table 1.1 shows one way of selecting applicants for interview – it's a section from what's called a comparison matrix, matching applicants against the person specification.

As CVs or application forms are scrutinized, the information is entered on the matrix to see how well it fits. The six applicants with the best match will be called for interview, the next six best will be kept in reserve in case any of the first choice can't come, and the rest will probably be sent a rejection letter.

As you can see from Table 1.1, a matrix helps to make information clear, even if the decisions aren't always clear cut. Paul Atkins, for example, has excellent knowledge and experience, but his specific abilities are less good, and his disposition is only fair. He probably wouldn't reach the interview stage.

In contrast, while John Dean's education and training are only fair, he has excellent experience, the specific aptitudes required and an excellent disposition for the job. Depending on how much weight the employer gives to education, and the reasons for his lack of formal training, John Dean has an excellent chance of being interviewed, where he will probably be asked person-specific questions about his educational background.

TABLE 1.1 Matching applicants against the person specification

Applicant	Training and Education			Knowledge and Experience			Specific Aptitudes			Disposition		
	1	2	3	1	2	3	1	2	3	1	2	3
Paul Atkins		✔				✔		✔		✔		
Helen Brown			✔			✔		✔				✔
John Dean	✔					✔			✔			✔
Carol Dyer			✔		✔			✔			✔	

Grade 1: fair; 2: good; 3: excellent

Now that you know how interviewers prepare interviews, let's look at how you can use this information to prepare for your own interview.

EXPERT QUOTE

I've had 20 years' experience in human resources. During that time I've seen it move away from very formal interviews to more relaxed informal ones. There's no point putting people on the spot or intimidating them; we want them to relax and be at their best. You get more out of people when they feel at ease, and you can make a more accurate assessment when you can see the natural person.

Gail Milne, HR Manager, Teddington Controls

2
Prepare yourself
What you need to know before the interview

Now that you know how the interviewer prepares the interview, you can begin to understand what they want to know and to anticipate what questions they'll ask. You know that:

They have a job description and a person specification.

They read your CV or application form to see how well you match.

Therefore, you can expect that:

They'll ask searching questions about all the skills, qualifications and personal qualities mentioned in the job advertisement and the job description.

They'll probe those areas of your CV where the match is less good or less clear.

As well as that, they will expect you to know something about the organization and the job you're applying for, and to be able to offer convincing reasons why you want the job.

Make sure that:

- you understand what skills, qualities and experience are required to do the job;
- you know what skills, qualities and experience you have that match those requirements;
- you can give examples of how, when and where you've demonstrated those skills and qualities;
- you can present those examples concisely and confidently.

What should you prepare?

As you can see from the information above, preparing for interviews is actually quite straightforward in theory, if quite demanding in practice. You need to present your case clearly. Like a top-rank lawyer presenting a case in court, you need to have your 'exhibits' ready:

Exhibit 1: evidence that you meet their needs with regard to skills, qualities and experience;

Exhibit 2: reassuring answers and satisfactory explanations for those areas of your CV where you don't quite match or where there might be some other problem;

Exhibit 3: some knowledge of the industry or business sector, and the interviewing company in particular;

Exhibit 4: sound reasons why you are applying for the job.

Let's look at each of these in more detail.

Exhibit 1: Evidence that you meet their needs

This will form the major part of the interview, so how do you set about preparing evidence that will convince them? You need examples of occasions when you've successfully displayed your skills and qualities and which demonstrate your areas of experience. These are known collectively as your competencies – the things you're competent doing because you've done them before.

Reread the advertisement and the job description

The first and most obvious thing to do is to reread the original job advertisement. Next, take a look at the information that came with the application form. There's usually a detailed job description, and some companies send out quite a comprehensive information pack. If you don't have anything, look on their website or contact the company to see if there are any additional details about the job you could use. Add any specific requirements to your list. The more information you have, the more thoroughly you can prepare.

Study the information carefully. You must make absolutely sure that you know exactly what the job entails; and that you know exactly what skills, qualities, experience and qualifications are required.

Find examples

Once you know what they want, you need to review what you've got. Make sure that:

you have the skills and qualities required;

you can give examples of how, when and where you've demonstrated them in the past;

you can present those examples confidently and enthusiastically.

Go about this systematically and actually write things down. It's easy to think to yourself, 'Oh, I've done this' or 'Yes, I can do that.' What you are looking for, and what you will have to present to the interviewer, is *evidence*.

Work through the job ad and job description (and any other relevant information), underlining the key points:

- specific skills;
- areas of experience;
- responsibilities;
- qualifications and training;
- knowledge areas;
- qualities and characteristics;
- abilities.

Make a list of all the requirements.

Make notes that show how, when and where you've had experience of each requirement. Think of examples from:

- your current job;
- previous jobs;
- unpaid positions: voluntary work, community associations, organizations and sports teams;
- your personal life.

Study your notes and jot down the details of specific occasions that show you using each particular competency. For example, the ad asks for someone who is calm under pressure. You note down the occasion when an order had to be completed in half the usual time along with details of how you kept calm, organized yourself and prioritized the workload so you could meet the deadline, saving the company a large penalty charge.

Sort and polish your notes until you have at least one good example for each requirement.

If you ever watch chat shows, you'll recognize that some people interview well and others don't. The worst people either give one-word answers or else go on at great length to no particular point. The best people offer interesting, concise anecdotes that answer the question and expand on it to good effect.

Turn your basic information into anecdotes that give the interviewer the full story. For example, if they ask *'How would you cope with an aggressive customer?'* rather than say just 'I would do x, y and z,' give them an anecdote to show how you actually dealt tactfully and successfully with an aggressive customer in a real-life situation.

Arm yourself with as many of these stories as are relevant to the job in question. Polish them until you are certain they reflect your true abilities.

Bring benefits

Employers particularly like to know that the person they're employing will be of benefit to the company. It's very important, therefore, to prepare examples and anecdotes about the occasions when you:

increased:

- profits;
- production;
- turnover;
- sales;
- efficiency;
- market opportunity.

decreased:

- staff turnover or absenteeism.
- risk;
- the time taken to do something or process something;
- potential problems;
- costs;
- waste.

improved:

- competitive advantage;
- marketability;
- organization;
- information flow or communication;
- staff performance;
- teamwork and staff relationships.

Practise

Memorize these answers and practise delivering them until you feel comfortable and at ease. Nerves are guaranteed to make you forgetful, so, like an actor learning lines, rehearse your key answers until they come easily to you. Role-play them with a friend or colleague if possible, so you get used to telling your anecdotes to an audience.

Exhibit 2: Reassuring answers and explanations

Few people exactly match the job description, but remember that you must come pretty close or they wouldn't be interviewing you. You may need to answer a few nagging doubts, however, and being prepared will make it a lot easier.

Look at your CV or application form with an employer's eye and match it to the job description and job ad. Are there any obvious mismatches such as:

shortage of relevant skills or experience;

shortage of experience in certain areas;

lack of qualifications.

You can be certain that you will be questioned about these inconsistencies. There's no reason to be worried by questions about these things if, as above, you prepare your evidence before the interview and can put their mind at rest.

We will be looking at these issues in much greater depth in Chapter 14, Tackling the difficult questions, so don't let them worry you too much. Many people find this aspect of the interview intimidating; indeed, some find it puts them off even applying for jobs in case they are asked questions about difficult areas of their career history. Employers are often much more flexible than you think, and if they have asked you to an interview, they are willing to be convinced.

Briefly:

If you have simply missed skills or experience off your CV not knowing they were relevant, simply reply positively with good back-up anecdotes to demonstrate your knowledge.

If you genuinely lack workplace experience in a particular area, they are possibly right to worry about how you will manage when faced with it at work. Your best way to reassure them is to find the nearest experience you have to it – either from work or from outside interests or voluntary work – and show, with appropriate anecdotes, how you coped then and how you relate this to your future role.

If you lack qualifications or training, does your practical experience make up for this? If so, explain how. Many older people, for example, manage very well having been promoted into jobs that would demand a degree from a new starter..

Are you currently undergoing training or education that will fill a particular gap? Or are you willing to train, possibly in your own time or at your own expense, to remedy the situation? Again, it would help to offer an anecdote about how quickly you've picked things up in the past, or how well you managed to work and train at the same time before.

The other thing to look for on your CV or application form is anything that suggests you've had problems with employment in the past. In the interviewer's mind, this means:

any gaps in employment;

frequent job changes;

moves backwards or sideways;

abrupt career changes;

inconsistent choices of work.

If any of these things leap out from your CV, you should seriously look at giving it a revamp. However, it can't be too bad or they wouldn't be interviewing you. You still have to answer their worries, though, and, as above, we will be looking at this in great detail in Chapter 14, Tackling the difficult questions.

Have your story ready. You can't lie outright, but you can think about how to present any problems in the best possible light and prepare your answers accordingly.

You may have very good reasons for employment gaps or job changes. If so, explain them clearly. If, for example, you have a year-long gap because of travel, explain this and offer a brief anecdote focusing on what you learnt during that time that will be relevant to the job – how you got on with people from all walks of life or coped with potential disaster, for example. You also need to make it clear that the travel bug, or whatever caused the gap, is out of your system now, and you won't be disappearing from this job at a moment's notice.

If you have no good reasons, just explain any contributing factors without sounding as if you are making excuses for yourself. What you *must* do in this case is emphasize that you are a very different person now, and give them anecdotes to back this up. Describe how you've now found your true niche in life, how you stuck to your last job despite difficulties, how you overcame something that would formerly have made you leave, etc.

Exhibit 3: Industry knowledge

We've already looked at how important getting a detailed job description is, and how useful it is for preparing your interview answers. The next most important information you need is anything about the industry and, specifically, the company doing the interviewing.

Imagine going on a date with someone who says they've always longed to meet you, are absolutely fascinated by you and are really enthusiastic about future dates. Yet, when you question them, they know absolutely nothing about you and don't seem particularly interested in finding out, either. Would you think them genuine, or a total sham? Well, companies can be just as sensitive.

The more senior the position, the more they'll expect you to know, but at any level industry knowledge wins you gold stars at interview. A good grounding in company background also helps your confidence and enhances your performance.

How do you find out?

The simplest way is to ring the company and ask for information. You don't have to pretend to be an investor or a customer; just explain that you have an interview and you'd like some information about the organization to read beforehand. You should fairly easily be able to get hold of:

sales, marketing and advertising brochures;

the annual report;

any customer newsletter or magazine;

any in-house staff newsletter.

Other sources of information

The internet

You should be able to find:

company websites;

news and chat groups;

professional organization and society websites.

These should give you detailed information as well as background data on your chosen area for both your own country and abroad. You can also perform a company search by entering the name into a search engine to see if it crops up in any articles, etc. In addition, versions of many journals and publications are available on the internet.

Business journals and trade publications

Trade and business directories will give you information about specific companies, from how long they've been going to the number of people they employ.

Every industry and virtually every type of job has its own newspaper or journal that will tell you what is happening in that particular sector. If you don't know about the ones in your field, there are online directories for trade-related journals and publications that will help you find them. They can tell you about professional or trade associations that are relevant to you and that will also have useful information. They'll also tell you about interesting and useful websites that could give you more information.

People

Do you have friends, current or former colleagues, or business contacts with information about the company or industry, or can you get to meet people through them? Informal inside information is valuable and would definitely increase your confidence. Without digging for company secrets or gossip, insider knowledge can help you gauge the company culture and direction as well as giving you an employee-eye view of the organization.

People who have business contacts with the company could also provide information, so always nurture good relationships with customers, suppliers, representatives, sales people, etc when you get the opportunity.

Use your library

One of the best places to start looking for information is your public library. It will, of course, have full internet access available for your online research, and you should be able to find many of the directories, journals and other publications mentioned above. It will also be able to help you find out about professional associations and other organizations that could be useful to you, such as local business groups where you can network.

What are you looking for?

While you are gathering all this information, what are you actually looking for? What do you need to know?

Apart from getting a general feel for the company and some idea of the corporate culture, background and direction, some specific questions you might want answered are:

What does the company do?

- What are the company's products and/or services?
- What is its profile in the marketplace? How does it like to be seen?
- How and where are goods or services produced?
- How are they provided or distributed?

Who does it do it for?

- What is the market for these goods or services?
- Who are the actual customers?
- Is the market expanding or contracting?
- What is the company doing about it in either case?

How is it organized?

- How big is the company?
- Is it a single company or a conglomerate?
- Is it multinational?
- Are there lots of subsidiaries and divisions, or is everything centralized?
- How is your particular part of it structured?

What's the competition?

- Who are its competitors?
- What are they currently doing?
- How does it position itself against them?

What's its history?

- Where did it come from, when was it established, how did it start out and how was it built up?
- What are its biggest achievements?
- Was it bigger or smaller in the past?
- Is the area you are entering increasing or decreasing in size, prestige, etc?
- Have there been takeovers, mergers, buyouts, downsizing?
- What has changed radically over the years?

What's its future?

- What is the company's vision? Does it have a mission statement, for example?
- What are the current priorities?
- What are its prospects?
- What are its major current and future projects (as far as you can legitimately find out)?
- What is the biggest threat currently facing the company and/or the industry as a whole?
- What is the greatest opportunity confronting it?

Although these sound like very detailed questions, they are the sort of thing you can pick up quite easily and which will quickly build into a clear picture of the place where you are hoping to work.

The level of detail you will want to go into depends on the type of job and the level of seniority you are applying for. An executive, for example, would need to demonstrate a high degree of company and industry knowledge. But even if you are only applying for the most junior job on the lowest rung of the hierarchy, you should have a clear idea of at least what the company does and whom it does it for.

Exhibit 4: The reasons you want this job

Well, why *do* you want this job?

Don't be vague about your reasons. You need to have a clear idea of how this position fits in with your career progression and overall goals. Above all, you need to show how well you fit the job profile, and how this post is a natural progression from your current job. You need, in other words, to show that this job could have been made for you or, from the employer's point of view, that you could have been made for the job.

Think in terms of what you can bring to the job, rather than what you can get from it. It does no harm to prepare and rehearse an answer, showing how the job:

matches your skills and abilities;

follows naturally from your existing experience;

gives you the chance to use those skills and talents for the company's benefit;

presents you with challenges you have the background and experience to tackle successfully;

gives you the opportunity to play a key role in an organization or industry you respect.

EXPERT QUOTE

Prepare. Do some background research on the job and the company. We send out an information pack which includes the job description and the person specification. People coming to an interview should at least have read that. It shows some interest and enthusiasm.

Gail Milne, HR Manager, Teddington Controls

EXPERT QUOTE

Do your preparation and make sure you know what the job entails. Read the advert and the job description word for word; all the key points are made in there. Match your skills and experience to the job's needs; don't make the interviewer do all the work. I'm afraid no preparation often means no job.

Tina M Buchanan, Group HR Director, Hamworthy Combustion Engineering

3
Answering questions
What the interviewer will ask and what you need to tell them

This is the main part of the book. From here on, you will find examples of the sort of questions asked at interview along with helpful ideas and suggestions for answering them.

Before we get on to what to say, however, let's look at how you say it. In this chapter we'll look at some general points about answering questions and how to put your answers across with confidence and enthusiasm.

Make a good impression

Overall impressions count for a lot at interview. Later, in Chapter 20, we'll look at creating a good first impression through how you dress, your body language and dealing with nerves. In this chapter, we look at creating the right impression through how you respond to questioning.

When you go into the interview, you have a full set of cards in your hand. They may be good cards, or not so good, but it's up to you to see you play them all and play them well. They are:

your skills and abilities;

your background and experience;

your qualifications;

your enthusiasm for a new opportunity;

yourself – your personality and how you present yourself.

The interviewer already has an idea of your skills, qualifications and experience, and these are impressive enough for them to want to see you. What they don't have such a clear impression of are the last two items on the list: your personality and your enthusiasm. These are difficult to express on a CV or application form; you need to get them across at the interview.

Don't put on an act and pretend to be some super-confident, super-bubbly or hard-nosed high-flyer if that's not the natural you. Be yourself, but be your best self. You know what you're like when you're happy, confident, vibrant and alert, and you know what you're like when you're crabby and stressed. They're both authentically you, but which one do you want to present at interview?

There are some key qualities that are always highly valued and which will help you a lot if you can express them at the interview. They are:

openness;

enthusiasm;

confidence;

energy.

Openness

You probably feel more comfortable with people who are friendly and open than with those who are reserved and stiff, and interviewers are no different.

Most employers want employees who are open, accessible and communicative. They are much more pleasant to work with and get on with their colleagues better, so, naturally, employers will be looking for these traits during the interview.

Be forthcoming; don't make the interviewer dig the information out of you. Avoid one-word, yes–no answers if you possibly can, and always give a full reply including relevant anecdotes as illustrations to key points. By being open and responsive, you will have a head start in presenting yourself well at interview.

You also need to be able to volunteer positive information about yourself and your abilities. In other words, you need to be able to blow your own trumpet. After all, they won't know how good you are unless you tell them. How do you put your points across without sounding as if you're bragging all the time? When you start to feel uncomfortable with 'I am...' and 'I can...', try ringing the changes with:

'I would say that I...'

'I believe I am...'

'My past record suggests...'

'My experience tells me...'

'People have told me I...'

'Colleagues tell me that...'

'My boss would probably say...'

'Friends say that I...'

Enthusiasm

Enthusiasm for the sort of work you do and enthusiasm for the job you're applying for are essential. Interviewers look more kindly on people who they feel will give 100 per cent than on those who may be better qualified on paper, but appear less wholehearted.

You don't have to gush; just be interested in what the interviewer is saying. Listen, smile and nod when they tell you things. When you answer, let your enthusiasm show in your anecdotes and illustrations, and in your questions to the interviewer (which we'll look at in Chapter 17). Genuine interest, sincerely shown, will increase your chances at interview enormously.

Confidence

Confident may be the last thing you feel when you go into the interview. Nevertheless, confidence is one key quality you must project. You needn't come across as pushy, smug or arrogant, but you do need to project a quiet confidence in yourself and your abilities. The employer needs to be able to trust you to do the job. If you sound hesitant or uncertain, you undermine that trust.

Always answer positively. People tend to take you at your own estimation, so don't put yourself down or apologize for what you see as shortcomings.

Example

The interviewer says, *'This job requires an understanding of spreadsheets. Would you say you had that?'*

You could put yourself down by replying: 'I'm sorry, I've used them to do the household accounts, but that's all, I'm afraid.'

Or you could give a positive impression by saying: 'Yes, I would. I use Microsoft Excel to do all the household accounts, so I'm quite used to it. I'm sure I could quickly become familiar with its commercial use.'

However nervous you are, make sure your voice sounds confident:

> Pause and take a full breath before speaking. This relaxes your vocal cords and steadies your voice.

> Speak a little lower than normal, projecting from your diaphragm rather than your throat. This stops your voice sounding shrill and strangled.

> Speak a little slower and more clearly than you normally do. It stops you gabbling and saying things without thinking, and it gives you *gravitas*.

> Remember to smile a few times during the interview; it warms up the voice and also helps you to relax your lip and cheek muscles.

Energy

Sit up straight, look alert, speak clearly, smile and make eye contact. When you appear energetic and lively, the interviewer sees someone positive, assured, optimistic and constructive – someone who will tackle a problem rather than add to it, and someone who will be pleasant to work with.

Three cardinal rules

When answering the interviewer's questions, remember three cardinal rules:

> Stick to the point.

> Illustrate your answers with real-life anecdotes.

> Don't waffle. When you've answered the question, stop talking.

Stick to the point

Listen to the question and make sure you answer it. Keep your answer relevant to the job you are interviewing for and don't go off at a tangent. Remember, most people have a two-minute attention span at the most, so practise keeping your answers shorter than this.

On the other hand, avoid simple yes–no answers unless the question clearly calls for no more than that.

If you're not sure you've understood the question, or you're not sure you've heard it properly, it's perfectly all right to ask the interviewer to repeat or rephrase it. It's much better to do that than to give an irrelevant answer.

Illustrate your answers with real-life anecdotes

Don't just say you can do x, y or z. Support your claim with concrete examples (see Chapter 2). Remember to stick to the point as outlined above – be concise and pick anecdotes that are appropriate for the job in question.

Don't waffle

When you've answered the question, stop talking. Don't let silence draw you into irrelevancies or, worse, negative revelations about yourself. When you've finished, add something like 'I hope that answers your question' or 'Does that cover all the points you need to know?' Then smile and wait for the next question.

One more cardinal rule: it always helps to imagine the words 'RELEVANT TO THIS JOB' after every question.

In the next chapter we'll look at the first few minutes of the interview – the welcome and the interviewer's opening questions. Knowing what to expect from the outset will help you to relax and put you at your ease so that you can concentrate on giving your best performance with confidence and style.

EXPERT QUOTE

I want to know how people react to things, what they do in certain situations. I want them to draw on their life experience. So when I ask what they would do in a crisis, for example, I don't want them to say 'I would do this; I would do that...' I want them to say 'I *have* done this; I *have* done that...'

Mark Colton, Business Development Team, Jobcentre Plus

EXPERT QUOTE

People are hired for their skills. Don't let modesty prevent you from telling the interviewer about yourself, what you've done and the value of what you can do. Know yourself, what you're good at, and be comfortable and articulate talking about that.

David Giles, Resourcing Manager, Westland Helicopters Ltd

4
Starting the interview
What to expect from the interview and how to begin confidently

This is it: you're in the interview, sitting opposite the interviewer. What happens now? We'll talk about how you got there – entering the room, shaking hands with the interviewer and lots of other details about making a good impression – in Chapter 20, Looking the part. But for now, let's look at how the interviewer will start the interview and their opening questions to you.

Your interviewer will probably open the interview with a brief introductory chat about the company, the job, the form the interview will take, etc. There will also be general 'social' questions designed to break the ice:

'Did you have a good journey?'

'Was the traffic OK?'

'Did you find the building/your way here all right?'

Beware. The impression you give in these first few minutes will linger throughout the rest of the interview. Although the questions are genuinely meant to put you at your ease, your responses will still form a picture of you in the interviewer's mind.

Don't:

Gabble feverishly. You should have got there in enough time to regain both your breath and composure. If nerves are a problem, see Chapter 20 for tips on dealing with them.

Clam up. On the other hand, try to give more than a terse, one-word answer.

Complain. However bad the traffic, however difficult the office was to find, don't make an issue of it: 1) you'll be seen as a moaner; 2) they'll wonder how you cope with other minor problems and irritations; 3) you'll be making the same journey every day if they employ you, so are they going to have to listen to you complain every time?

Blame. Don't pick faults in their directions or instructions even if you could improve on them.

Ramble. This is not the time for lengthy answers about routes, timetables, maps, etc.

Put yourself down. You don't need to explain how disorganized you are or what a poor sense of direction you have.

Use problems as an excuse. They won't see being stuck in a traffic jam that morning as a reason for doing badly in the interview.

Do:

Smile. Do your share of the ice breaking by smiling and making eye contact.

Answer warmly and pleasantly. Behave as you would in any somewhat formal social situation.

Give a positive response. Whatever the circumstances, give the impression of being calm and in control.

See Chapter 20 for more tips on creating a good first impression.

After putting you at your ease, the interviewer will sometimes lead into the main part of the interview by asking you an open question such as *'Tell me about yourself'* or *'Tell me about your current job.'* They want to know about your competencies, so this is your invitation to sell your ability and experience. Think of it as a mini-interview in which you briefly introduce topics that the interviewer can explore in greater depth with their subsequent questions.

Q 'Tell me about yourself.'

This is as open as a question can be. Remember that from the very outset of the interview, your aim is to demonstrate your suitability for the job. Consequently, it's up to you to set the boundaries and make sure you stick to points that are informative and relevant. The interviewer wants you to include things like:

your current position;

your background, education and training;

the skills and strengths that make you good at your job;

your experience and accomplishments;

the high points of your career so far;

what attracted you to your particular field and how you got into it;

your goals for the future.

You need, of course, to tailor your answer and take into consideration the skills, strengths, aptitudes and experience – the competencies – required for the job.

Example

'I'm a [give a concise, pithy description of yourself in 15 words or less]. I'm an experienced [what you are] with an extensive knowledge of [your relevant knowledge area] including [a key point] and [another key point]. My main skills or qualifications are [give two or three of your most relevant skills or your key qualifications].

'I also have experience in [go on to your next most relevant skill or knowledge area], including [develop one or two key points].

'My achievements to date include [two or three of your major achievements]. The benefits to my current employer have been [outline the benefits – what you've increased, decreased or improved]. I believe the position you're offering would allow me to [what you want to go on to do or develop].'

Example

'I'm a computer science graduate with a keen interest in the practical application of information systems. I'm an experienced computer programmer with an extensive knowledge of robotics including 3-D modelling and components assembly. My main skills are programming methodologies and microelectronics.

'I also have experience in artificial intelligence, including Popll and Prologue.

'My main achievement to date has been to write a geographical database using a GIS package, which allowed NHS patient data to be mapped for the entire West Midlands region. This greatly improved allocation of resources to high-density areas, and reduced patient waiting time by 11 per cent overall. I believe the position you're offering would allow me to continue to develop my problem-solving skills and I feel I could contribute skills and experience that would be of value to you.'

Q *'Give me an outline of your current position.'*

This question focuses more closely on your actual job. It is practically asking for your current job description to see how well it matches the job you're applying for. The interviewer wants to know things like:

  what your tasks and responsibilities are;

  the skills required to do your job;

  the strengths and personal aptitudes you bring to it;

  the key objectives of your job;

  targets and result criteria;

  whom you answer to – your position in the company hierarchy and level of authority.

Base your answer on the example above, incorporating all the relevant information.

Q *'What does your current job entail? Describe a typical day to me.'*

With this question, the interviewer is looking for a more personal interpretation of your job. They want to see how you view your tasks and responsibilities. They want to know:

  what you see as the prime purpose of your job;

  the tasks and responsibilities your job entails;

  the skills, strengths and aptitudes you employ;

  the problems you routinely encounter and how you deal with them effectively;

  how you work with others – as part of a team, dealing with staff, meeting customers or clients, etc;

  what you enjoy and find satisfying about your job.

After hearing your answers to these sorts of open questions, the interviewer will usually go on to ask other questions to fill in more details – *'Tell me more about x,' 'Can you say a bit more about y?'*

Answer in more detail, bearing in mind the relevance of your points to the job you are interviewing for, and supply anecdotes to illustrate and support what you are saying.

Example

Q 'Can you tell me more about how you get the best out of your team?'

'I believe that people work best when they're given responsibility. For example, we had a problem meeting sales targets in the Colchester area. Rather than just harassing the team to get better results, I put it to them as a group problem and asked them to come up with a workable solution. After a couple of brainstorming sessions, they came up with a member-get-a-member scheme based on the upcoming festival. They were responsible for implementing it while I saw they had the back-up needed from Head Office. Sales increased by 40 per cent over the festival, and subsequently steadied to 22 per cent, well within target.'

Example

Q 'Can you tell me more about how you fit into the organization? You work alone currently, don't you?'

'I'm at the selling end of the operation, representing the company to the public. But, even though I work alone, I still see myself as part of a wider team. I have strong links to Head Office and really appreciate the help and support they give. I'm also ready to support them in any way I can. For example, when stocktaking was done recently, Head Office decided it would be quicker and more efficient if it was done in teams of three rather than each of us doing just our own. I thought this was a good idea and was happy to travel to another branch in return for help with my own stocktake. It made what could have been a rather long and tedious job much quicker and more enjoyable.'

These more probing questions lead naturally into the main part of the interview. We'll discuss this in detail in Chapter 6 onwards, with examples of questions asked at interviews for different types of jobs along with suggestions for the best ways of answering them – from the straightforward ones to the decidedly tricky.

First, though, let's look at the questions they ask everybody – those general questions that seem to crop up at interview after interview – and how you can use them to your advantage.

EXPERT QUOTE

Listen to the question before you try to answer it. You've got two ears and one mouth; they're in that ratio for a reason.

Janet Hembry, Head of Education and Skills Policy,
Government Office for the South West

5

Questions they ask everybody

Standard questions you should prepare for

In the rest of this book we'll be looking in detail at the questions asked during interviews for different types of jobs and the best ways of answering them. In many cases, even when the questions are the same, the answers – and what the interviewer is hoping to find out – will have a different emphasis, so it's worth having different sections that focus exclusively on the requirements of each particular sort of job.

There are some questions, however, that are pretty much the same for everyone, whatever the job is. Look at the ones here and consider how you would reply. The answers given here and throughout *Ultimate Interview* are intended to get you thinking about your own particular circumstances. You don't have to learn them parrot-fashion; adapt them to your own style of speaking so that you can say what *you* want to say. They do, though, cover the main points that you will need to think about. They can help you plan your responses ahead of the interview so that you are rarely, if ever, caught unprepared.

It's unlikely you'll be asked all these questions, or that they'll be phrased in precisely these words, but being prepared means you'll be able to answer any similar questions confidently.

Q 'Why do you want to work here?'

If you've done the preparation suggested in Chapter 2, you should have a clear idea of how this job fits into your career plan and why the company is the right one for you. Good reasons to concentrate on are those things that allow you to work at your best.

These include the company structure, reputation, conditions, management methods, opportunity, challenge, etc. Follow up with the positive things you will be able to contribute to the company under those conditions.

Example

'I believe [company name] is a progressive company providing a challenging, stimulating and supportive environment for its employees and their achievements [or whatever else you value – the opportunity for rapid advancement, creative freedom or technical innovation]. I have x years' experience in [your field of work] and my time at [the company you work for] has shown me I have a talent for [a skill or ability highly relevant to the job you're applying for]. I think I've demonstrated that by [mention achievement]. I am now looking for the opportunity to continue to achieve at that level and beyond, in a company that will help me develop professionally. I believe your company offers just such an opportunity.'

Example

'I take pride in my work and like to be fully involved with the whole process rather than just my little bit of it [for example]. I believe the team-based structure employed by [the interviewing company] and your use of performance bonuses [for example] encourage a greater involvement and demand more of a sense of responsibility both individually and as a team member.'

Example

'I'm looking for a position where I can use my [a relevant skill, aptitude or area of experience]. I believe this job would allow me to make the most of my [a talent, aptitude, skill or ability] along with [another skill, personal quality or ability]. I see it, above all, as a natural development from [your experience, further qualifications or training].'

Q 'What interests you most about this job?'

Concentrate on what you will bring to the job rather than what you believe you can get out of it. The interviewer needs to know you are enthusiastic about using your skills, abilities and experience to benefit the company. In answering the question, remind them of the skills that mean you *can* do the job and the personal qualities that mean you *will* do the job. Add your reasons for wanting to change jobs, and your reasons for wanting to work for the company if those questions haven't already been dealt with.

Example

'I'm looking for a position where I can use my [one or two of your key abilities] to the full. I believe this job would allow me to make the most of those along with my [another skill or personal quality]. I see it as a natural development from [your experience and achievements]. I've enjoyed working in [your current job], especially [mention a key feature], but they're a small company and unfortunately there's no opportunity for advancement with them in the near future [for example]. I believe an expanding company [for example] such as yours offers a greater range of challenges and opportunities, in particular [a key responsibility or competency mentioned in the job description that you would like to develop further].'

Q 'What experience do you have for this job?'

The interviewer wants to know you fully understand what the job requires. They also want to be sure you're capable of taking over the job smoothly without a long, disruptive adjustment period. If you've done your homework, you'll have already matched your skills, strengths and experience to those required in the job description, and be ready to point out how good a match you are.

Example

'I have x years' experience working in [your relevant background]. My achievements include [give examples]. My background in [the relevant experience you've had or positions you've held] and familiarity with [a process, piece of equipment, working environment, for example] would allow me to contribute to the job from the start. I understand [one or two key things from the job description that demonstrate you know what the job involves], and the importance of [a personal quality from the job description]. These have been essential elements in my current job and I appreciate their importance. In addition, I have an excellent record of [a key ability you've found essential to carry out your work effectively]. For example, [give a short anecdote demonstrating this skill or quality, and its benefits].'

Q 'How has your job changed since you've been there?'

The interviewer really wants to know if your responsibilities have increased, so tell them about any extra tasks or responsibilities you've taken on, and any skills and qualities you've developed or training you've undertaken. They also want to know how you respond to change – do you adapt well or do you resent it? It's unusual for any job to stay the same, so tell them what changes have happened in your job, including different working methods, different tasks, different management, etc. Emphasize that you adapted to the changes easily and found them beneficial. Give the impression that you are prepared to be flexible.

Q 'Do you have more responsibilities now than when you started?'

Q 'Have your responsibilities increased while you've been doing your current job?'

Tell the interviewer about any extra tasks or responsibilities you've taken on and, especially, any promotions you've received. Even if your duties haven't increased officially, it's almost certain that you've taken on more responsibilities as you've got to know the job and become more confident.

Example

'Yes, my responsibilities have increased substantially. When I first started, my supervisor [manager, boss] had to instruct me about every job and check my work at each stage. I made mistakes in the beginning, naturally, but it meant I learnt how to [do what you do] thoroughly, and I learnt how to work efficiently and to a high standard. With time, I became more confident about what I was doing and took responsibility for [list some of your tasks], and eventually [name something you became responsible for]. These days, my supervisor just gives me the work schedule [or whatever] and I plan the work order and carry it out [for example]. I believe the confidence my supervisor now has in my ability shows how I've developed in the job, and that I'm now ready to take on greater responsibilities.'

Q 'What has your current job taught you?'

Q 'What did you learn from your last job?'

Most companies like a level of maturity and flexibility in their staff. They like to know that you are capable of learning from experience and can accept constructive advice. Reflect this in your answer and choose a key point from each of the following:

a personal quality you've developed or realized the value of;

a responsibility you've taken on;

a practical skill you've developed.

Pick a brief anecdote that shows you using them. Remember, too, that what you've learnt must be relevant to the job you're applying for, not just the one you've been doing.

Example

'I'm always happy to learn on the job and I believe my last position taught me a number of things. I learnt how to [include a skill] and I developed [another skill or ability] further. I also developed [a responsibility or role you took on]. I would say that in that job I also learnt the importance of [a personal quality or workplace skill you learnt the value of]. For example, [give a brief anecdote].'

Q 'Do you prefer working alone or with others?'

You will know from the job description whether the job involves primarily working alone or in a team, so tailor your answer accordingly. However, whatever job you do, you have to get on with others and there will be times, even as a team member, when you have to work on your own. Reassure the interviewer you'd be happy in either role.

Example

'I've worked as a team member in [give a specific situation], and I've worked on my own in [give another situation]. I'm happy to do either depending on the requirements of the job. I've found, though, that working in [whichever the job requires] allows me to [give some positive benefit of either working with others or alone].'

Q 'How well do you work in a team?'

Presumably, you'll be working in a team if you get the job or they wouldn't ask. Therefore, your answer is that you work very well in a team. Anyone can claim that, though, so illustrate your answer with an anecdote about a time you successfully worked in a team and enjoyed it. If you can't give an example from the workplace, use a sport or other activity to illustrate your answer.

Example

'I would say from past experience that I enjoy being part of a team. I like the camaraderie and that feeling of all working together towards a common goal [for example]. I believe a good team member should be [see the list in the next question for a selection of positive qualities] and I try to demonstrate these qualities when working with others. For example, in my last job, [give your example of working well in a team, demonstrating at least one key quality from the list].'

Q 'What makes a good team member?'

Good team members are:

communicative;

supportive of the other members;

flexible – they can fit in with others and adapt to changing demands;

unselfish – they put the needs of the other team members on a level with their own;

interested in the success of the team as a whole, and making a positive contribution to that, not just their own performance.

As above, illustrate your answer with times when you've displayed these qualities.

Q 'Why do you want to change jobs?'

Q 'What were your reasons for leaving your last job?'

You must have a positive answer ready. If the interviewer asks you this question, they are trying to find out if there's anything that should sound alarm bells for them:

Are you changing jobs because you've been sacked?

Are you leaving because of a personality clash with your boss or a colleague?

Have you been passed over for promotion or some similar reason?

Negative reasons such as that you didn't get on with your boss, or were asked to leave for any reason except job redundancy, will go down badly. Even just being vague might make the interviewer wonder if you are prone to changing jobs on a whim.

Good reasons for changing jobs are:

Challenge. You want more demanding tasks and responsibilities.

Reputation. As long as you don't cast a slur on your present employer, applying to a more prestigious company is an acceptable reason for wanting to change jobs. If you're proud of your skills, why not use them for the best in the business?

Promotion. If the job you're applying for is a step up from your current one, naturally you'd go for it, especially if the structure of your present company doesn't allow you to develop further.

Opportunity. You want the chance to work on something different or develop in a particular way.

Security. This can be a convincing reason for some jobs. There's no harm in wanting a more secure job with a more stable company as long as 'challenge' and 'ambition' weren't key words in the job description.

Location. If the company you're applying to is in a better or more convenient place, you could mention this as a contributing factor, but try not to make it your main reason.

Money. Your salary may no longer reflect your experience or value to the company. Again, though, try not to give this as your main or only reason.

Start by saying that you enjoy your current job and give brief details of what you enjoy and why. Go on to explain why, despite that, you want to change, using the reasons above as a guide.

Example

'I've enjoyed working [where you work or what you do], especially the opportunity they've given me to [mention something you've achieved]. They're a small company, though, [for example] and unfortunately there's no opportunity for advancement with them in the near future [the promotion reason].'

> **Example**
>
> 'I enjoy my job as a [what you do], and I've enjoyed working at [where you work]. I've particularly appreciated [mention a few key points about your role or the working conditions you've benefited from]. However, I've developed my bookkeeping skills [for example] over the past year or so, and I now find this side of the job more appealing. Unfortunately, a suitable position using these skills is unlikely to arise in the near future so I'm looking for a post where I can develop them more fully [the opportunity reason]. I believe this job offers just such an opportunity.'

The next eight chapters focus on questions for specific types of job. Different jobs demand a different set of abilities, and the interviewer's questions take this into account. Interviewing is becoming more of a science than an art. In an increasing number of interviews, you'll find the process stripped right down to its basics. The interviewer will have a list of the six or seven key competencies – skills, abilities and experience – specified for the job and will ask you six or seven questions about times when you've demonstrated exactly those competencies: *'Give me an example of when you've done x.' 'Tell me about a time when you demonstrated y.'* Although they may ask further questions to clarify points or draw out more details from you, those six or seven questions constitute the interview. It is essential that you:

read the job description and the job ad thoroughly;

list the competencies asked for in them;

have ready real-life examples and anecdotes of times when you've used them.

Whatever the job and however the interviewer sets about interviewing you, your key task *always* is to demonstrate your suitability for the job.

Find the chapter that relates most closely to the sort of work you're interviewing for – clerical, technical, practical, creative, etc. Read the questions and prepare your answers. Although they may not be worded in exactly the same way, the questions are typical of the sort asked. Even if you aren't asked these exact questions, preparing the answers will take you through key points so you'll be well equipped to answer confidently, whatever form the questions take. You may not use all the answers you've prepared, but having gone through them and knowing the information is there at your fingertips will give you the sort of confidence that shines through at interview.

Prepare your answers, then practise, practise, practise delivering them so that you can do it even in the stress of an interview. Friends or family can help – even better if they can reword the questions so that you don't know exactly what's coming and have to think about your response. It will help you to be flexible and able to think on your feet without losing your nerve.

EXPERT QUOTE

My advice to anyone would be: think; don't rush. Stop and take in the question. Make sure you understand what the interviewer wants to know and think about the answer. Make sure you answer the whole question.

Maggie Fellows, Project Manager, TUC

6
Questions for practical jobs

Core question: 'Are you reliable?'

Typical jobs:

- maintenance worker;
- warehouse worker;
- catering worker;
- assembly worker;
- driver;
- carer;
- appliance repairer;
- construction worker;
- service engineer;
- mechanic;
- fitter;
- dental assistant;

grounds keeper;

furniture maker;

animal handler;

health and safety;

heating engineer;

horticulturist;

hospital porter;

machinist.

Businesses need reliable people to do the practical jobs such as building maintenance, deliveries, security and line work.

They need to know that the nuts-and-bolts hands-on jobs will be done dependably. If they aren't, other employees won't be able to do their own work. If there's no one to carry out these key roles accurately, effectively and efficiently, the whole organization quickly falls apart. Consequently, dependable, trustworthy people are absolutely vital for practical jobs.

The key thing the interviewer will be trying to find out is: *'Are you reliable?'* They need to know if you'll be able to do the job competently and dependably. In other words, are you a safe pair of hands? Keep in mind the key qualities needed for most practical jobs. These are:

knowledge and hands-on experience of the job;

competence and reliability;

self-reliance as well as the ability to follow instructions accurately;

flexibility and adaptability;

recognized training such as NVQ or City & Guilds qualifications.

The interviewer wants you to demonstrate clearly that you know *what* needs to be done and that you know *how* to do it. One of the most important things to emphasize, therefore, is your experience. When you're going through the questions and preparing your answers, focus your attention on:

The sort of experience you have. Look at the work you have done in the past and in your current position. Focus particularly on the tasks and responsibilities. Look at the experience you have gained in each job, the specific responsibilities you have had, and the skills you have developed through doing it.

Your key skills. Concentrate on the practical skills that you need for your job and that have proved useful in the past. Make it clear that you understand what the job requires and that you know how to deliver it. If you have training, or if you have specific qualifications – an HGV licence, for example, or a Hygiene Certificate – don't forget to mention them in your answers.

Your personal qualities. You know which qualities have proved useful in your job – things such as patience or confidence in dealing with the public, for example. Mention them and how useful they have been to you in your work. Provide anecdotes about when and where you've used them. You'll also need anecdotes that clearly show your:

- competence and dependability;
- self-reliance;
- flexibility;
- ability to follow instructions accurately and find out further information where necessary.

Keep these important points in mind when thinking about your answers to the questions that follow.

Q *'What are your greatest strengths?'*

Q *'What are your best qualities?'*

When you're looking for a practical job, focus on your practical qualities. Ideally, one of your greatest strengths will be your experience, and another your reliability. Give some solid examples of how, where and when you've demonstrated these qualities. Stick to three or four key points and put them across strongly.

Example

'I would say my greatest strengths with regard to this job are my experience, my reliability, my [a skill] and my [a personal quality]. I have x years' experience working in [your relevant background] and my knowledge of [tasks you've done or responsibilities you've held] and familiarity with [a relevant process or piece of equipment] mean that I would be able to do the work competently and efficiently. I believe my current/previous employer would agree that I can be relied on to do the job even under difficulties/pressure. For example, [describe a time you did that].'

> **Example**
>
> 'I believe that my [your most relevant skill] would be valuable in this job. It would allow me to [explain why this skill is important]. Another strength I can bring to the job is my [your key personal quality]. I've found it to be of great importance in my current/previous job as it means that [explain why this quality has been helpful to you in the past].'

Q 'Why should I hire you?'

The interviewer might throw this question in as a challenge. React calmly and consider your answer.

> **Example**
>
> 'I think you should hire me because I believe I have the skill and experience to do the job reliably and dependably. (If you haven't already covered them, now is a good time to outline your key strengths. See the previous question for more details about doing that.)'

Q 'What are your qualifications for this job?'

Give any qualifications you have, along with any training. Don't forget vocational qualifications and on-the-job training as well, as this can often be more useful than classroom-based training. Follow up with a brief rundown of your experience as this is often more important in practical jobs than paper qualifications.

> **Example**
>
> 'I have [your qualifications – NVQ, ONC, HNC, HND, etc]. I've also been trained in [any relevant on-the-job training]. I believe, though, that my best qualification for the job is my x years' experience. I have [give your relevant employment history]. My practical knowledge of [the tasks you've done or responsibilities you've held] and familiarity with [a relevant process or piece of equipment], along with my training, mean I would be able to do the work competently and efficiently.'

Q 'What would you say makes a good... [what your job is]?'

Q 'What makes you a good... [what your job is]?'

You've read the job description, so you know what *they* think makes a good whatever your job is. Match this to your own skills, strengths and personal qualities. Emphasize your practical abilities and reliability.

Q 'How well do you work without supervision?'

If they ask you this question, it's likely the job involves working without supervision for large parts of the time. Your answer must therefore be positive. They want to know if you will:

get on with the job even when no one's looking over your shoulder;

take responsibility for your work;

make appropriate decisions;

take action in everyday situations;

solve everyday problems.

It's rare for someone to have never worked unsupervised and have no experience to draw on. However, even if you have little experience, there are sure to have been times in your personal life when you've successfully completed tasks or projects on your own that you can refer to.

Examples

'In my previous job as a [what you did], I often worked alone without direct supervision for long periods of time because [explain why – you worked off-site, you had no direct line manager]. I would consult [whoever you consulted] when there was a technical problem [or other problem outside your responsibility], but otherwise I planned my own work and handled everyday problems and decisions myself.'

'In my previous job as a [give your work experience], I worked without direct supervision for short periods of time when [explain the circumstances]. However, I'm an experienced DIYer [for example] and have carried out many home projects without supervision, so I'm used to planning my own work and handling practical problems and decisions myself. For example, I have to [outline how you plan and organize your work].'

Q 'What qualities do you need to work unsupervised?'

As above, the underlying question is *'Can you work without supervision?'* The skills you need to work unsupervised are:

self-discipline – the ability to tackle tasks and meet deadlines and targets without being chased up all the time;

self-motivation – the ability to carry out your responsibilities without constant encouragement;

self-reliance – the ability to resolve everyday problems and make straightforward decisions on your own.

Mention these skills and go on to say when and where you've demonstrated them.

Q 'What kinds of decisions do you make independently in your current job?'

This is a straightforward question about your responsibilities, but it still helps to have thought about it before the interview. Most people underestimate what they do until they actually go through it all.

Example

'In my job as a [what you do] I'm responsible for everything to do with [what you're responsible for]. I consult [whoever you consult] when there's a technical problem [or other problem outside your responsibility], but otherwise I plan my own work and handle everyday problems and decisions myself. For example, [give examples of the sort of decisions you take in a normal day and how you deal with them].'

Q 'Have you ever had any problems with supervisors?'

Obviously, the answer is 'No'.

Example

'No, I've never had any problems that I can think of. Supervisors are there to see that the job gets done and I understand that it sometimes entails guidance and constructive criticism.'

Q *'Would you say you follow instructions well?'*

Even though the question invites it, avoid saying just 'Yes' or 'No'. Illustrate your answer with an anecdote or example.

Example

'Yes, I would say I take instructions well. Like most people, I prefer it when I'm given reasons and explanations for things, and my current supervisor is usually very good about that, although I realize it's not always possible under pressure. I make sure I've clarified the information before I carry out the task, and I feed back the results to my supervisor afterwards if necessary. For example, [give an example of a time you did that].'

Q *'What have you done that shows initiative?'*

Ideally, as well as following instructions, you should be able to think for yourself and act on your own initiative when the need arises. Think of a time when you acted responsibly and resolved a problem or made a decision. Choose an occasion when you acted responsibly and avoid anything that makes you look rash or impulsive.

Q *'How do you decide when it's appropriate to use your initiative or better to refer to your manager?'*

In other words, how do you balance following instructions with thinking for yourself? You need to give a balanced answer in response.

Example

'On the whole, the company I currently work for sets out clear guidelines about what decisions I can make and what options are practical [you are used to making everyday decisions]. They also have clear procedures for most circumstances and I would generally follow those [you can understand and follow instructions]. However, if a situation arose where there were no guidelines, it was urgent or I was unable to contact my supervisor, I would do my best to make a decision based on the facts, using my experience of similar circumstances. I would keep a record of my actions and inform my manager as soon as possible. For example, [tell them about a time when you did that].'

Q *'Do you get bored doing routine work?'*

The job has a high proportion of routine work or they wouldn't be asking you, so the answer is 'No'. Avoid the simple one-word answer, though.

> **Example**
>
> 'No, I don't really get bored. I have a methodical approach to things and enjoy doing a thorough job.'

Q 'Are you reliable?'

Yes, of course you are – one of the key things they're looking for is reliability. Illustrate your reply with an anecdote demonstrating your dependability.

> **Example**
>
> 'I believe that I am and I think my present company would agree that I am, too. I have an excellent timekeeping and attendance record, and I take my responsibilities seriously, completing [what it is you have to do] on time and to a high standard. I have to be reliable in my work as a [what you do], because if I don't do my job other people can't do theirs. So it's important to me that I do a good job even when it takes extra effort. For example, [give an example of when you had to overcome a problem or setback and make an extra effort to get a job done, and the resulting benefit to the company].'

Q 'Do you think speed or accuracy is the more important?'

They want both, so you need to convince them that you are both fast *and* accurate.

> **Example**
>
> 'I believe both are important. I try to manage my workload so that both are achievable. Fortunately, my experience means that I am able to work to a high speed while maintaining quality.'

Q 'What are some of the problems you encounter in your job?'

Q 'Tell me about a problem you've had to deal with.'

All jobs involve a degree of problem solving, but they don't just want to know what the problems are; they want to know how you resolve them. Stick to practical problems and avoid anything that suggests a problem getting on with people, difficulties with management, or anything that could be seen as a criticism of your current employer. When you tell them how you dealt with the issue, include the following points:

You stayed calm.

You were clear-headed.

Experience and common sense helped you find the solution.

You kept your supervisor/manager informed.

Example

'Every job has its problems, of course. In [the sort of work you do] common difficulties include [mention some of the everyday practical difficulties that crop up in your job – breakdowns, malfunctions, hold-ups]. My supervisor relies on me to resolve everyday problems in the course of the work. For example, [give an example of how you resolved one of these problems – choose something that displays the points set out above]. On another occasion, [give an example of how you saw a problem coming and took steps to prevent it].'

Q 'What are your views on health and safety?'

The interviewer wants to know if you:

are aware of the importance of health and safety;

know about health and safety issues relevant to your job;

understand and follow regulations;

have any health and safety training.

Cover each of these points in your answer.

Q 'Have you ever had to bend health and safety rules to get a job done?'

On absolutely no account should you ever ignore health and safety regulations. If you've had an experience in the past where it looked as if a job couldn't be done because of the rules but a safe and legal way round it was found, then include that in your answer. Otherwise, just keep off the subject.

> **Example**
>
> 'I've never found it necessary to bend the rules, and I wouldn't expect to be asked to.'

Q 'What would you do if someone on your team wasn't pulling their weight?'

The interviewer wants to be sure you can handle day-to-day problems yourself as well as knowing when to refer them to a supervisor.

> **Example**
>
> 'It depends on the reason for it. If there were health and safety issues, if they were drinking on the job for example, I would discuss it with the supervisor. If they were just being lazy, I'd joke them out of it until they got the message [for example]. [Tell them about a time when you successfully resolved a similar situation in a way that kept everybody happy.]'

Professional knowledge

As well as the questions above, you can expect to be asked specific things about your current job and the job you're applying for. It's not possible to cover all the questions that might come up; they are too individual. You know your own work, however, and should be able to anticipate what they'll be. They will include things like:

how you deal with actual situations that arise in your work;

your experience of using particular machinery or equipment;

your understanding of specific processes used in your occupation;

how you set about certain tasks commonly occurring in the job;

what you would do in specific circumstances likely to occur in the job.

Give full, detailed answers based on your real-life experience.

EXPERT QUOTE

Don't try to give the 'right' answer; give an honest one. Because some of the processes can be dangerous, we need people who can judge the situation and act accordingly, but we also need people who can act on their own initiative. It's not really a trick question, but something we do is to ask a couple of questions about situations the interviewee should be able to handle themselves, followed by one where they should clearly call in expert help. Some people have a real struggle admitting they'd pass the problem on rather than tackle it themselves, but that's what we want them to do.

Senior Chemical Engineer, chemical plant

7
Questions for creative jobs

Core question: 'Will you deliver?'

Typical jobs:

product designer;

feature writer;

video maker;

photographer;

graphic artist;

copywriter;

website designer;

architect;

interior designer;

window dresser;

musician;

producer;

director;

screenwriter;

game designer;

illustrator;

fashion or textile designer;

model maker.

Creative people provide solutions to problems. It's their job to use their technical skill, talent and expertise to achieve tangible results with originality and flair. Businesses need to know that their creative people, whether designers, artists, writers or whatever, will come up with innovative solutions, on time and to budget. If they don't, the business will suffer as a result.

The most important thing the interviewer needs to know is: *'Will you deliver?'* In other words, they need to know not just that you're creative, but that you'll be creative *for them*, and also that you'll be creative on demand – within reason.

'Creativity' is a difficult thing to measure objectively. Proof of your *ability* to deliver will largely rely on your reputation, portfolio and past record. Your *willingness* to deliver, however, is more nebulous. Things the interviewer will be looking for include:

a thorough understanding of your specific field;

your previous ability to come up with effective and creative solutions to problems;

the drive and ambition to produce top-quality work every time;

your ability to work both individually and with a team to achieve results;

the ability to undertake action, rather than passive observation;

your desire to achieve results over and above the original requirements.

The personal qualities they will be searching for include:

self-motivation;

innovation;

flexibility;

energy and enthusiasm;

resilience;

professionalism.

Before you get to the interview, make sure you have thoroughly reviewed, and have a clear knowledge and understanding of:

Your career history. Review your current position and the work you've done previously. Focus on your experience of analysing and solving creative problems. Assess the skills you've developed in different jobs, the specific challenges you have encountered and the expertise you have developed through overcoming them. Look at the proficiency you have gained in each job.

Your key achievements. Creative jobs are results orientated – you need to be able to talk about your successes fluently and enthusiastically. The interviewer will want achievement to mean success in both creative and practical terms – that is, work that has fulfilled its creative brief inventively, completed to deadline and within budget, and that has actively contributed to the company's success.

Your key abilities. Practical ability and technical competence are basic requirements in creative jobs. It's only when these fundamental elements are present that style and originality can develop over and above them. Make sure you can outline the full range of skills you have that are appropriate to the job you're interviewing for, and how they've contributed to your achievements. Good foundation skills will help an employer assess the likelihood that you'll repeat your successes in the future.

Above all, you need to know what you are good at. You need to understand what your specific creative skills are; and the personal qualities that allow you to perform your skill to a professional level. For example, an artist's specific skill might be their feel for colour, their draughtsmanship or their daring use of composition. A writer's skill may lie in their innovative use of language or their acute observation of human behaviour. Understand what your own particular strength is, along with the other supporting skills that make up your own particular skill profile. Prepare examples and anecdotes for your interview that clearly demonstrate their importance and your proficiency at employing them.

Understand, too, the personal qualities that support your talents. Pick two or three to focus on in your interview with examples and anecdotes. Make sure they are key qualities that genuinely help you to do your job, and are relevant to the job you want. They might include things like:

energy;

flexibility;

thoroughness;

patience;

confidence;

drive;

communication skills;

focus;

enthusiasm;

attention to detail;

dedication;

honesty and integrity;

ability to get involved;

dogged determination.

Keep all these points in mind while you prepare your answers to the questions that follow.

Q 'What do you know about our company?'

Naturally, you've done your homework and you know quite a lot about the company. Start with general comments and then focus in on your own area. For example, start with the company's key products or services, its mission statement, main sites, etc. Include background history, current plans and future projections. Next, move on to your own area of interest – its position in the market, for example previous marketing campaigns, future considerations. Finish up by saying why all this interests you and why working for the company appeals to you.

Q 'Why should I hire you?'

Treat this question like the challenge it is meant to be. The core answer is 'Because I can provide first-rate creative solutions to your problems.' If appropriate, recap your achievements, your strengths, skills, abilities and personal qualities.

> **Example**
>
> 'Because I can solve your [design, website, direct marketing] problems. I have/am [recap your achievements]. I have x years' experience working in [continue as appropriate depending on the detail given in previous answers].'

> **Example**
>
> 'I believe I could make a significant contribution to your company. I can deliver [first-rate copy, top-quality artwork] as shown by [recap your key achievements]. I have x years' experience working in [continue as above].'

Q *'How would you define your profession?'*

Q *'What makes a good... [what your job is]?'*

The interviewer wants to know what you believe the crucial areas of your job are. If you have read the job description, you'll be aware of what they consider the key points to be and you can plan your answer around these, highlighted with your own individual beliefs and experience.

Q *'What can you do for us that no one else can?'*

This looks like an impossible question, but all they're asking really is *'What can you do for us?'* Ignore the bit about no one else doing it; it's just testing your self-confidence – as a creative person, you have to believe that you're unique. Emphasize your key strengths and talents, along with your existing achievements.

> **Example**
>
> 'I don't know about no one else being able to do it, but I believe I can bring to this job [key points mentioned in the job description]. I am [outline your key talents] and have [your key skills and abilities]. To date, I have [mention your biggest achievements]. I believe I have [personal qualities relevant to the job description]. In addition, I understand [a relevant factor of the job], which I believe would allow me to [make some significant contribution to the company].'

Q *'What would you do if we gave you a completely free hand?'*

If you're applying for a creative job, it does no harm to consider this question. It would probably be asked if you were going in at a certain level – head of department, for example – or were being asked to take on a specific project. If you're interviewing at this level, think about this in detail beforehand, as it could be the main point of the interview.

On the other hand, some interviewers are simply interested in the scope of your creativity. To give a convincing answer, you need to know about the company, what it has done in the past, what its market is and what its future direction is. This means doing your homework. Whether you would continue in the company tradition or break out into new areas is down to your own personal style, but you need to able to:

outline your proposals clearly;

explain why you would make the decisions you suggest;

describe how they would benefit the company.

Q *'How do you keep up with changes/innovations in your profession?'*

The question is really *'Do you keep up with changes and innovations?'* Your answer would ideally include as many as possible of the following:

professional, trade and business magazines;

online professional groups;

business contacts;

professional associations;

trade fairs, shows and exhibitions;

suppliers and clients;

courses and seminars.

Example

'Keeping up with new [products, ideas, trends] is, naturally, very important in this job. I [say what you do to keep up]. It takes a bit of commitment, but I've found it to be essential. For example, [give an example of how knowing something ahead of time benefited you, your job and the company].'

Anticipate a follow-up question: *'What do you see as the future trend right now?'* Make your answer optimistic, mentioning key developments and the opportunities these present, especially to the creative person.

Q 'What are your greatest strengths?'

Q 'What are your outstanding qualities?'

Your greatest strengths are your creative skills and your ability to deliver those skills on time and to budget. They are demonstrated through your greatest achievements. It's best to pick two or three really strong points and put them across powerfully. Stick to the ones most relevant to the job you are applying for.

Example

'I would say my greatest strengths with regard to this job are my [pick your most relevant creative ability], my [pick your most relevant professional skill] and my [pick your most relevant personal quality and say why it's important]. I have x years' experience working in [your field of work] and my knowledge of [a key, relevant area] means I would be able to make a significant contribution from the beginning [or at an early stage]. My track record includes [state your major achievements], which I believe [outline why they are relevant to the company you are applying to]. Finally, I believe my current employer would agree that one of my key strengths is my ability to do the job even under difficult conditions. For example, [describe a time you successfully completed a job to a high creative level under pressure].'

Q 'What are your greatest achievements?'

Creative jobs are results orientated. The final product – video, website, exhibition, magazine, ad campaign, whatever – either works or it doesn't. You need to have achievements and you need to be able to talk about them fluently. Focus on your biggest successes, obviously, but it also helps to show yourself as a rounded person if you can also include an example of:

recent achievements rather than things that happened early in your career;

success you achieved as part of a team;

a time when achievement was snatched from the jaws of probable defeat (especially if it displays your personal qualities as well as your creative ability);

a time when you helped someone else achieve success (in a mentor role, perhaps, or a back-room contribution).

Any of these will help to show that you are a current achiever, have a generous nature, can work well with others or can function effectively under stress – all good things in an employee.

Q *'What are the reasons for your professional success?'*

This may sound like *'What are your greatest strengths?'* or *'What are your greatest achievements?'* but it's actually subtly different. The interviewer wants to know if *you* know how you work. They're looking for self-awareness. If you shrug and say you've just been lucky, although you may sound charmingly modest they may wonder what happens when your luck runs out. If, however, you can give reasons based on real skills and qualities, you will probably continue to deliver the creative goods. Base the reasons for your success on:

   natural abilities that you've developed and enhanced;

   creative skills that you've built on systematically;

   the personal qualities that have formed your professional attitude;

   the support you've received from others – bosses, colleagues, etc;

   the opportunities you've made good use of.

Q *'What are you looking for in a job?'*

Q *'What are you seeking in an employer?'*

As a creative person, what you are looking for is the chance to deliver some great work. The job you're applying for provides just that opportunity.

Example

'I'm looking for the opportunity to accomplish my best work. My experience at [the company you work for] has shown me I have a talent for [something relevant to the job you're applying for]. I believe that it's demonstrated by [give your achievements using that talent or skill]. I am looking for the opportunity to continue to achieve at that level and beyond, and a company that will help me continue to develop professionally. So, I suppose I would say that what I'm looking for is a progressive company that will provide a challenging, stimulating and supportive environment for its employees and their achievements (be as specific as possible). I believe your company offers just such an opportunity.'

Q *'Under what conditions do you work best/produce your best results?'*

You have to be honest about this, for your own peace of mind if nothing else. If you say you relish the cut-and-thrust environment that particular company prides itself on when you would actually find it intimidating, you are not going to enjoy working there and you will not produce good work. Otherwise, go for balance – you're happy to work in a team, but equally able to be a self-starter; you function well under stress but appreciate a harmonious environment; you're happy to work closely with your boss when required, but are self-motivated and independent, etc. Add to this some specific quality of the company you're applying to that would enable you to produce good results.

Example

'I'm fairly equable. I've worked in a variety of environments [mention a couple] so I've learnt to adapt. As a result, I'm happy to work in a team [for example], but equally able to work independently given a free hand. I function well under stress when necessary, but, like most people, I appreciate a harmonious atmosphere. I've found that on the whole I work best when [give your preferred conditions, matching them as far as possible to what you know about the company]. I believe that [mention some aspect of the company you're applying to] would enable me to produce good results, which is one of my reasons for applying.'

Q 'What would you say your attitude to challenge is?'

Few creative people actively avoid challenge; most relish it and find it stimulates some of their best work. You need to get your appetite for a challenge across to the interviewer. You also need to make it clear that, when you take on a challenge, you intend to succeed. Base your answer on anecdotes about challenges you've take on in the past and how you've met and overcome them. Include the benefit your success brought to the company.

Q 'What is your attitude to risk?'

Risk is one of those double-edged swords – you don't want to be considered un-adventurous, but on the other hand you can't be seen as reckless. Risk in a creative job is different from risk in more practical jobs. It's unlikely that your risk would endanger life or limb. It's quite probable, however, that your risk taking could cost the company money or prestige. The ideal answer shows you know how to calculate risk and take appropriate action. If in doubt, ask them what sort of risks they have in mind.

Example

'While I would never take a risk that would compromise the reputation of the company, most creative work entails going out on a limb from time to time. For example, [give an illustration of a time you took a risk that paid off. Include details of how you analysed the risk, weighed the options, came to the decision it was worth it, and kept your employer in the picture. Include how the risk paid off – for the company or client, not only for you]. On another occasion, however, [give another brief anecdote about a time you were faced with taking a big risk but came up with a solution that avoided it but was just as innovative].'

Q 'Would you say you are innovative?'

This question is best answered with anecdotes about the times when you've displayed your talent for new ideas, how you made them workable, how they were successful and their benefit to the company.

Q 'How well do you interact with people at different levels?'

You will probably be asked this question if the job you are applying for involves you working with two sets of people with different needs, for example a designer who has to take the requirements of production staff into consideration as well as those of management and clients, while still being able to put their own view across. Your answer needs to demonstrate that you can communicate confidently and effectively with everyone involved.

Example

'I haven't experienced problems at any level. In my current job [or whatever experience you are using if you don't have workplace experience] I have to work with [the different groups you deal with]. I'm expected to [outline the dealings you have – presentations, discussions, reports, etc – and at what level – departmental, board, client]. For example, [give an illustration of how you communicated confidently and effectively with people at different levels of the company hierarchy].'

Q 'How do you approach a project?'

They want to know if you are methodical and systematic in your approach, rather than flying by the seat of your pants. The latter approach they see as unreliable and likely to cost them money and/or prestige when you fail. Tell them how you undertook a typical project, taking into account:

creative planning – how you generate and refine ideas;

resource planning – what you need to get the job done: tools, materials, people, equipment, etc;

time planning – scheduling what must be done when, if the completion date is to be met;

budget planning – allocating money, time and resources to each stage of the project;

contingency planning – what you'll do when things go wrong, including time and cost overspends.

Q *'Are you sensitive to criticism?'*

Q *'Describe a situation where your work was criticized. How did you respond?'*

Unless you intend to play safe all the time, criticism is inevitable in most jobs and especially creative ones where you have to take risks. The interviewer wants to know if you're going to be difficult every time and make life unpleasant for everyone. On the other hand, you don't want to give the impression that you can't stand up for your ideas. Give an answer that shows you are open-minded and mature. If asked to describe a situation, choose one from early in your career that doesn't show you in too bad a light and where the consequences weren't too disastrous.

Example

'I believe I'm mature enough to handle constructive criticism. It's essential, in fact, if I want to continue to improve my performance. I remember early in my career, [describe the event and how it arose. Who did the criticizing?]. I listened to what they said and [when the circumstances were explained] I could see that they had a point. We discussed it and [go on to describe how you came to a mutually agreeable solution]. I learnt that [mention something that was useful to you subsequently].'

Q *'How do you handle rejection?'*

This question, like the one about criticism above, looks at your resilience. Companies need their staff to be emotionally tough, buoyant and quick to recover from setbacks. Not all ideas are accepted and they want to be sure that you will accept rejection robustly and come up with new and better suggestions.

Example

'Unfortunately, rejection is sometimes a part of being a [what you are] when you have to come up with so many [ideas, designs, etc]. Experience has taught me that the next idea will be better, so I just get on with it. For example, [give an illustration of how, after an initial idea was rejected, you went on to put a twist on it that turned it into a success].'

Q *'Have you ever failed to meet a challenge?'*

The only safe answer here is 'No'. Illustrate your answer with an anecdote showing how you rose to a challenge against all the odds and the benefit to the company of doing so.

Q *'Describe a difficult problem you've had to deal with. How did you handle it?'*

This is a good opportunity to show off. Pick a difficult problem and describe the skills, talents and personal qualities you used to overcome it brilliantly. Don't forget to say what the benefit to the company was. As you're applying for a creative job, make the problem a creative one that shows off your flair and innovation. Don't choose problems that involve not getting on with other people or disobeying management decisions, as these rarely reflect well on the interviewee.

Q *'Have you done the best work you're capable of doing?'*

This question is double edged. If you say 'No', the interviewer will wonder why you haven't tried harder. If you say 'Yes', they'll think you've nothing more to offer. Your best bet is to tell them that you've done some terrific work in the past, but the job you're applying for offers the opportunity to do even better.

Example

'I've done some great work [briefly recap your achievements], but the conditions in your organization would give me the opportunity to do even better [specify what they are and how they would improve your performance].'

Q *'What are you like with deadlines?'*

Every company fears the person who has a brilliant creative mind, but who never delivers on time. As a newspaper editor once said, 'I don't need it perfect; I need it Tuesday.' Lost deadlines mean lost clients, lost money, lost reputation and so on. Consequently, your answer needs to be that you have never missed a deadline. Include a couple of anecdotes showing how you've met tight deadlines successfully. Include one, if possible, about how you achieved this against the odds, demonstrating your determination.

Professional knowledge

In addition to the questions already covered, you will almost certainly be asked about specific aspects of your work and professional knowledge. It's almost impossible for an outsider to guess what these questions will be, as they are often of a highly specialized nature. You, however, know exactly what your job entails and should be able to foresee what the interviewer will ask. They will include things such as:

details about specific campaigns or projects – how you prepared, the issues involved, how you overcame problems, the reasons for your creative decisions and so on;

your understanding of specific processes;

your experience of using particular equipment, specialist programmes, etc;

your actual areas of experience in detail;

the extent of your knowledge and skill;

how you deal with actual problems and situations that arise in your occupation;

how you approach tasks and responsibilities common in your job.

Your answer should be fully based on your actual experience. Let your interest and enthusiasm for the everyday details of your job shine through.

EXPERT QUOTE

What I'm really looking for is enthusiasm. I can train anybody to do anything, but, if that initial spark isn't there, forget it. It isn't going to work.

HR Manager, engineering company

EXPERT QUOTE

Because of the sort of organization we are, we appreciate a high degree of interest and commitment in the people we interview. We're looking for examples of how they've done certain things in the past, how they've overcome difficulties, for instance, but we're also interested in why they want the job and how they see it fitting into their overall career plan.

Maggie Fellows, Project Manager, TUC

8

Questions for clerical and administrative jobs

Core question: 'Are you efficient?'

Typical jobs:

financial administrator;

records administrator;

clerical assistant;

office manager;

secretary;

personal assistant;

accountant;

medical administrator;

bank clerk;

bookkeeper;

bursar;

auditor;

securities analyst;

legal executive;

admissions clerk;

bilingual secretary;

cashier;

accounting technician.

Clerks and administrators ensure the smooth running of an organization. Offices and departments can virtually grind to a halt if their administrative staff aren't competent. The interviewer wants to be sure you'll fit in and get on with the job reliably and efficiently with the minimum of disruption.

The key question they are trying to answer is: *'Are you efficient?'* Someone who is efficient is:

well organized;

competent;

resourceful;

proficient;

capable;

professional;

helpful.

The most important things the interviewer will be looking for in someone applying for a clerical or administrative job are:

organization;

dependability;

a methodical approach;

specific technical skills – the ability to use certain computer programs, for example;

experience in specific areas – data handling, for example;

the ability to work with others.

When you're preparing for your interview, make sure you've thoroughly assessed your:

Key skills. Many clerical, administrative and secretarial jobs require specific skills such as word-processing, language or bookkeeping skills, use of particular sorts of software, familiarity with specific equipment such as a particular sort of switchboard, or knowledge of a specific process. Review all your relevant skills, especially those that match the job description of the job you're applying for.

Key experience. Review the general experience you have had such as supervision and planning that will be relevant to most positions. Focus on specific experience relevant to the job such as payroll procedures, data handling, etc. Relevant experience in a specific field is also an advantage. A computer services administrator, for example, will have very different areas of knowledge and expertise from someone working in personnel administration, even where the basic requirements of the job are the same. As the interviewer is looking for someone who will take the job over with the minimum of disruption, go over any relevant experience or knowledge you have.

Hold all these points in mind while working through the following questions.

Q 'What do you know about our company?'

Having done your homework, as suggested in Chapter 2, you know quite a lot about the company. Start with general points – what it does, background history, etc. Then, if possible, focus in on the aspects of the company that have a bearing on your own job.

Q 'What makes you a good... [what your job is]?'

The answer is your efficiency. Focus on that and add details of what contributes to that efficiency:

your proficiency in specific skills and/or processes;

your experience;

your competency and resourcefulness;

your professional approach;

your organizational skills.

Include anecdotes that illustrate these points.

> **Example**
>
> 'I would say that my efficiency is the greatest contributing factor to being a good [what your job is]. For example, [give some brief examples of your efficiency including their benefit to your employer]. I have x years' experience of [a relevant area] and am highly proficient at [two or three of your skills]. These together with my [two or three of the personal qualities that help you do your job well] ensure that I can do my job competently and professionally.'

Q 'What are your greatest strengths?'

Your greatest strengths are the same as those in the answer above – your efficiency and the skills and qualities that make you efficient.

Q 'Why should I hire you?'

This is often asked as a bit of a challenge to see if you can stand up for yourself under mild pressure. Show how unflappable you are, stay calm and give an answer that says, in effect, 'Because I can take over the job smoothly and efficiently with as little disruption as possible.' If you haven't already mentioned them, assure the interviewer of your competence, knowledge and proficiency. Demonstrate that you understand what the job requires and that you can deliver it.

> **Example**
>
> I believe that my background in [your relevant experience] and familiarity with [a relevant process or professional area] mean that I would pick up the job quickly and make a significant contribution from the start.'

Example

'Because I have x years' experience working in [the relevant area] and would be able to take over the job smoothly and efficiently with as little disruption as possible. [If the following points haven't been covered in previous questions, now is the time to introduce them.] I understand [choose two or three relevant tasks or responsibilities from the job description that demonstrate you know what the job involves] and the importance of [the skills and qualities important in the job]. These have been essential elements in my current job and I appreciate their importance. In addition, I have an excellent record of [a key skill or quality that you've needed to carry out your work efficiently]. For example, [give a short anecdote demonstrating it].'

Q 'Have you worked without supervision?'

Q 'What qualities do you need to work unsupervised?'

The skills you need to work unsupervised are:

- *self-motivation* – the ability to undertake tasks and responsibilities without outside motivation;

- *self-discipline* – the ability to meet responsibilities, deadlines and targets without constant monitoring;

- *self-reliance* – the ability to sort out routine problems and use your own judgement appropriately.

If they ask you this question, expect to be working without supervision for large parts of the time. Your answer must therefore be positive if you want to maintain your image of efficient capability. Even if you haven't done it at work, it's rare for an adult to have never worked unsupervised and have no experience to draw on. There are sure to have been times in your personal life when you've successfully completed tasks or projects on your own that you can refer to.

Example

'In my current job as a [what you do], I often work alone without direct supervision. This is because [explain why – it's simply expected of you; you have no direct line manager; your supervisor is working on other projects, etc]. I consult [whomever you consult] when there's a [problem outside your responsibility], but otherwise I plan my own workload and handle everyday problems and decisions myself. For example, [describe a time you did that, mentioning the qualities outlined above].'

> **Example**
>
> 'In my previous job as a [insert your work experience], I worked without direct supervision for short periods of time when [explain the circumstances]. However, I'm an experienced party planner [for example] and have carried out several projects without supervision, so I'm used to planning my own work and handling practical problems and decisions myself. The sort of things I have to do, for example, [tell them about what you do, bringing in the qualities outlined above].'

Q 'What kinds of decisions do you make in your current job?'

This is a question about your level of responsibility. Most people find they under-estimate what they do until they actually think about it, so it helps to go through it all before the interview.

> **Example**
>
> 'In my current job I'm responsible for everything to do with [whatever you're responsible for]. I consult [whoever you consult] when there's a [problem outside your responsibility – give some very brief examples], but otherwise I plan my own work schedule [for example] and handle everyday problems and decisions myself. For example, [give an idea of the sort of decisions you take in a normal day].'

Q 'Have you ever had any problems with supervisors?'

The only answer you can sensibly give is 'No'.

> **Example**
>
> 'I've never had any problems that I can think of. Maybe I've been lucky with the people I've had supervising me, but I believe that supervisors are there to see that the job gets done efficiently and I understand how feedback and constructive criticism are sometimes necessary to achieve that.'

Q 'What have you done that shows initiative?'

You need to have an illustration ready for this question. Think of a time when you acted responsibly on your own initiative to solve a problem or to stop a problem arising. Remember to say how the company benefited from your action.

Q 'How do you decide when to use your initiative and when to refer to a supervisor/manager?'

The interviewer wants to know that you can balance following instructions with thinking for yourself. Give a balanced answer that shows you can take responsibility when necessary, without acting rashly.

Example

'The company I currently work for has clear procedures for most circumstances and I usually follow those [you can understand and follow instructions]. They also set out clear guidelines about what decisions are my responsibility under normal circumstances and what options are possible [you are used to making everyday decisions]. However, if a situation arose where there were no guidelines and it was urgent or I was unable to contact my supervisor, I would do my best to make a decision based on the facts, using any experience of similar circumstances. I would keep a record of my actions and inform my supervisor as soon as possible. For example, [tell them about a time when you did that successfully].'

Q 'Would you say you are reliable?'

Of course you would. Don't just give a 'Yes' or 'No', though; illustrate your answer with an anecdote demonstrating how reliable you've been in the past.

Example

'I believe I am and I think my present supervisor/manager would agree that I am, too. I have an excellent timekeeping and attendance record, and I take my responsibilities seriously, [doing what it is you have to do] on time and to a high standard. I have to be reliable in my work, because if I don't do my job [say what the negative result would be]. So it's important to me that I do a good job even when it takes extra effort. For example, [give an example of when you had to overcome a problem or setback and make an extra effort to get a job done, and the resulting benefit to the company].'

Q 'Do you like analytical tasks?'

If the job you're applying for includes a high proportion of analytical tasks, then you have to give a positive answer to this one. As above, a 'Yes' or 'No' answer is less convincing than one that offers an illustrative anecdote.

Example

'I enjoy doing analytical tasks. I believe I have [the personal qualities that contribute – an eye for detail, patience, methodical approach, numerical aptitude, etc] necessary for the task, and I've developed this further [say how – qualifications, training, experience]. I believe they are valuable skills. [Give a brief illustration of a time your analytical skills have been of benefit to the company.] I've used these skills [how, when and where], and my decision to apply for this job is [to some extent or to a large degree, depending on your own tastes and the nature of the job] influenced by that.'

Q 'Do you get bored doing routine work?'

A lot of clerical and administrative work entails a high proportion of routine, so suggesting that you do get bored won't go down well. However, implying that you love doing routine work makes you look dull and lacking in initiative. Try to strike a reasonable balance in your answer.

Example

'Every job entails a degree of routine. I'm lucky in that I have a methodical approach to things and can do routine jobs thoroughly and efficiently.'

Q 'Do you like doing detailed work?'

A lot of clerical and administrative jobs require attention to detail. If they ask you this question, attention to detail is probably an important feature of the job you're applying for.

Example

'I enjoy doing detailed work. I have a methodical approach and can do that sort of work thoroughly and efficiently. I believe I also have [the personal qualities that contribute – eye for detail, patience, logical approach] necessary for the task and have used these skills [say how and where you've successfully done detailed work, whether in your job or in some other capacity].'

Q *'Do you prefer routine tasks and regular hours?'*

This can be a slightly tricky question. You can't say you don't like routine work and regular hours because that's what clerical work largely entails (see above). However, if you say you prefer them, you could seem to be lacking in ambition and, even worse, such a preference could indicate that you might go to pieces or make a fuss if they ask you to work extra hours or carry out a non-routine task. Your answer has to strike a balance.

Example

'I appreciate that [the type of work you're applying for] largely entails routine work and regular hours. I'm used to that; that's the sort of job it is, most of the time. However, there have been times, as there are in all jobs, when the work has been far from routine and the hours very irregular. I believe, and I'm sure my current/previous employer would agree, that I've risen to those occasions and met the demands efficiently and effectively. For example, [tell them about a time when you've done so, including the benefit to the company].'

Q *'Can you follow instructions?'*

The interviewer wants to know if you can deal efficiently with instructions, that is:

understand them;

clarify any problems;

carry them out;

feed back results.

They also want to know if you follow instructions willingly, without argument or resentment. Cover both interpretations in your answer.

Example

'Yes, I would say I follow instructions well [give an outline of how and when you do in your current job or on other occasions]. I listen carefully, make sure I understand what's being asked for and clarify anything I'm not sure about. I keep my supervisor informed at key stages and give feedback of the results. For example, [give an example bringing in all the points mentioned]. Like most people, I prefer to be given reasons and explanations for things, and my current supervisor is very good about that. However, I realize that it's not always possible when under pressure.'

Q 'Would you say you are organized?'

You have to say 'Yes', of course. Back up your claim with a brief anecdote illustrating your organizing skills and naturally organized nature.

Q 'Do you work well under pressure?'

Rather than just saying 'Yes', use this as an opportunity to demonstrate how well you've worked under pressure in the past.

Example

'Yes, I believe I work well under pressure, and I believe my supervisor/manager would agree. I've experienced [mention some situations such as urgent tasks, unexpected events, limited resources, short notice]. My priorities in a stressful situation are to stay calm, assess the situation, assess the resources available to me, decide the best course of action and act promptly and efficiently [or whatever else you've found works well]. I've found that pressure can reveal unexpected strengths, and achievement in those circumstances can bring a lot of satisfaction. For example, [illustrate with a brief anecdote].'

Q 'Do you think speed or accuracy is the more important?'

In clerical work, both are equally important, so don't imply that you would willingly sacrifice one for the other. You are both fast *and* accurate.

Example

'I believe both are equally important, which is why I aim to manage my workload so that both are achievable. Fortunately, my experience and [specific skill] mean that I am able to work at a high speed while maintaining quality. For example, [give a brief, supporting anecdote].'

Q 'What are some of the problems you encounter in your job?'
Q 'Describe a difficult problem you've had to deal with.'

They don't just want to know what the problems are; they want to know how you resolve them. Choose practical problems and avoid anything that suggests you don't get on with people or have difficulties with your manager or supervisor. Ideally, when describing how you resolve difficulties, include the following points:

You stayed calm.

You were clear-headed.

Experience and common sense helped you find the solution.

You kept your supervisor/manager informed.

Example

'Every job has its problems, of course. In [the sort of work you do] common difficulties include [mention some of the everyday practical difficulties that crop up]. My supervisor relies on me to resolve everyday problems in the course of the work. For example, [tell them how you resolved one of these problems – include the points set out above]. On another occasion, [give an example of how you saw a problem coming and took steps to prevent it].'

Q 'What would you do if a chatty colleague was interrupting your work?'

The interviewer wants to know if you can handle minor problems and the inevitable personality clashes without letting them disrupt your work or grow out of proportion. Assure them you would solve the problem yourself without either causing offence or involving management in minor personal irritations.

Example

'I'd probably smile and say I was sorry but I was up to my eyes in work at the moment and why don't we meet for coffee during the break when I'll be all ears [or whatever suits your own personal style].'

Example

'I had just that problem a little while ago. I [say what you did to resolve it tactfully].'

Professional knowledge

As well as the questions we've already looked at, there will almost definitely be some about your professional knowledge. Expect to be asked specific details about the practical aspects of your job. Although it's not possible to cover these highly specialized questions here, you should be able to anticipate what will be asked from your own personal knowledge of the job. Expect them to include:

your areas of experience in detail;

your knowledge of specific processes;

your experience of using particular pieces of equipment;

your experience of using different software programs, etc;

how you deal with specific circumstances that arise in the job;

how you approach everyday tasks;

your understanding of the responsibilities of the job.

Give full, detailed, knowledgeable answers based on the full range of your experience.

EXPERT QUOTE

I know people are nervous so I don't expect them to be word perfect in an interview. If I ask someone about a time they've displayed a certain skill, personal effectiveness, perhaps, and nothing comes readily to mind, I don't mind if they say, 'I can't think of a good example at the moment; can I come back to that later?' Don't be afraid to go back to previous questions, and don't be afraid to change or correct anything you've said, either. It's better than giving the wrong impression.

Robert Johnson, Area Director, ACAS South West

EXPERT QUOTE

I'd rather someone said 'Sorry, that's outside my area of experience,' so I can go on to a back-up question, rather than waffle on and waste those valuable 45 minutes.

Janet Hembry, Head of Education and Skills Policy,
Government Office for the South West

9
Questions for sales and marketing jobs

Core question: 'Can you sell?'

Typical jobs:

- sales;
- telesales;
- retail;
- marketing;
- media sales;
- insurance sales;
- financial marketing;
- public relations;
- recruitment;
- sales trainer;
- advertising sales;
- technical sales;

export sales;

sales agent.

People actively dealing with the public might want to look at Chapter 12, too. Media and marketing people might find some of the questions in Chapter 7 useful.

Sales people ensure that a company sells its products and makes a profit. The key skill the interviewer is looking for is, quite simply: *'Can you sell?'*

The qualities that most interviewers want in the people they interview for sales jobs include:

the ability to sell;

energy, commitment and enthusiasm;

tenacity and perseverance;

competence and integrity;

the ability to get on with others.

You need to be able to get across the certainty that you will be able to sell this company's goods or services and increase its profits. The clearest way of doing so is to emphasize your success in doing this for your current and previous employers. Therefore, before the interview make sure you review:

Your key achievements. Make sure you have plenty of anecdotes illustrating each of your achievements – meeting or exceeding targets, contributing to increased turnover and profits, increasing orders, winning new customers, increasing repeat orders, etc. Where possible, put facts and figures to your successes, emphasizing your benefit to the company bottom line.

Your career history. Remind yourself of the areas you have covered in the past and the sort of experience you've had. Experience outside sales but relevant to the job you're applying for can be very useful – companies know that buyers like to feel they are talking to someone who speaks their language.

Build your success story as you think about your answers to the following questions.

Q *'What do you know about our company?'*

For this sort of job, you really do need to know a lot, especially about the markets and products you will be dealing with if appointed. Ideally, read the catalogue or product/service guide when you apply for the post as well as getting a broader perspective from the company website, company report, etc (see Chapter 2). Think about what you read and prepare a short but comprehensive outline, ending up with why the company and its product or service interest you, and why you want to work there.

Q 'What do you think the key trends in the industry are?'

You need to be up to date with what's happening in your field to be able to answer this one. Sales can be very sensitive to market changes. Keep an eye on the trade journals, marketing magazines, etc (see Chapter 2), as well as the newspapers. Outline the key trends as you see them, keeping your views optimistic and focusing on the opportunities these developments offer.

Q 'What are you looking for in a job?'

Most sales people are looking for challenge and opportunity. Think in terms of what you can give rather than what you can get – the challenge of increasing orders and exceeding targets, the opportunity to make sales and increase profits as well as earning commission.

Example

'I'm looking for the opportunity to make sales. My experience at [the company you currently work for] has shown me that I have a talent for [what you do – sales, marketing, telesales, etc]. I believe that's clearly demonstrated by [your main sales achievements]. I'm looking for the opportunity to continue to achieve success at that level and beyond, in a company with a first-rate product/service [or whatever the key attraction is for you] that will give me the support to develop professionally. I believe your company offers just such an opportunity.'

Q 'What are your greatest achievements?'

The interviewer is inviting you to make your sales pitch; don't let them down. Pick three or four of your biggest successes to go into in detail, backed up by a couple of others that show your range. Sales jobs are result orientated, so keep your achievements sales based and emphasize the benefits to the company, quoting actual figures wherever possible.

Q 'What are your outstanding qualities?'
Q 'What are your greatest strengths?'

The interviewer is chiefly interested in the strengths and qualities that will be of use in the job. Your greatest strength is your ability to sell, of course. Your outstanding qualities are the personal characteristics that contribute to that ability. They often include qualities or skills such as:

energy;

enthusiasm;

perseverance;

drive;

initiative;

confidence;

integrity;

communication skills;

attention to detail;

reliability;

diplomacy;

interpersonal skills;

determination;

industry knowledge;

approachability;

product knowledge.

Example

'I would say my greatest strength is my ability to sell. I have experience in [outline some specifics – types of sales, specific sales skills, etc]. Within the past [couple of years, few months] I have [give some brief examples of your achievements]. I believe this was possible because of my [pick your most relevant sales ability], my [pick your most relevant professional skill] and my [pick a couple of your most relevant personal qualities].'

Example

'I have x years' experience working in [your field of work] and my knowledge of [a key relevant knowledge, product or market area] means that I would be able to make a significant contribution from the beginning. I am [outline your chief abilities] and because of that I have [give your key achievements]. I believe my current/previous employer would agree that one of my key strengths is my ability to do the job even under difficult conditions. For example, [describe a time you succeeded under difficulties and the benefit to the company that resulted].'

Q 'What are the reasons for your success in this profession?'

Q 'What makes you a good... [what your job is]?'

Give solid reasons. The job description will indicate what the company you are applying to thinks some of the key factors are, and you can also include:

your specific sales skills;

your experience and proficiency;

your competence and resourcefulness;

your professional approach.

Example

'I would say my experience and proficiency make me a good salesperson. I have x years in [your field of work] and am experienced/have experience in [outline some specifics – types of sales, specific sales skills, etc]. My knowledge of [insert a key, relevant knowledge, product or market area] means that I can make a significant contribution to your company from the beginning. Finally, I believe my current/previous employer would agree that one of the reasons for my success is my ability to do the job even under difficult conditions/pressure. For example, [describe a time you succeeded against the odds. Don't forget to include the benefit to the company].'

Q 'What can you do for us that no one else can?'

If you ignore the bit about no one else doing it, this question is simply asking *'What can you do for us?'* Emphasize your achievements and your key selling strengths and qualities.

> **Example**
>
> 'I don't know about no one else being able to do it, but I believe I am [outline your key strengths] and have [insert your key abilities]. To date, I have [mention your biggest achievements]. I believe I can bring to this job [key requirements mentioned in the job description]. I have [relevant personal qualities and/or experience]. In addition, I understand [a relevant factor of the job], which I believe would allow me to [make a significant contribution to the company].'

Q 'Why should I hire you?'

As a sales person, your core answer needs to be something like 'Because I can increase your profits' or 'Because I can make you money.' Think of yourself as a product and pinpoint your key features and benefits. After all, if you can't sell yourself, how will you sell anything else?

Q 'How long do you think it would take you to make a contribution to this company?'

Unless this is your first experience of doing this type of job, most companies expect you to be doing a reasonable job within a few weeks and making a significant contribution with some substantial achievement within the first six months. You can say that this is what was expected of you in your last job and that you fulfilled that target satisfactorily. Give details of what you did and how you achieved it.

Q 'Would you say you have good influencing skills?'

Q 'Would you say you are persuasive?'

This question is best answered with an anecdote demonstrating your skill. Pick something with a win–win outcome and avoid anything that might make you look devious.

Q 'Are you a leader or a follower?'

This question isn't as easy as it first looks. It's natural to assume that they would prefer someone who is a strong leader – someone confident and dynamic with a strong personality. They probably *do* want that, but they may also want that balanced with someone who can listen to customers and be guided by their requirements. Show this balance in your answer.

Example

'I would say that I am, by nature, a leader and I think most people who know me would agree with that. I [give some examples of your leadership skills in action, either in the workplace or outside it]. However, I've found that, to be a good sales person, it sometimes pays to be a follower, rather than a leader. For example, [give an illustration of a time when listening to the customer, being empathic, etc were beneficial. Go on to describe how you used gentle influencing skills and gentle motivation in either that situation or another to make the sale]. So, on the whole, I would say that it pays to be versatile.'

Q 'Are you ambitious?'

By saying that you are ambitious, you are suggesting that you are hard working, focused, goal orientated and dedicated, but it can also suggest that you are cut-throat and competitive. Your answer should reflect the positive qualities.

Example

'Yes, I would certainly say I am ambitious. I have the drive, enthusiasm and [add your own qualities] to make a significant contribution to the company I work for. For example, [give an anecdote that demonstrates your ambition in a favourable way – overcoming difficulties to achieve a goal, for example, either in the workplace or outside it]. I'm very clear about where I want to be and what I want to do.'

Q 'Would you say you are determined?'

They're asking if you will become demoralized and give up in the face of discouragement and rejection – everyday situations in most sales environments. Answer this question with a couple of anecdotes that demonstrate your determination in action. One of them should be from the workplace, but you could also include something from outside work if this illustrates your determination better. Make the outcome one worth the effort, and don't forget to include the benefit to the company in the work-related situation.

Q 'How do you rate your confidence?'

You have to be able to rate it highly without coming over as smug or bumptious. This is possible if you give sound reasons for your confidence.

Example

'I would say that I'm a confident person. I'm certainly confident of my ability to sell, and that confidence is based on my [pick your most relevant sales ability], my [your most relevant professional skill] and my [your most relevant personal qualities]. Within the past [couple of years, few months] I have [give some examples of your achievements]. I believe [outline briefly how your qualities have contributed to these successes]. Having worked x years in [your field of work], I believe my confidence to be well founded on experience.'

Q 'What is your attitude to challenge?'

Q 'What's the biggest challenge you've faced?'

You need an appetite for challenge in sales jobs. You also need to make it clear that, when you take on a challenge, you intend to succeed. Base your answer on anecdotes about challenges you've taken on in the past and how you've met and overcome them. Include the benefit your success brought to the company.

Q 'What is your attitude to risk?'

This is not an easy question. One person's calculated risk is another's reckless behaviour. Risk in a sales job is different from risk in more practical jobs, though, and it's unlikely that any risk you take would physically endanger anyone. However, it's quite probable that your risk taking could cost the company money or reputation. The ideal answer shows you know how to calculate risk and take appropriate action. If in doubt, ask them what sort of risks they have in mind.

Example

'While I would never take a risk that would compromise the reputation of the company, I'll admit I've had to go out on a limb from time to time. For example, [give an illustration of a time you took a risk that paid off. Include details of how you analysed the risk, weighed the options, came to the decision it was worth it, and kept your employer in the picture. Include how the risk paid off – for the company or client, not just for you]. On another occasion, however, [give another brief anecdote about a time you were faced with taking a big risk but came up with a solution that avoided it but was just as successful].'

Q 'This job needs someone passionate about business improvement. Does that describe you?'

Sales and marketing are key factors in business expansion. The interviewer wants to know you appreciate that and can take on the responsibility for ensuring, as far as you are able, that the company does more business this year than it did last; that customers return year after year; that customers recommend the product to others; that the company opens new markets and that it reaches more clients. The key words are 'passion' and 'improvement'. Let your enthusiasm show as you tell them about the improvements you've made in the past to sales figures, customer retention, company reputation, etc. Include actual figures where possible.

Q 'How do you handle rejection?'

Rejection is a common occurrence in sales. The interviewer wants to know if you're robust enough to bounce back quickly and without a loss of confidence or self-esteem that will damage your effectiveness. A good answer shows that you accept rejection as part of the job without taking it personally and, in fact, it just makes you more determined.

Example

'Rejection is simply part of the job; some people simply don't want what I'm selling, I don't take it personally. If anything, it makes me more determined. For example, [give an anecdote where you were rejected and it made you more determined to succeed. If possible, describe how it made a positive difference – made you look for a new market or new clients, change your approach, or maybe even how you tried a new approach with the same client and were successful].'

Q 'How do you handle tension?'
Q 'How do you deal with pressure?'

Selling is often a stressful job. Companies want sales people with drive and enthusiasm, but they don't want people who are going to crack up with stress. At a time when workers are suing employers for stress-related illness, the interviewer wants to know that you are stress-hardy and able to look after yourself.

> **Example**
>
> 'I've always been good with stress. Even during exams at school/college, I was the one who stayed calm. I believe it's because I'm good at planning and organizing. I [describe some of the things you do to organize your work and schedules]. It means the practical things rarely get on top of me or drag me down, which leaves me free to put all my energy into [the most important part of the job, face-to-face selling, for example]. I think I need a degree of tension to focus me anyway. I like to feel that tingle [or however you would describe it] when I [go in to see a client, meet a customer, pick up the phone, etc]. Life would be flat without that.'

Q 'Have you ever failed to reach your target?'

If you did, it was long ago, you didn't have the skill and experience you've got now and there were extenuating circumstances. Follow up with how you or your behaviour changed as a result.

> **Example**
>
> 'I successfully meet all my current targets, but I remember, when I first started with [an early employer], I didn't have the experience I have now and I came close to missing my targets once or twice. I had to [describe the extra efforts you had to go through to meet them]. I learnt as a result to [include something you learnt – how to plan your time, how to focus your efforts, not to procrastinate].'

Q 'When was the last time you felt angry?'

Q 'Do you ever lose your temper?'

If you lose your temper with a colleague, you'll cause friction and unpleasantness. Lose your temper with a client and you could lose the company thousands of pounds, not just for that order but from any order they might have placed in the future, the orders from people they've told about your outburst and so on. Reassure the interviewer that you are not the sort of person who ever loses their temper.

> **Example**
>
> 'Oh, I get angry about [something reasonable but slightly vague – world hunger or injustice, for example], just like everyone else, but I can't say that everyday pressures affect me much. I can't remember the last time I actually lost my temper.'

Q *'How many hours a week would you say you work currently?'*

You need to balance your answer between putting in enough hours to get the sales and heading for a breakdown from overwork.

Example

'It's variable. I put in the time that it takes to meet my targets and my own high standards. I plan my time effectively and I'm good at scheduling, so I believe I work efficiently, but there are always times when something crops up or you spot an opportunity. That's when it's worth putting in the extra hours.'

Q *'How do you plan your workload?'*

Q *'How do you schedule your sales trips?'*

Ideally, you want to spend as much time as possible on productive work, and minimize, as much as possible, necessary but non-productive things like record keeping, travelling to appointments, etc. Explain how you achieve this and illustrate it with a typical example.

Q *'Describe a difficult problem you've had to deal with.'*

Q *'Describe a difficult sale you've made.'*

This question offers you the opportunity to show yourself in the best light. Pick a difficult or problematic sale and describe the skill, experience and personal qualities you used to overcome all the hurdles successfully. Avoid, however, anything that suggests you have a problem getting on with people or following management decisions, as these will sound alarm bells for the interviewer. Don't forget to emphasize the benefit to the company of your success, along with facts and figures where possible.

Be prepared; the interviewer might try to take the wind out of your sails with the follow-up question, *'Now tell me about a time when you were less successful.'* Have an anecdote ready from the early part of your career and include the valuable lesson you learnt from the experience.

Q *'What do you think is the key to successful negotiation?'*

Q *'What is your approach to selling?'*

You will have your own views on this one. The trick is actually to have an answer, rather than um and er about it. Good answers currently include something about cooperation, motivation, customer-led negotiation and win–win formulas. Follow up with an anecdote about a time when you applied your principles with great success.

Q 'What are your views on customer service?'

The interviewer is looking for a positive attitude and the assurance that customer service is high among your priorities, no matter how difficult, demanding or unreasonable the customer might be.

Example

'I would say I put customer service at the top of my priorities. Happy customers buy; unhappy ones don't. For example, [give a couple of anecdotes about times you've dealt successfully with difficult, demanding or angry customers or clients].'

Q 'What motivates you in your job?'

In selling, money is an acceptable motivation, which is why so many jobs work on a commission basis. It's nice, however, to be able to give some broader motivation – it shows your depth of character.

Example

'I like winning [for example]. When I do my job well, listen to clients, meet all their needs and objections and make that sale, I feel an enormous sense of achievement.'

Q 'How do you find out what your competitors are doing?'

How do you keep ahead of the competition? Your answer would ideally include as many as possible of the following:

professional, trade and business magazines;

online professional and business groups;

business contacts;

professional associations;

trade fairs, shows and exhibitions;

suppliers and clients;

seminars.

Example

'Keeping ahead of the competition means keeping up with new [products, ideas, trends, etc]. I believe that's very important in this job so I [say what you do to keep up]. It takes commitment, but I've found it's been extremely valuable. For example, [tell them how knowing something ahead of time benefited you, your job and the company].'

Anticipate the follow-up question: *'What do you see as the future trend right now?'* which was covered earlier in this chapter.

Professional knowledge

You can also expect to be asked questions that explore specific details of your professional knowledge. These questions are too varied and too individual to be gone into here, but as a sales professional you should be able to anticipate what the interviewer will ask. The questions will be based on things like:

   your detailed knowledge of products, markets, etc;

   your understanding of specific sales and marketing techniques;

   your areas of experience and any specialized knowledge you have;

   how you approach specific situations;

   how you handle specific tasks and assignments.

It's possible you may also be asked to sell something to the interviewer to check your confidence and technique – *'Sell me this pen,'* for example.

In all your answers, however basic or practical, make sure you get your enthusiasm and energy across to the interviewer.

EXPERT QUOTE

When you've answered the question, stop talking. Remember, an interview is meant to be a dialogue, not a monologue. If you go on at length it restricts the number of different areas that the interviewer can explore in the time available. At the end the interviewer is likely to feel frustrated that they don't know enough about you other than that you talk a lot.

Robert Johnson, Area Director, ACAS South West

EXPERT QUOTE

If you look at the interviewer and talk *to* them rather than *at* them, you'll see if they're interested or not. If their eyes start to glaze over, stop talking.

David Giles, Resourcing Manager, Westland Helicopters

10
Questions for technical jobs

Core question: 'Can you do the job?'

Typical jobs:

engineer;

system controller;

technician;

computer programmer;

design engineer;

draughtsperson;

applications programmer;

laboratory technician;

biomedical engineer;

medical technologist;

chemical technician;

civil engineer;

systems analyst;

dietician;

electrical engineer;

metallurgist;

surveyor;

clinical psychologist.

People heading large teams or managing projects might find some of the questions in Chapter 11 useful as well.

Technical personnel are responsible for carrying out production methods or processes with precision, accuracy and efficiency. As they are often the most knowledgeable people with regard to that method or process, they are often expected to be problem solvers as well.

Staff changeovers in technical posts can mean loss of money in downtime for the company. The more quickly a new employee can take up the reins, the smaller the loss. The interviewer needs to know that you have the technical expertise, knowledge and experience to do the job and are able to fill the vacancy with as little disruption to the department as possible. As the work is often complex, demanding and highly skilled, the interviewer's main concern is: *'Can you do the job?'*

The key qualities they are looking for when interviewing for technical positions are:

specific technical skills;

qualifications that guarantee those skills;

experience in specific areas;

dependability and accuracy;

a methodical approach;

organization;

the ability to work with others.

You need to be able to generate confidence in the interviewer that you have the competence, experience and technical expertise to do the job effectively and thoroughly. Prior to the interview, review your career history with a special focus on:

Your key skills. Emphasize your knowledge and competence in applying that knowledge. Look at your skill areas and your experience. Put together anecdotes about situations requiring the use of those skills and the benefits to your employer resulting from them. Be clear too about the benefits of your qualifications and training. What do they mean you can *do*, how do they make you more competent in the job and how does that benefit your employer?

Your career history. Experience brings knowledge, competence and proficiency. Concentrate on the areas of responsibility you've covered, the skills you used and the experience you gained.

Keep these important points in mind while you think about the questions that follow.

Q 'What do you know about our company?'

You need to know about any products or processes that you will be involved with if appointed. Find out as much as you can from the company website, company report, etc, as well as getting a broader perspective from industry journals, etc (see Chapter 2). Think logically and intelligently about what you read and outline a short but thorough summary, ending with why the company, its products and its technical procedures interest you, and why you want to join it.

Q 'What do you think the key trends in the industry are?'

Technology changes almost daily, and companies can't afford to lag behind their competitors, so you need to be up to date with what's happening in your field. Keep an eye on the professional journals, trade magazines, etc (see Chapter 2), as well as the newspapers. Outline the key trends as you see them, keeping your view optimistic and focusing on the interesting opportunities these developments offer.

Q 'How do you keep up with developments in your profession?'

Your answer should ideally include as many as possible of the following:

  professional, trade and business magazines;

  online professional groups;

  business contacts;

  professional associations;

  trade fairs, shows and exhibitions;

  suppliers and clients;

  courses and seminars.

> **Example**
>
> 'Keeping up with new [products, ideas, trends, etc] is, naturally, very important in this job. I [say what you do to keep up]. It takes a bit of commitment, but I've found it to be essential. For example, [tell them an anecdote about how knowing something ahead of time benefited you, your job and the company].'

Q 'Describe how your current job relates to the overall goals of your department or company.'

In other words, can you see the wider picture? Technical people, because their jobs are often so specialized, can sometimes become a bit remote from the rest of the company. Explain the relationship between:

  your job and the department;

  your department and other departments;

  your department and the company as a whole.

Explain how your job goals contribute to the company's goals and how you perceive they fit into the company vision and, where appropriate, mission statement.

Q 'How do you keep aware of what's happening in other departments?'

Give a brief description of what you do to keep yourself aware of the bigger picture within your company and how you maintain communication through things such as:

  newsletters;

  internal memos;

  departmental and interdepartmental meetings.

Q 'Do you like analytical tasks?'
Q 'Would you say you have good analytical skills?'

Not uncommonly in technical jobs, the post you've applied for includes a high proportion of analytical tasks, so you have to give a positive answer to this question. A simple 'Yes' is less convincing, though, than an answer that offers a descriptive anecdote.

Example

'I enjoy doing analytical tasks. I believe I have [the personal qualities that contribute – eye for detail, patience, methodical approach, numerical aptitude, etc], and I've developed this further by [training, experience]. I believe they are valuable skills; [give a brief anecdote about a time your analytical skills were of benefit to the company]. My decision to apply for this job is [to some extent, to a large degree, depending on your own tastes and the nature of the job] influenced by that.'

Q 'What are your qualifications for this job?'

Give the interviewer an outline of your relevant qualifications and then follow up with your experience, which shows your qualifications in use.

Example

'I have [give your key qualifications]. I also have [relevant in-work training] and [any training you've undertaken on your own behalf]. This means that [explain why these mean you can do the job and why they are of benefit to the company]. In addition to my qualifications, I also have [give your relevant experience]. Because of this experience, I have a [thorough, working or practical] knowledge of [a relevant area, process, technology] and am familiar with [another relevant area or process], which means that [show how this makes you suitable for the job, and how the company will benefit].'

Q 'What makes you a good... [what your job is]?'

The answer is your thorough knowledge of whatever your field is. Focus on that and add details of what contributes to it:

your experience in specific areas;

your proficiency in specific skills and/or processes;

the personal qualities that allow you to exercise those skills effectively;

your problem-solving abilities;

your qualifications and training;

your competence and resourcefulness, reliability and precision;

your methodical, organized approach.

Include anecdotes that illustrate these points.

Example

'I would say I am a good [what your job is] because I know [your relevant area] inside out owing to [your training] and [outline your experience]. For example, [give a couple of anecdotes about using the depth and breadth of your knowledge to solve problems, and the benefit to your employer].'

Example

'I have x years' experience of [relevant area in which you have experience] and am highly proficient in [two or three of your major skills]. These together with my [two or three of the personal qualities that help you do your job well] ensure that I can do my job thoroughly and expertly. For example, [give a relevant illustration].'

Q 'What are the crucial aspects of your job?'

Q 'How do you define doing a good job in your profession?'

The interviewer is asking what your key tasks and responsibilities are and if you know what your performance indicators are. They also want to know if they are at the forefront of your mind when working. Give the standard criteria you are expected to work to and then follow these up with a more personal definition.

Example

'The most important part of my job is [your key tasks and responsibilities]. The standard performance indicator in [an engineering project, for example] is getting the project complete on time, within budget and to the standard outlined in the project documentation. For me, doing a good job means [give your personal criteria for success].'

Q 'Why should I hire you?'

The basis of a good answer might be 'Because I know [xyz] inside out and have an excellent track record of [whatever is important in your job – technical solutions, business solutions, problem solving, etc].' Clarify with specific, relevant details.

Q 'What are your greatest strengths?'

Q 'What are your outstanding qualities?'

Your greatest strengths are your technical skills and your ability to use those skills to solve problems and complete projects on time and to budget. Pick a couple of really strong points and put them across powerfully. Choose the ones most relevant to the job you are applying for.

Example

'I believe my greatest strengths are my technical skills and my ability to use those skills to solve problems and complete projects on time and to budget. For example, [tell them what you've achieved in the past].'

Example

'I would say my greatest strengths with regard to this job are my [pick your most relevant technical skill], my experience in [most relevant experience] and my [your most relevant personal quality and say why it is important]. I have x years' experience, and my knowledge of [a key, relevant knowledge area] and familiarity with [a relevant process, technology, etc] mean that I would be able to make a significant contribution from the beginning. I also believe my current employer would agree that one of my key strengths is my ability to do the job even when things get tough. For example, [describe a time you completed a job or tackled a problem under difficult conditions and the resulting benefit to the company].'

Q 'What are your greatest accomplishments/achievements?'

Successful technical people have a track record of practical achievement. After all, the product or process they develop either works or it doesn't, so you need to be able to talk about your achievements confidently. Focus on your success in problem solving, but it also shows you as a well-rounded person if you can include brief examples of:

recent achievements rather than things you did years ago;

success you achieved as part of a team;

a time you succeeded in the face of probable defeat, particularly if it shows personal determination as well as your technical skills;

a time you helped someone else achieve success, perhaps in a mentor role.

These will demonstrate that you're a current achiever, can work well with others and can work well under pressure – all positive traits.

Q 'What is your attitude to challenge?'

Think of your answer in terms of problem solving. Show how you relish such challenges and how they spur you to find innovative yet practical and workable solutions. Base your answer on anecdotes about challenges you've taken on in the past and how you've used your skill, knowledge and experience to meet and overcome them. Include the benefit your success brought to the company.

Q 'What is your attitude to risk?'

Challenge and risk are two different things. 'Risk' is one of those double-edged words – nobody wants to be considered unadventurous, but on the other hand you can't afford to be seen as reckless. Risk taking in a technical job can, at worst, be a danger to life and, at best, will probably cost the company money, time and reputation. The ideal answer shows you know how to anticipate risks and take appropriate action to avoid them. If in doubt, ask them what sort of risks they have in mind.

Example

'I would never take a risk that would compromise the safety of the staff or the reputation of the company. For example, [give an illustration of a time you were faced with a big risk and used your problem-solving skills to come up with an innovative solution that avoided it].'

Q 'What are your views on health and safety in your job?'

Some technical jobs involve potentially hazardous processes or working in dangerous environments. The interviewer needs to know that you:

are aware of the importance of health and safety;

know about health and safety issues relevant to your job;

understand and follow regulations;

have any health and safety training.

Cover these points in your answer.

Q 'Have you ever had to bend health and safety rules to get a job done?'

On absolutely no account should you ignore health and safety regulations. If you've had an experience in the past where it looked as if a job couldn't be done because of the rules but you found a safe and legal solution, then include that in your answer. Otherwise, don't rise to the bait.

Example

'I've never found it necessary to bend the rules, and I wouldn't expect to be asked to.'

Q 'How do you deal with criticism?'

Managers sometimes find it difficult to criticize or even question the work of technical personnel. Because technical knowledge can be so specialized, it's difficult to assess performance unless the manager is in the same field. The interviewer wants to know if you are going to be difficult or easy to manage in this respect. They are looking for a mature, open-minded answer that shows you can accept constructive criticism while still standing up for your ideas and principles and, where necessary, pointing out technical aspects that may have been overlooked or misunderstood. Provide an anecdote from early in your career that shows you accepting suggestions and learning from them.

Example

'I believe I'm mature enough to handle constructive criticism. It's essential, in fact, if I want to continue to improve my performance. I remember early in my career [describe the event and how it arose. Who did the criticizing?]. I listened to what they said and [when the circumstances were explained] I could see that they had a point. We discussed it and [go on to describe how you came to a mutually agreeable solution]. I learnt from that [something useful in the rest of your career].'

Q 'Would you call yourself a problem solver?'

Q 'Would you say you are innovative?'

Answer this question with a couple of anecdotes illustrating your problem-solving skills. Describe the problem and how you used your skill, knowledge and experience to arrive at an elegant, workable solution. Don't forget to include the benefit to the company.

Q 'Can you work under pressure?'

Q 'What kinds of pressures arise in your job?'

Everybody has to work under pressure at some time. The question here is whether you can maintain your competence, expertise and accuracy while doing so.

Example

'The nature of my job means that I've had to work under pressure [very often, quite often, fairly often, occasionally]. The sort of things that can arise are [give some examples]. I don't find working under pressure a problem; I've learnt to [say what practical things you do to manage it]. I've found that can actually be constructive; there's a tremendous sense of satisfaction when you succeed. For example, [give some examples of when you worked successfully under pressure. If possible, include at least one occasion when the need to maintain accuracy was paramount, and how you achieved that].'

Q 'How do you approach a project?'

They want to know if you are methodical and systematic in your approach. If you aren't, they could see you as unreliable and likely to cost them money and/or reputation when you fail. Take into account:

your problem-solving approach to the project;

resource planning – what you need to get the job done: tools, materials, people, equipment, etc;

time planning – scheduling what must be done when, if the completion date is to be met;

budget planning – allocating money, time and resources to each stage of the project;

contingency planning – what you'll do when things go wrong, including time and cost overspends.

Q 'How do you interact with people at different levels?'

This question will come up when the job you are applying for involves working with two sets of people with different needs and constraints, for example taking the requirements of production staff into consideration as well as those of management, while still being able to put your own view across. Your answer needs to show that you can communicate confidently and effectively with both groups. If you haven't experienced this at work, use an example of interacting successfully with different people on a project in your personal life.

Example

'I can't say I've had problems at any level. In my present job [or whatever experience you are using] I have to work with [the different groups you deal with]. I'm expected to [outline what you do – presentations, discussions, reports – and at what level – departmental, board, client]. For example, [give an illustration outlining how you communicated confidently and effectively with people at different levels of the company].'

Q 'What would you do if your opinion differed from that of your boss?'

The interviewer is assessing how assertive you are. You may be the only person with the specialist technical knowledge. If your boss is about to make a decision that you know won't work, you have a responsibility to tell them that and suggest an alternative. Can you think independently, and can you disagree and get your point across tactfully?

Example

'My current manager is very good about discussing problems and issues and values my experience, so I always have an input into the analysis [it does no harm to say how you expect to be treated]. If my opinion differs from theirs, I try to find out why – what angle they're approaching it from that gives them a different point of view. I then explain the reasons why I think as I do, and in the discussion we usually find a mutually acceptable solution. For example, [include an illustration of a time when that happened].'

Q 'Have you ever had to supervise people more qualified than you?'

This is a not uncommon occurrence in some fields. If the answer is 'Yes', explain the circumstances and go on to describe how you successfully established a sense of rapport and cooperation with them, how you motivated them and how you possibly even learnt from them in an environment of mutual understanding and respect.

If the answer is 'No', explain how you would go about establishing the same conditions as above, drawing on outside experience for examples wherever possible.

Q *'Would you object to being supervised by someone less qualified than you?'*

The inclusion of this question possibly means that your prospective boss is less qualified than you are, so your answer has to be 'No'. Illustrate your reply with any positive examples you have of doing so, drawn from either your working or personal life.

Example

'I did work for someone less technically qualified at [say where and when, in what circumstances]. I don't believe either of us found it a problem. This person was very experienced and an excellent manager and team motivator and we had a very good relationship.'

Q *'Have you written any technical, procedural or training manuals for your company?'*

Q *'Are you involved in writing procedures, specifications, tenders, etc in your current job?'*

They want to know if you can write effectively, clearly and comprehensibly, so that a layperson can understand it. Ideally, if you know the job includes writing manuals, take a couple of examples of anything similar you've written to show the interviewer. If the answer is 'Yes', show your examples and explain how you prepared and wrote them – the planning, things you had to take into consideration, whom you consulted, etc. If the answer is 'No', find the closest thing you can that shows you can write:

confidently;

clearly;

articulately;

with the reader/user in mind.

Describe any tasks in your current job that involve writing – instructions, reports, operating procedures, etc. Include any relevant experience you've had outside work and express your confidence in your ability to apply that experience to the workplace.

Q 'Have you made any presentations in your current job?'

... because you probably will in the one you've applied for. As above, if the answer is 'Yes', give details of the circumstances and describe how you prepare and how you ensure you give a professional presentation. If the answer is 'No', describe any experience you have had of speaking to groups of people, including how you prepared for it and made sure it was proficiently delivered. If presentations are an important feature of the new job, you will probably be asked to give a short example at the interview. You will almost certainly be warned beforehand, so make sure you prepare adequately. See Chapter 19, Interview extras.

Q 'Have you done the best work you're capable of doing?'

If they ask you this question, they are probably looking for high achievers or people who will go on to be high achievers, so the interviewer is assessing your motivation and ambition. There isn't a simple answer to this. If you say 'No', the interviewer will wonder why not. On the other hand, if you say 'Yes', they might assume you've nothing more to offer. Give an answer that reflects your ambition. Tell them that, although you've done some very good work in the past, the position you're applying for now offers you the chance to develop further and do even better.

Example

'I've done some very good work for [your current employer]. For example, I've [briefly recap your key achievements]. However, I believe that [a specific condition of the job you're applying for] would give me the opportunity to do even better [specify how it would improve your performance].'

Q 'Describe a difficult problem you've had to deal with.'

The interviewer doesn't just want to know about the problem; they're much more interested in how you handled it. Pick a difficult technical problem and describe the skills, knowledge and experience that you used to resolve it. Describe how you approached the problem, the factors affecting your decisions and so on, finishing up with the benefit to the company. Don't choose any problem that involved not getting on with colleagues or management as these simply make you look 'difficult' and fail to demonstrate your technical expertise sufficiently.

Q *'How do you go about making important decisions?'*

Q *'Tell me about a difficult decision you had to make.'*

If the job involves a lot of decision making, the interviewer wants to be sure that you have reliable strategies in place. Think about how you make decisions and organize the process into a logical series of steps. Follow with a good example of how you used this strategy in practice.

Example

'When I have an important decision to make, there are four steps [for example] I follow to ensure I choose the best possible option. First, I get together all the facts I can. Secondly, I talk to the people involved in the matter and get their input as well. Thirdly, I examine all aspects and try to predict the possible outcomes. Lastly, I try to foresee any contingencies that might affect my decision along with any problems that might arise from it. When I have all that information, in my experience a clear option usually stands out. Taking into consideration factors such as timing, budget and so forth, it's then usually possible to make an appropriate decision. For example, [briefly outline a decision you made using these steps, its success and its benefit to the company].'

Q *'Are you planning to continue your studies?'*

Adding to your qualifications is usually seen as a positive thing in technical jobs. It shows that you intend to continue adding to and updating your knowledge. Tell them if you've already undergone additional training since leaving college or university, including any in-work training and accredited courses you've done. Reassure the interviewer that you won't be leaving work in the short term to go back into full-time education, but do tell them of any other plans you have to upgrade your value to the company.

Professional knowledge

As well as the questions outlined above, expect to be asked specific questions about your current job and the precise details of your professional knowledge. It's not possible to cover all the possible questions that might come up; they are too technically specific and individual to the job. You know your own work and area of expertise, however, and should be able to predict what they'll ask. They'll be based on things like:

precise details of your technical knowledge;

your understanding of specific processes;

your knowledge and understanding of special techniques;

your experience of using particular machinery or equipment used in your field;

your knowledge of technical software;

how you set about certain tasks commonly occurring in the job;

how you deal with actual situations that arise in your work;

what you would do in specific circumstances likely to occur in the job.

As your role is likely to be that of problem solver to at least some extent, you may also be given examples of possible technical problems to resolve or at least comment on as part of the interview.

As with all questions, give full, detailed answers based on your real-life experiences.

EXPERT QUOTE

Forty-five minutes, the length of the average interview, isn't long to make an impression. I want people who know what they're good at. I also want a sense of involvement and an understanding of how their experience fits our needs and can be of use.

Janet Hembry, Head of Education and Skills Policy,
Government Office for the South West

EXPERT QUOTE

It's all a matter of fit. Do your skills fit our needs? Do we fit yours? Ideally, I want *you* to tell *me* how well suited we are for each other and save me the effort of having to dig for it.

Director, manufacturing company

11
Questions for management jobs

Core question: 'Will you get results?'

Typical jobs:

- retail manager;
- financial manager;
- personnel manager;
- operations manager;
- customer services manager;
- marketing manager;
- sales manager;
- hotel manager;
- services manager;
- technical manager;
- IT manager;
- centre manager;
- brand manager;

account manager;

production manager;

estate manager;

purchasing manager;

public relations manager.

In addition to this chapter on questions for management jobs, managers may also find the questions for their own particular field useful – sales managers looking at the questions in Chapter 9, for example, or customer service managers checking the questions in Chapter 12.

As well as being well versed about your own particular field, you also need to have specific management skills. The interviewer is looking for someone who can:

organize and run a department;

develop and lead a team;

motivate people;

develop the potential in people;

inspire, lead and support;

manage change;

devise and implement strategy;

make decisions and solve problems.

Managers see to it that things happen according to plan within the company. It's the manager's job to ensure that their staff carry out their own jobs effectively and efficiently, and if not to understand what the problem is, devise a solution and implement it.

The key question the interviewer is asking is: *'Will you get results?'* It's essential that the interviewer believes you will be an effective manager, able to do the things listed above. The best way to establish this is to give plenty of examples of when, where and how you've demonstrated these abilities, especially your ability to get results.

When preparing for the interview, remind yourself of:

Your achievements. It's important that the person interviewing you has faith in your ability to be a successful manager, someone who can make a positive difference to performance. Make sure you have plenty of anecdotes illustrating your achievements to date. Where at all possible, include actual figures – profits, costs, percentages, etc.

Your career history. Whether you are currently in a management position or whether this will be your promotion into management, assure them that you will be able to perform the management tasks listed above by giving them plenty of illustrations of occasions when you've successfully demonstrated these abilities and got results. Your experience of interacting effectively with people, as well as encountering and solving problems, is of prime importance.

Your personal qualities. The personal qualities valued in managers are:

- tenacity and perseverance;
- drive and motivation;
- energy, commitment and enthusiasm;
- well-founded confidence;
- reliability, honesty and integrity.

Make sure you have a fund of anecdotes illustrating the times you've demonstrated these qualities.

Your management skills (or potential management skills). Along with the technical and professional skills needed for the type of work you do, certain other skills are required by managers. They are:

- analytical skills: the ability to weigh up the facts in a situation and make an appropriate decision;
- problem-solving skills: the ability to assess options and benefits and arrive at a solution;
- communication skills: the ability to receive and relay information at different levels;
- interpersonal or leadership skills: the ability to motivate, influence and persuade people.

Again, ensure you have compelling anecdotes that demonstrate occasions when you've displayed these skills.

Keep these in mind when you look through the questions that follow.

Q 'What do you know about our company?'

If you're planning to manage a part of it, you'd better know a lot. Get a broad perspective from the company website, company report, newsletter, product/service guide, etc before focusing down on your own particular area of interest. Know where the company is coming from (its background and history) and where it's going (its mission statement, future prospects, current opportunities and so on). You should be able to gather enough information to prepare a SWOT analysis of the company:

  its *strengths* – what it does well, its past and current achievements, its reputation, positive practices, etc;

  its *weaknesses* – no need to parade these at this stage; just make sure you're aware of them;

  its *opportunities* – changes affecting it positively such as potential markets, new prospects, changing environments, technical innovations, workplace changes and legislation, etc;

  its *threats* – negative changes, competitors, diminishing markets and so on.

Use this to prepare a succinct but comprehensive outline, ending up with why the company and its products or services interest you, and how you can contribute, in a management role, to their future growth.

Q 'What do you think the key trends in the industry are?'

As a manager, it's your job to manage change in your department, so you need to be aware of what those changes are likely to be. Keep yourself up to date with what's happening and outline the key trends as you see them. Keep your opinion positive and optimistic, and focus on the potential opportunities these developments offer and how these are likely to affect your department.

Q 'How do you keep up with what's happening in your field?'

This could be a follow-on question from the one above. Include as many as possible of the following methods in your answer:

  professional, trade and business magazines;

  online professional groups;

  business contacts;

  professional associations;

  trade fairs, shows and exhibitions;

  suppliers and clients;

  courses and seminars.

> **Example**
>
> 'Keeping up with new [products, procedures, ideas and trends] is, naturally, very important in this job. I [tell them what you do to keep up]. It takes a bit of commitment, but I've found that it's essential. For example, [give an example of how knowing something ahead of time benefited you, your job and the company, allowing you to anticipate and manage change effectively].'

Q 'How do you manage/have you managed change?'

As a manager in charge of a department or even just a team of people, you will need to deal with everyday changes and adjustments to work patterns, targets and outcomes, procedures and staffing, as well as the big, structural changes organizations have to go through at regular intervals if they are to remain competitive. You not only have to be able to adjust to change yourself; it's your role to make the changes workable and acceptable to your staff.

Rather than try to answer it in the abstract, your best strategy is to answer this question with a real-life example. If you have no workplace experience, use an example from outside work. Outline the situation and then describe how you:

analysed the situation and identified the changes to be made;

stated the actions to be taken;

persuaded the people involved to accept change, especially those reluctant or dubious about the need for it;

supervised the implementation of the actions.

Don't forget to say what positive difference the change made, and the benefit to the organization and the team. If possible, include how you dealt with unforeseen problems and what you learnt from that.

Q 'How would you define your profession?'

Management is a tricky profession; the job title covers so many responsibilities. Read the job description thoroughly to see where the company places the most emphasis – are they chiefly looking for a problem solver or team motivator? Construct your answer around their requirements and perceived needs, building in lots of illustrative anecdotes.

Q 'What can you do for us that no one else can?'

Again, the job description will probably tell you what they *need* you to do for them. Don't worry about no one else being able to do it; the interviewer just needs to see that you are able to match your unique combination of skills, qualities and experience to their specific needs.

Example

'I believe I have the [outline your key strengths and abilities] needed to manage [what it is you will be managing]. To date, I have [mention your relevant achievements]. If I've read the situation correctly, you need someone who [very briefly summarize the job description] and I believe I can bring to this job [key requirements mentioned in the job description]. I have [personal qualities or experience relevant to the job description]. For example, [outline some of your experiences]. In addition, I understand [a main factor of the job], which I believe would allow me to [make some significant contribution to the company].'

Q 'How would you define a conducive working atmosphere?'

It will be your responsibility, as a manager, to create and maintain a conducive working atmosphere for your staff. On the whole, a conducive working atmosphere is one in which the team is productive. Prepare an outline of what you believe encourages the optimum productivity in your experience. You might include things like:

a cohesive team with a united vision;

clear roles and responsibilities within the team;

clear goals and outcomes;

a degree of independence and autonomy for team members;

supportive management;

positive feedback;

whatever else you feel is important.

The next question, of course, is how you have gone/would go about establishing and sustaining such an atmosphere. This is a direct question about your management skills – how you will apply your:

analytical skills;

communication and interpersonal skills;

leadership and motivational skills;

planning, organizational and problem-solving skills.

Example

'I believe the key factors in establishing a productive atmosphere are [whatever you believe them to be]. They are important because [explain why they are necessary in practical terms]. In my experience, [give an anecdote illustrating your successful use of these factors to improve your team's performance].'

Q 'Why should I hire you?'

See the answer to 'What can you do for us that no one else can?' and bear in mind the core question the interviewer is asking and make sure the clear message in your answer is 'Because I can get results.'

Q 'What makes you a good manager?'
Q 'Why do you believe you would make a good manager?'

The job description will tell you what the interviewer thinks some of the key factors to being a good manager are. Make sure you cover all your relevant skills and experience in your answer.

Example

'I think a good manager is someone who [say what you think is the hallmark of a good manager – can develop potential, motivate staff, devise strategy, inspire the team, juggle priorities, etc]. I believe I am/would make a good manager because of my ability to [pick your most relevant management ability], my [your most relevant professional skill] and my [your most relevant personal quality]. Within the past [couple of years, few months] I have [give some examples of your management-relevant achievements]. I believe [outline how your qualities and skills have made these successes possible].'

> **Example**
>
> 'I have x years in [your field of work] and have experience of [outline some specifics, handling both problems and people]. My [skills and abilities] and my knowledge of [a key relevant product, process or management skill] mean I could make a significant contribution to your company from the beginning. I believe my current/previous employer would agree that one of the reasons for my success is my ability to [do the job, motivate the team, produce results, handle problems, whatever your key skill is] even in difficult circumstances. For example, [give an anecdote describing a time you succeeded under difficulties and the resulting benefit to the company].'

Q 'What would you do if we gave you a free hand?'

Unless you are a very senior executive, they are probably not about to give you carte blanche. However, they might genuinely be looking for innovation, and the interviewer might be interested in the extent of your vision, especially if you are being called in to take on a specific project. It does no harm to consider this question before the interview. To answer it, you need to know about the company and the department you'd be managing, what they've done in the past, what their goals are and what their future direction is, which comes down to doing your homework and developing a SWOT analysis as before. Whether you would continue in the company tradition or develop into new areas is a matter for you and your own personal style, but you need to able to explain clearly:

what you would do;

why you would take the decision you propose;

how this would benefit the company.

You also need to do this without being seen to criticize the company or its current methods. It's difficult balancing enthusiasm about both the status quo and potential changes, but if they are looking for a dynamic 'new broom' it could be a rewarding exercise.

Q 'What kinds of decisions are most difficult for you?'
Q 'How do you deal with difficult decisions?'
Q 'Describe a difficult decision you've had to make.'

Management jobs involve a lot of decision making, and this is a two-pronged question. The interviewer finds out what you consider to be difficult decisions; they also find out how you resolve them. Be careful which decision or problem you choose and think of the implications; what kind of decisions will you be making in the job you're applying for? Rather than saying outright what you find difficult, you can hedge a little in your answer. Carry on swiftly to outline how you deal with decisions, and give an example of your successful decision making.

Example

'I've found that decisions that look difficult on the surface often just need more careful consideration. When I have to make an important decision, I use four steps [for example] to make sure I choose the best option. First, I gather all the facts. Secondly, I talk to the people involved and get their opinion. Thirdly, I look at everything and try to predict the possible outcomes. Finally, I try to envisage any problems that might affect my decision along with the eventualities that might develop from it. In my experience, once I have all that information a clear option usually emerges and it's possible to make a decision, taking into consideration factors such as timing, budget and so forth. For example, [briefly outline a decision you made using these steps, its success and its benefit to the company].'

Q 'Describe a difficult problem you've had to deal with.'

As above, choose your problem with regard to the problems you'll be dealing with in the new job, and pick one that shows off your most relevant management skills at their best. Describe the skills, knowledge and experience you used to resolve the problem. Describe how you approached it, the factors affecting your decisions, how you put the solution into effect and so on, finishing up with the benefit to the company.

Having listened to your answer, the interviewer may follow up with *'Now tell me about a time when the outcome was less successful.'* They want to know how you cope with adversity and disappointment. Choose an event from the early part of your career – when you were young and foolish – and emphasize the valuable lesson you learnt from it.

Q 'What would you do if I told you your presentation earlier was terrible?'

Don't worry, your presentation was probably fine – this is a stress question designed to unsettle you. Don't rise to the bait. The question the interviewer is really asking is *'How do you respond to criticism?'* Prove that you are a mature, open-minded individual who can accept and act on constructive criticism to improve their performance, while still standing their ground.

> **Example**
>
> 'Well, I'm always grateful for advice that will improve my performance. Perhaps you could tell me which aspects of my presentation you weren't happy with. If you could point out where you feel the problem lies, I can clear up any misunderstandings.'

Q 'How do you respond to criticism?'

As in most jobs, your performance is going to be assessed and this could lead to criticism – the suggestion that you could do something better or at least differently. For managers who are used to being in the leadership role, this can be difficult. The interviewer wants to know if you are going to be one of the difficult ones. As above, demonstrate that you are an emotionally mature person who can take advice yet still stand up for their ideas and principles. A good way to do this is to give an anecdote from your early career that shows you accepting suggestions calmly and reasonably and learning from them.

> **Example**
>
> 'I don't take it personally if that's what you mean. I believe I'm mature enough to handle constructive criticism. In fact, it's essential if I want to continue to improve my performance. I remember earlier in my career, [describe the event and how it arose. Who did the criticizing?]. I listened to what they said and [when the circumstances were explained] I could see that they had a point. We discussed it and [go on to describe how you came to a mutually agreeable solution]. I learnt from that [describe the lesson you learnt and how it was useful to you in the future].'

Q 'What are your greatest strengths?'

Q 'What are your outstanding qualities?'

Q 'What would you say are the reasons for your success?'

Your greatest strength is your ability to get results. That's the key quality required in a manager, and it's the point you should highlight in any question asking about your strengths, qualities or achievements. Pick out the skills and qualities that support this ability.

Example

'I would say my greatest strength/outstanding quality with regard to this job is my ability to get results. For example, [tell them about the results you've achieved and how you've achieved them].'

Example

'I believe my present employer would agree that one of my key strengths is my ability to get results even in difficult circumstances. For example, [describe what you did and how you did it and the benefit it was to the company].'

Q 'What are your greatest accomplishments/achievements?'

Successful management people are usually achievers. They are, after all, people who get results. You need to be able to talk about your achievements fluently and confidently. Focus on your successes in tackling problems, but it's also useful if you can also include examples of:

  an achievement against the odds, especially if it demonstrates your personal qualities or leadership skills;

  a time when you helped someone else achieve success in a management or mentor role;

  a team success rather than a solo achievement;

  achievements that are recent rather than past glories.

These will show that you are an achiever who works well with a team and functions effectively under pressure.

Q 'What are you looking for in a job?'

Q 'What motivates you?'

Think in terms of what you can give rather than what you can get. Most people in management are looking for the opportunity to use their skills and experience to put their own stamp on an organization and make a significant contribution.

Example

'I'm looking for the opportunity to make a difference. My experience at [the company you work for or the work you currently do] has shown me that I have a talent for [what's relevant to the job you're applying for]. I believe that's clearly demonstrated by [your principal achievements]. I am looking for the opportunity to continue to achieve success at that level and beyond, in a company with a first-rate product/service/reputation [whatever the key attraction is for you] that will give me the support to develop professionally. I believe this company/position offers just such an opportunity.'

Q 'When was the last time you lost your temper?'

As a manager, you're allowed to get a little more worked up than other professions, but only in the right way for the right reasons. You must be able to remain calm in the face of provocation, but it's important to show that you're no mild-mannered pushover.

Example

'I can't remember the last time I actually lost my temper. Everyday irritations don't affect me that much; there's always something you have to deal with. It's just a part of life. However, I take a very strong line with my staff over [something important – honesty, customer courtesy, bullying, etc]. For example, [give an anecdote about a time you had to tackle someone about this problem. Show how you dealt with it reasonably and fairly and maintained a good working relationship as well as your temper].'

Q 'What is your attitude to challenge?'

Q 'What is your attitude to risk?'

Managers need to be able to face up to challenges and even take calculated risks, should the need arise. What the company doesn't need is a reckless maverick with a thirst for danger. Use anecdotes to show typical challenges and risks you've met and overcome in the past. Present the challenge in terms of problem solving, demonstrate the range of skills you used to resolve it and make it clear that when you take on a challenge you intend to succeed. If in doubt, ask the interviewer what sort of challenges or risks they have in mind.

Example

'I believe that meeting and overcoming challenges is the way to grow and develop. For example, [outline the problem that challenged you. Include details of how you analysed the problem, weighed the options and came to a decision about what to do, and the skills you used to carry it out]. As a result, the company/team [state what the positive benefits were] and I learnt [how you developed positively because of the challenge]. Since then, I've gone on to [how you've continued to develop since].'

Example

'I've would never endanger the reputation [or whatever else is important] of the company, but I admit circumstances have demanded that I take a risk from time to time. For example, [give an anecdote about a time you took a risk that paid off. Include details of how the circumstances arose, how you analysed the risk, weighed the options, came to the decision it was worth it, and kept your employer in the picture. Say how the risk paid off for the company, not just for you]. On another occasion, however, [give another anecdote about a time you were faced with taking a big risk but came up with a solution that avoided it that was just as innovative].'

Q 'Would you say you are confident?'

You want to be confident, not cocky. You can put that across by focusing on how you have earned that confidence and how you have built firm foundations for it.

Example

'Yes, I would say that I'm a confident person. I'm certainly confident of my ability to [undertake the key responsibilities of the job]. My confidence is based on my [relevant abilities], my [relevant professional skill] and my [relevant personal qualities]. Within the past [couple of years, few months] I have [give examples of your achievements]. I believe [outline briefly how your qualities have contributed to these successes]. Having worked x years in [your field of work or specific skills], I believe my confidence to be well founded on experience.'

Q 'This job needs someone who is passionate about business improvement.
Is that you?'

The interviewer wants to know that you feel committed to the company, fully involved
with its development and responsible for ensuring the company's success. You need
to demonstrate clearly that you believe your job to be a fundamental component
of that overall achievement, and that you are able to look at the wider picture rather
than just focusing on your own narrow goals. Use anecdotes to demonstrate that
improving business has always been one of your top priorities and when, how and
where you've actually achieved that. Let your enthusiasm shine through as you talk.

Q 'Would you say you have authority?'

A manager who considers other people's views is one thing. One whose staff or team
argue with every decision or instruction is another. As a manager, you need to have
authority, but without being authoritarian and domineering. Your answer needs to show
that you can gain the respect of your staff while still being pleasant and supportive. If
in doubt, ask the interviewer if they have a particular situation in mind.

Example

'I don't have problems with authority in my current job. I foster an attitude of mutual respect
within my team and I'm certain they could come to me if they had any doubts or uncertainty
about anything I've asked them to do. I set clear goals and targets and, where it's appropriate,
encourage full discussion and keep them informed of the reasons behind my decisions [or
anything else you do]. At the end of the day, though, I expect them to respect my decisions and
act on my instructions, and I'm happy to say no one has let me down yet. For example, [discuss
a time when you tactfully and successfully exerted your authority].'

If the follow-up question is *'Have you ever had any trouble exerting your authority?'*
give an example from early in your management career and say what you learnt from
the experience.

Q 'Are you ambitious?'

Demonstrate you have the right sort of ambition – focused, hard working and goal
orientated rather than back-stabbing.

> **Example**
>
> 'Yes, I would certainly say I am ambitious. I have the drive, enthusiasm and [add your own qualities] to make a significant contribution to the company I work for. For example, [give an anecdote that demonstrates your ambition in a favourable way – overcoming difficulties to achieve a goal, for example, either in the workplace or outside it]. I'm not saying that I would ever trample over a colleague to reach my goals – that's usually very unproductive anyway – but I'm very clear about where I want to be and what I want to do.'

Q 'Would you say you are innovative?'

Innovative people come up with new ideas and new solutions to problems. Your best answer to this question is to give an anecdote about a time when you used lateral thinking to come up with a creative and successful approach to a challenge that benefited the company.

Q 'Would you say you are determined?'

They're asking if you will become demoralized and give up in the face of discouragement – not a great virtue when you have to lead and motivate others. Answer this question with a couple of anecdotes that demonstrate your determination in action. One of them should be from the workplace, but you could also include something from outside work if this illustrates your determination better. Make the outcome one worth the effort, and don't forget to include the benefit to the company in the work-related situation.

Q 'Would you describe yourself as a problem solver?'

Of course you would. Illustrate your answer with an anecdote demonstrating your problem-solving skills. Describe the problem, explain how you used your knowledge and experience to resolve it and say what the resulting benefits to the company were.

Q 'How do you interact with people at different levels?'

Managers often need to deal with, and be able to communicate effectively with, all levels within the company. They can sometimes be pig in the middle, too, mediating between employees and senior management. Show that you have experience of interacting effectively with many different types of people either at work or outside it.

Example

'I have no difficulty working with anyone at any level. In [my current job, past career, voluntary position] I've had to [give some examples of the people you've worked with]. I'm used to dealing with a broad range of people. For example, [give an example of a project you worked on, for example, that engaged a wide range of participants. Say how you interacted with them confidently and effectively and what the positive outcome was].'

Q 'Why do you feel developing people is important?'

One of the responsibilities of a manager in a good company is to ensure that staff are developed to their full potential, enhancing their usefulness and value to the organization, as well as increasing motivation and job satisfaction.

Example

'I believe that people are the company's most important asset. They are vital to effective performance and success [and whatever else you believe to be key factors]. Developing their potential is an important element in maintaining motivation and job satisfaction [and anything else you think is important], which are key elements in productivity. With my own staff/team, I make sure I understand their career aims, identify the skills they would benefit from and would like to learn, and put together a programme to make that achievable using available resources. I ensure they're supported while they're learning and give them every opportunity to use the new skills they're developing [or anything else you do]. Would you like me to go into more detail about training?'

If the answer is 'Yes', provide the factual details about what you do and how you do it, and then give an anecdote illustrating the success it's been and the value to your company.

Q 'What do you regard as the essential skills for motivating people?'
Q 'How do you get the best from people?'
Q 'How important do you think motivation skills are for a manager?'

As a manager, you can't just demand a good performance from people; you have to motivate them to deliver it. The interviewer wants to see that you have the necessary motivational skills to get the best from your team. Give examples of what you do and how you do it, either from work or in a motivational role outside the workplace.

Example

'I think good motivational skills are essential for a manager. Getting the members of a team/ department working together towards a common goal with enthusiasm and purpose [or whatever else you value] is vital for performance. I make sure my team have clear goals and targets, and understand how those contribute to the overall aims of the company. They know why their role is important and how it fits in with the rest of the organization. All the members are kept informed about developments and, where appropriate, involved in discussions and contribute to the decision-making process [and whatever else you do that motivates your staff]. I also make the effort to understand the personal motivations of my staff, be they recognition, challenge, responsibility or whatever. As a result my staff are, I believe, well motivated and work well both individually and as a team. For example, [give an example demonstrating your motivational skills and your team's resulting achievements – excellent productivity rates, high rates of promotion, good bonuses, award-winning team, etc].'

Follow-up questions could ask you for specific details of events, such as *'Tell me about a team member you had difficulty motivating. What did you do about it?'* or *'Tell me about a difficult team member you had to deal with. How did you handle them?'*

Q *'What makes a good leader in your view?'*

Q *'Do you see yourself as a leader or a follower?'*

Managers need good leadership skills, so it's natural to assume that the interviewer is looking for someone who is a strong leader – dynamic and confident with a strong personality. They probably *do* want that, but a manager may also have to be a good negotiator and mediator. The employer might want strong, dynamic leadership balanced with someone who can also listen, empathize and be guided by the requirements of others. The job description should tell you what it wants, so you can show the appropriate balance in your answer.

Example

'I believe being a good leader is a matter of motivation. Good leaders are people who can keep a team enthusiastic and committed to success despite difficult and challenging conditions. I would say that I am, by nature, a leader and I think most people who know me and work with me would agree with that. I [give some examples of your strong leadership skills in action, either in the workplace or outside it]. However, I've found that to be a good manager it pays to be as versatile as possible, depending on the situation. For example, [give an anecdote about a time when listening to someone, being empathic, etc was beneficial. Go on to describe how you used negotiating skills, influencing skills and gentle motivation rather than forceful dynamism to get a result].'

Q *'What are the key factors for a successful team?'*

Q *'What skills do you feel are essential to team building?'*

The difference between a good team and a bad team can mean the difference between profit and loss for a department and even the company as a whole. It's not enough that you can do the job; you must be able to inspire the rest of your department or team to do their jobs as well. Building a good team that runs smoothly with high productivity is an essential management skill.

Example

'I believe a successful team is one where the members are committed to each other and to the successful achievement of a worthwhile goal [for example]. I believe it's up to me as the team leader to ensure that the team is more than just a collection of people working on the same project but a real team pulling together with a strong sense of cohesion. I ensure this in my own team [in the workplace or in some other role] by seeing that everyone knows what their role is within the team and how important it is to the overall outcome. I make sure that individual skill and input are valued and appreciated not just by me, but by everyone concerned. I encourage team members to support each other to complete tasks rather than focusing exclusively on their own responsibilities, and reward the group collectively when they achieve team goals [or whatever else you do to encourage a team spirit]. I also [tell them about anything else you do to support team unity – group activities, group bonuses, social and bonding activities, etc]. I believe I have a strong and unified team. Over the past [few months, year, couple of years] we have [give some examples of the things your group has achieved].'

Q *'How do you prioritize your workload?'*

The most important thing is that you *do* prioritize your workload – almost any method will do; it doesn't have to be spectacular. Most systems include things like:

listing tasks;

identifying them as one of the following:

- – urgent and important;
- – urgent but not important;
- – important but not urgent;
- – neither urgent nor important;

deciding on an order for dealing with the first two classes of tasks as your highest priority;

scheduling, delegating or deleting, as appropriate, the second two classes of task.

You might also be asked, as a follow-up question, how you decide which tasks are important, which urgent and so on. You need to be clear what your key objectives are, and what your tasks and responsibilities are in order to be able to answer.

Q 'How many hours a week do you currently work?'

This is not as easy as it first appears. Few management jobs these days have set 9-to-5 hours, and your answer needs to strike a balance between putting in enough time to get the work done and burning out from overwork.

Example

'I find it's variable. I put in the hours that it takes to cover the workload and to meet my own high standards, and there are always times when something unexpected crops up. I plan my time effectively, though, and I'm good at scheduling and prioritizing, so I believe I work efficiently.'

Q 'How do you handle stress?'

Q 'How do you work under pressure?'

Management is often stressful, so the interviewer wants to be reassured that you are stress-hardy and able to look after yourself. Show in your answer that, while you have drive and enthusiasm, you're not likely to crack up from stress.

Example

'I've always been good with stress. I was always the one who stayed calm during school and college exams. I believe it's because I'm good at planning and prioritizing. I [describe some of the things you do to organize your workload]. It means that everyday things rarely get on top of me, and it leaves me free to put my energy into [the most important part of the job]. A degree of tension gets the adrenalin going, anyway. I think life would be a bit flat without it.'

Q *'What kinds of pressures do you face in your current job?'*

Everybody in management has to work under pressure at some time. The question here is whether you can maintain your competence and exercise skill and good judgement while doing so.

Example

'The nature of my job means that I have to work under pressure [very often, quite often, fairly often, occasionally]. The sort of things that can arise are [give some examples]. I've found that working under pressure can actually be quite constructive. Having to call on untapped strengths and inner resources can be very stimulating and, of course, there's a tremendous sense of satisfaction when you succeed. For example, [give an example of when you worked successfully under pressure. If possible, also include an occasion when you had to keep a team together under pressure, and how you achieved that].'

Q *'What are you like at influencing and persuading?'*

Give some anecdotes to illustrate your skills. Avoid seeming manipulative and Machiavellian by choosing situations where you were persuading someone to do something that was either to their advantage or best for the group or organization as a whole. Describe the skills you used to get on their wavelength and outline the benefits of your proposal to negotiate a win–win outcome.

Q *'How long do you think it would take you to make a contribution?'*

As a rough guide, most companies expect you to have picked up the reins and be doing a reasonable job within a couple of months, and making a substantial contribution with a significant degree of achievement in around six to nine months. Explain that's what is expected in your current job, and give details of how you have met those targets satisfactorily.

Professional knowledge

As well as the questions detailed above, there will also be questions that ask you about specific practical aspects of your job and the job you're applying for, as well as details of your professional knowledge. You know your own responsibilities and tasks best, so anticipate what might be asked and how you can respond concisely, informatively and effectively. Expect precise, detailed questions on:

your areas of experience in detail;

your knowledge of specific management techniques;

your experience in handling common problems;

your approach to specific situations arising in the job;

your understanding of the responsibilities of the job.

The sort of questions asked might include things like:

'What are the main factors to consider when planning for growth?'

'What conflicts do you anticipate between the needs of the shareholders and those of employees, and how would you balance them?'

'Tell me about some of the projects you've worked on.'

'What methods do you use to predict future workloads?'

'What sort of training methods do you use to develop your staff?'

'Have you used MBO (management by objective) techniques before?'

'Are you familiar with Total Quality Control? Do you use it currently?'

'What software packages do you currently use for project management?'

'Could you tell me more about [anything you've mentioned on your CV or application form]?'

'What type of training do you think is most effective?'

'How do you go about recruiting a new member for the team?'

'How do you make sure meetings run to time?'

'What type of appraisal systems do you use?'

'How do you organize and plan for major projects?'

Give full, detailed, knowledgeable answers that demonstrate the full range of your experience and show your enthusiasm for the nuts and bolts of the job.

EXPERT QUOTE

Don't oversell yourself. Don't be too pushy, take over the interview or lecture the panel. Be sincere about the skills and experience you have to offer.

Helen Cole, Learning Services Coordinator, South West TUC

EXPERT QUOTE

Look the interviewer in the eye and smile but don't be too brash. Don't use their first name, for example, unless they actually ask you to.

HR Manager, retail company

12
Questions for customer relations jobs

Core question:
'Are you customer focused?'

Typical jobs:

sales assistant;

receptionist;

market researcher;

customer services;

customer relations;

telephone helpline;

cabin staff;

waiter or waitress;

demonstrator;

leisure and tourism;

consumer researcher;

travel agent;

travel rep;

hospitality worker.

People working in sales may find the questions in Chapter 9 helpful too. Those with an administrative role as well may find it useful to look through the questions in Chapter 8.

Customer relations jobs are those where the main focus is on dealing with people – the general public, clients or customers. This can be face to face or on the phone, and can mean making sales, answering queries, dealing with complaints or offering help and advice. Customer relations staff are the 'face' of the company, the part of the company the public deal with, and most employers want their customer relations staff to be:

friendly, outgoing and approachable;

confident;

helpful, cooperative and obliging;

articulate;

knowledgeable.

The key question for anyone applying for a job in customer relations is: *'Are you customer focused?'* So the questions the interviewer asks are designed to find out if you:

enjoy dealing with people;

have a positive approach to customer service;

have good influencing and persuading skills (especially in sales jobs);

have good interpersonal and communication skills;

can behave with courtesy, tact and diplomacy;

are calm under pressure.

Before the interview, review your:

Experience of dealing with people. Experience brings confidence. Assess all the different dealings you've had with people, in any capacity – at work or through a people-focused hobby or voluntary role – looking for experiences you can draw on. How have you handled difficult people in the past? How have you established rapport? How have you told someone something difficult that they didn't want to hear? Think about what you did that was successful, and what you learnt from each experience. Build up a rich fund of anecdotes about your actual experience ready for the interview.

Personal qualities. Look at the qualities and characteristics that make you good at dealing with people in a positive way. Gather together examples of when and how you've demonstrated these qualities. Keep these examples in mind as you go through the following questions.

Q 'What do you know about our company?'

If you're appointed, you'll be representing the company. You'll be customers' first contact with it, possibly their main contact when they're angry or have a problem. It's important that you display some interest and enthusiasm in the company by finding out who they are and what they do. As well as having some understanding of their products or services, it's important to be aware of how they want the public or their clients and customers to see them. Take note of the image they present, the reputation they promote, etc, and think about the market they're appealing to. Is their reputation for quality, innovation or value for money? Are they traditional or leading-edge? They'll want their values reflected in the attitude of their staff.

Q 'What do you see as the crucial aspects of your job/profession?'

Your top priority must be dealing with people, and your answer should cover things like:

customer satisfaction;

making sure the customer has a positive experience of the company;

establishing rapport;

listening;

whatever else you've found to be crucial.

Read the job advertisement for what other factors the company considers essential to the job you're applying for (efficiency, ability to work under pressure or attention to detail, for example) and structure your answer accordingly. Be prepared to answer any follow-up questions about when and where you've demonstrated these abilities, so have plenty of good, illustrative anecdotes ready.

Q 'What are your greatest strengths?'

Q 'What are your outstanding qualities?'

Q 'What makes you a good... [what your job is]?'

Your key strengths are your customer relations skills. Pick two or three really strong skills and talk about them confidently and enthusiastically, illustrating them with anecdotes from your past experience.

Example

'I believe my greatest strength for this job is my experience of dealing with customers. I have [outline your experience], which has developed [your key customer-service skills]. It means I can handle a variety of situations, such as [give some anecdotes about some of the things you've dealt with successfully, using skill and diplomacy].'

Example

'I would say my greatest strengths with regard to this job are my [pick your most important customer skills]. I believe I'm naturally [your most relevant personal quality – open, friendly, approachable], which means that [say why this quality is important]. I have x number of years' experience working in [your field of work] and have a thorough knowledge of [a key skill – answering complaints, giving help and advice, etc]. My track record includes [state your range of experience and achievements], which I believe [outline the relevance to the company you are applying to]. Finally, I believe my current employer would agree that one of my key strengths is my ability to do the job even in the most pressured circumstances. For example, [describe a time you achieved success under difficult conditions and the benefit to the company].'

Q 'What are your views on customer service?'

Your views need to be very positive. Show that you understand its value and importance and that it is top of your priorities with anecdotes from your experience that demonstrate that.

Example

'I believe customer service is of prime importance. In my last/current job, 60 per cent of sales were made to return customers rather than new clients [for example]. If they weren't happy with our customer service, they'd go elsewhere and that would mean an awful lot of lost sales for us. I believe that how you deal with [complaints, enquiries, queries or whatever is most relevant for your situation] is crucial and can make a big difference to the customer's experience of the company. For example, [give an example of how you dealt with a situation well or turned a situation around, so the customer was left with an enhanced, more positive image of the company].'

Q 'Do you enjoy dealing with people?'

Clearly, your answer must be 'Yes'. However, while it's easy to enjoy dealing with people who are reasonable and pleasant, you must also demonstrate that you get some satisfaction from working with people when they're difficult, angry or upset.

Example

'Yes, I enjoy working with people; it's one of the things that attracted me to work in [whatever your field is]. Of course, it's satisfying when people are pleasant and everything goes well, but I also enjoy the challenge of working with [difficult, angry, confused] people. For example, [give some examples of doing this, including the positive outcome you achieved for the customer or client].'

Q 'This position needs someone who is friendly and approachable. Is that how you would describe yourself?'

Q 'What do you think makes a person approachable?'

No one is going to say they're unfriendly or unapproachable. You need to convince the interviewer, though, that you're someone customers feel at ease complaining to or asking for help and advice. Illustrate your answer with anecdotes that demonstrate your qualities in this regard.

Example

'I believe I'm friendly and approachable, and I'm sure the people I deal with would agree. I try to put myself in the customer's shoes. I know when I've been on the other side of the desk and needed help myself, I've really appreciated [say what you've found helpful]. I've tried to introduce these things into my own approach with customers. For example, [give an example of dealing with a difficult customer, illustrating your friendly approachability, how you achieved this and what you did to reach a positive outcome].'

Q *'How do you get on with different types of people?'*

You get along well with all types of people in all conditions. Illustrate your answer with brief anecdotes demonstrating the range of your positive experiences with people. Make them as wide and as different as possible – mention your experience of travelling abroad, for example, and how you got on with people there, or your experience of working with children or elderly people. Especially useful are examples of your flexibility and ability to learn. Tell the interviewer how you overcame language difficulties to achieve mutual understanding, or how you realized people have different preferences – that older people sometimes appreciate a more formal and respectful approach, for example.

Q *'Would you say you are confident?'*

Working in customer relations, you have to be comfortable with people and able to make them feel comfortable with you, encouraging trust and belief in your ability to help them. You have to appear confident. As well as behaving confidently at the interview, the best way to confirm your confidence is to say how you achieved it. Give reasons for your confidence along with anecdotes about how you gained maturity and confidence through experience.

Example

'Yes, I would say that I'm a confident person. I do everything I can, though, to support my natural sense of confidence – knowing the product thoroughly [for example], preparing carefully for meetings [for example] and [other things you do to make sure you're well informed and prepared for your work]. I've always been outgoing and self-assured, and my confidence in dealing with people has developed naturally with maturity. I've learnt a lot, too, through experience. For example, [give a brief anecdote describing an occasion where you gained confidence through understanding, leading to a positive outcome].'

Q *'What skills do you think are especially important when handling people tactfully?'*

Q *'How do you react when approached by someone who looks angry?'*

If it's your job to deal with complaints, you will need to be able to handle disgruntled customers with tact and diplomacy. Give your views on what you believe are the most valuable skills for doing this well. Include things like:

listening attentively;

using open body language;

taking their problem seriously;

being calm and polite;

being constructive and helpful.

Illustrate your answer with an anecdote about a time when you used these skills successfully with an angry customer and reached a positive conclusion with them.

Q *'How do you behave under pressure?'*

Q *'How do you react to stress?'*

Q *'How do you handle tension?'*

If they ask you one of these questions at the interview, the work is going to be pressured, make no mistake. If they employ you, they need to be sure that you can take the stress without it affecting either your performance or your health. Assure the interviewer that you:

are experienced at working under pressure – saying how, when and where;

cope with it well – saying how you respond, how you maintain your equilibrium and your strategy for managing emergencies;

have sensible methods for handling stress and tension over the long term.

Example

'I would say I'm pretty stress-hardy. I have a lot of experience working under pressure [tell them when and where, including the reasons for the pressure – seasonal rush, tight deadline, urgent order]. I've found it can be really energizing. Having to call on untapped potential is very satisfying when you succeed. If I find myself getting overstressed, I [say what you do to calm down – something quick, simple and effective]. If I know there's a rush [for example] coming up, I [say what practical steps you take to prepare for it]. Long term, I combat any effects of stress by [taking sensible measures such as eating well, taking exercise, etc].'

Q 'When was the last time you got angry?'

In customer relations, you can't afford to lose your temper however much stress you're under or however difficult the customer is being. Reassure the interviewer that you are one of those rare people who never get angry, at least not with customers.

Example

'I suppose like most people I get angry about [something reasonable but somewhat vague like injustice, cruelty to animals, world hunger], but I don't find everyday irritations affect me. I've learnt that dealing with other people calmly and politely is more pleasant and less stressful for me as well as for them, so that now it's second nature. I can't remember the last time I actually lost my temper.'

Be prepared for a more specific follow-up question such as *'What would you do if someone was rude to you?'* Say what you would do to handle it calmly and politely, and give an example of just such a situation from your experience.

Q 'What are some of the problems you encounter in your current job?'

Q 'Describe a difficult problem you've had to deal with.'

Q 'Describe a difficult customer you've had to deal with.'

If your current job isn't in customer relations, briefly outline the sort of problems you have to take care of day to day; then focus in on those that are relevant, such as the ones that involve dealing with people, using interpersonal and communication skills. It's possible to be 'customer focused' in almost any job. If there are people who use your skills or services, they are your in-house customers. How do you balance their conflicting needs and priorities and keep everybody happy? How do you cope with unexpected demands? Include the sort of (practical, non-personal) problems people bring to you, and how you resolve them and send people away satisfied – a large part of customer relations involves coming up with solutions to customers' problems. The interviewer doesn't want to know so much about what the problems are as what you do to resolve them. Focus on *solving* problems.

If you do currently work with clients and customers, or you have a service-focused hobby or volunteer role you can draw on for experience, choose a problem that shows your interpersonal, communication, persuasion and negotiation skills to the full. Explain the circumstances, how they arose, what you did, the positive result and the value to the company or group as a whole.

This is another of those questions that might prompt a follow-up, asking you to recount a situation where you did less well. They want to see if you can learn from experience, so pick an example that shows you doing your best in difficult circumstances but not quite getting there. What did you learn from the experience and, most importantly, what did you do differently next time as a result?

Q 'What are you like at influencing and persuading?'

Q 'Tell me about a time you had to persuade someone to do something they weren't keen to do.'

You need to be persuasive and have good influencing skills, especially towards the sales end of customer relations, but in other positions too. Give a couple of anecdotes that show you using your powers of persuasion. Pick situations that show you persuading someone to do or have something that was for their own good or in their best interests, or the best interests of the company or group as a whole. This avoids you appearing Machiavellian and manipulative. Describe how you used your interpersonal skills to get on their wavelength, listened to their point of view, and then went through your proposal, emphasizing the benefits before arriving at a mutually satisfactory conclusion.

Q 'Describe how your current job relates to the rest of the company.'

They're asking if you can see the bigger picture. Explain how your job contributes to the company's goals and vision. Emphasize the value of customer relations to the company as a whole and explain the relationship between:

  your job and the department;

  your department and other departments in the company;

  your department and the company as a whole.

Professional knowledge

Expect to be asked questions that explore your professional knowledge and capabilities in specific detail. These questions are too varied and specific to be covered here, but with your knowledge of the job you should be able to anticipate what the interviewer will ask. The questions will be based on things like:

  how you deal with actual situations that arise in your work;

  how you handle specific tasks commonly occurring in the job;

what you would do in specific circumstances likely to arise at work;

your understanding of specific customer relations techniques;

your areas of experience and any specialized knowledge you have.

Make sure your answers are customer focused wherever possible, and make your enthusiasm and energy for even the most basic tasks clear to the interviewer.

EXPERT QUOTE

I need to probe people's skills, abilities and personal qualities in depth. I enquire quite deeply into particular incidents because I want to know how successful they feel they've been, what they've learnt from it, how they've changed as a result and what they might do differently in the future.

Tina M Buchanan, Group HR Director, Hamworthy Combustion Engineering

EXPERT QUOTE

I need to know what people have done in the past, not what they think they might do in the future. If I'm looking for a team player, for instance, I want to know exactly how the candidate performs in a team. I don't care if it was at work or not; I want to know *when* they worked in a team, *what* they did, *how* they did it, *why* they did it and how they felt about it. If they were a good team player then, I can be pretty sure they'll be one now.

HR Manager, insurance and finance company

13
Questions for school and college leavers

What to do if you don't have experience

So far throughout this book, the message has been to illustrate your skills and qualities with examples from your experience. The problem is, what if you don't have much workplace experience to draw on? This is the hurdle many school and college leavers face at interview.

The solution is to make the most of the experience that you do have. It doesn't matter if that experience was gained in very different sorts of work from that which you are hoping to do. It doesn't even matter if the experience was gained outside the workplace altogether. All that matters at this stage in your career is that you have the competencies required and that you can demonstrate, with well-chosen anecdotes, how, when and where you have used them in the past. If you've been asked to an interview, the company believes you have the potential to be useful to them. Your task is to make sure they have every reason to believe you will fulfil that potential by telling them about the times you've done so in the past.

Prepare for the interview by reviewing your:

Qualifications. Your education and training are important factors in this stage of your working life. Be clear what you have learnt, how that has affected and changed you, and how the theory fits in with the sort of work you're looking for. The actual process of learning and studying is important, too. The ability to ask the right questions to solve problems, for example, the discipline needed to study for exams, and the necessity of fitting in and getting on with people from different backgrounds are all elements to be looked at and mined for useful anecdotes illustrating your potential skills and qualities.

Achievements. Consider all your achievements, not just the academic ones. Think about any special tasks, duties or responsibilities you've had, and any team or individual challenges. Include anything that shows you as a well-rounded, responsible individual possessing determination, initiative and enterprise.

Work experience. Any work experience will show that you are familiar with the fundamental necessities of working life such as punctuality, following instructions, being responsible, getting on with others, etc. Include weekend and holiday jobs, voluntary work, work placements and work experience schemes. Think about the practical things you've learnt from your experience and how these skills could be transferred to any workplace situation.

Explore all your advantages fully, and keep them in mind when answering the questions that follow. Be aware also that the eagerness, open-mindedness and enthusiasm you should display as a fresh, new recruit to the job market are key points in your favour.

As well as reading this chapter, read the one relevant to the sort of work you want to do – practical, technical, customer focused or whatever – for more advice on the sort of questions you will be asked and how to answer them. Although you won't have workplace experience to refer to, you should still, in many cases, be able to base your answers on the examples given, drawing on your school/college/university experiences and outside interests for anecdotes to illustrate your statements.

Q 'Why did you choose the course/subjects you did?'

Try to relate the course or subjects you studied to the type of work you're applying for, as well as to your own interests and tastes. The interviewer is looking for:

clearly thought-out reasons that show you can analyse and evaluate information and come to a decision – useful qualities in an employee;

a considered course of action, and commitment to that course, rather than acting on a whim;

self-awareness about your strengths, interests and talents;

an appreciation of what education and your course in particular have taught you, for example the ability to reason, analyse, research and communicate, as well as specific theory and skills;

the ability to match future goals to current action;

the ability to meet challenges and find or develop the skills and qualities to overcome them – also useful qualities in an employee.

Cover as many of the points above as you can in your answer:

> Describe the process you went through to decide which subjects and/or courses were right for you.

> Outline all the relevant factors you took into consideration – how you researched information, talked to people and got their input, weighed the pros and cons and reached a.decision.

> Give four or five specific reasons why you chose the subjects/course you did. Focus on career-related aspects such as what they would enable you to do in the future and how they would develop your natural strengths and talents.

> Describe how the course challenged you and the skills and qualities you developed to meet those challenges.

Use the same process if they ask how you chose your college or university.

Q 'What were your favourite subjects?'

Q 'Which aspects of the course interested you most?'

Pick the ones that have some relevance to the job you're applying for. Don't ramble on at great length, but do speak enthusiastically – you're being invited to talk about something you enjoy. If possible, tell the interviewer about anything you did to develop your interest outside the course and follow it up in your own time. This shows you have initiative, energy and commitment.

Q 'Do you feel your education prepared you for the workplace?

Q 'What have you learnt that you think would be useful here?'

Make the most of your educational background, especially if you have little practical workplace experience to draw on:

> Give a concise outline detailing the knowledge and skills you learnt on your course that are relevant to the job.

> Explain that being in education has not only taught you specific facts, but has also taught you how to learn, how to pick up new skills and how to apply them.

> Describe briefly how your education has matured and developed you – opening your mind, presenting you with challenges, giving you a sense of responsibility, etc.

> Explain how it taught you practical considerations such as self-discipline, being organized, prioritizing work, meeting targets and deadlines, etc.

Describe how you developed useful communication and interpersonal skills – getting on with people from different backgrounds, taking part in discussions and putting your points across, giving presentations to classes or groups, following instructions, asking questions, clarifying information, etc.

Include any experience you have working with a team and/or being in a position of leadership.

Don't forget the useful computer skills you learnt.

Emphasize how eager you are to put the theory into practice, preferably in the job you are being interviewed for.

Illustrate any of the points above with brief anecdotes where appropriate.

Q 'What did you like about your weekend/holiday job/work placement?'

If the job was relevant to the one you're applying for, focus on the elements that match and will be useful in your work. If not, emphasize the more generally applicable things you enjoyed, such as:

doing a good job;

being part of a team;

learning new skills;

being given responsibility;

working with the public;

rising to a challenge or tackling a difficult task.

Illustrate your points with anecdotes to anchor them in the real world.

Q 'What did you like least about your weekend/holiday job/work placement?'

Avoid at all costs saying it was boring. You can hedge politely – recap briefly the things you enjoyed and believe will be useful in future jobs and then say how much you're looking forward to getting started in your intended career.

Q 'What are you looking for in a job?'

You're looking for:

the chance to start in your chosen career;

the opportunity to learn the skills required;

the opportunity to make a valid contribution even at a lowly level;

the chance to use the knowledge and skills you've acquired and put them into practice.

Explain why this position offers all those things.

Q 'Why do you think you would like this type of work?'

Q 'What makes you think you'll be successful in this field?'

You need to have read the job description thoroughly and to have researched the type of job. Match your talents, abilities, qualities and training with those required by the job.

Example

'It's my understanding that this job requires someone who is [give three or four of the personal qualities required], who has [give three or four of the key skills and abilities needed] and who has [give the training and/or qualifications asked for]. I believe I fulfil those requirements very well. I have [outline your personal qualities, skills and talents and illustrate them with examples of how, when and where you've demonstrated them]. I also have [outline your training], which has taught me [mention a key factor]. I am sure with the support and training of this company I could make a real contribution.'

Q 'How do you feel about starting at the bottom?'

Be realistic. However good your training, you still have to learn the ropes. The only possible answer has to be that you don't mind a bit.

Example

'I appreciate that everyone has to start at the bottom if they're to get a thorough grounding in [your chosen field]. So, no, I don't mind starting at the bottom. I certainly hope to work my way up, though.'

Q 'How do you feel about routine work?'

Again, this question is testing your realism. Most jobs involve an element of routine – entry-level jobs more than most. Show your willingness to master the basics before moving on.

> **Example**
>
> 'I understand that quite a lot of the work I'll be doing, if you appoint me, will be routine. I'm not unhappy with that; it gives me the chance to find my feet and get to know the job. I would hope that those routine tasks would become more responsible as I progress and develop and become more useful to the company.'

Q 'How do you get on with other people?'

The interviewer is worried that you've only ever mixed with people your own age, and lack the experience to get on with everybody else at work. You get on very well with people of all ages, status and background, of course, but you have to back up this assertion with some examples and anecdotes.

> **Example**
>
> 'I believe I get on well with other people and I think the people who know me would agree with that. I've had to get along with people from all different backgrounds in [give an environment where you've had to do this – college, travelling, voluntary work – and the sorts of people you've interacted with]. I feel I'm adaptable and open to new experience, which helps. For example, [give an anecdote about your ability to communicate in difficult or daunting circumstances – overcoming language difficulties abroad, for example, showing the chairperson of the school governors around, taking a group of under-10s on a play-scheme outing].'

Q 'Have you ever worked under pressure? How did you cope with it?'

You may think it's odd asking people who have just sat exams if they've ever been under pressure, but this question still gets asked of school and college leavers. Remember to focus on the second part, how you coped, rather than on how stressful you found it.

The interviewer needs to know that you:

have experience of working under pressure – outline briefly how, when and where;

are able to cope with it – explain how you keep your balance;

have tried and tested ways of handling stress and tension over the long term.

Example

'I would say I'm reasonably stress-hardy. I have experience of working under pressure [taking my A levels, sitting my finals, for example]. I kept the pressure manageable by [being organized, planning, prioritizing tasks, etc]. I find it very useful to [say what practical steps you take to prepare – reviewing what needs to be done, breaking it down into manageable steps and so on]. I've found, in fact, an element of tension can be quite energizing. Mobilizing untapped potential is very satisfying when you succeed [include a brief anecdote about a time you did that to succeed against the odds. Give a non-exam example if possible – a sport or some other challenge]. If I find myself getting overstressed, I [say what you do to calm down – something quick, simple and effective]. Long-term, I combat any effects of stress by [taking sensible measures such as eating well, taking exercise, etc].'

Q 'Where do you see yourself in five years' time?'

The interviewer wants to know what your career plans are. They also want to know if you have, on the one hand, a degree of drive and ambition and, on the other hand, a realistic idea of what to expect. If you've researched the job and the field of work you're entering, you should have a reasonable idea of the usual career progression and where you should be in five years.

Example

'In five years' time I would ideally like to be [say what you can reasonably expect to be doing]. I think I have the [skills and abilities] to achieve that, especially with [requirements such as further training, experience, specific professional qualifications]. I believe this position will help me achieve that goal because [give reasons, such as excellent training programme, opportunities for advancement, leading company in the field].'

Q 'What do you think influences progress within a company?'

They are trying to find out if you have a good idea of how business works. Base your answer on:

- constructive attitudes such as commitment, positivity, determination, willingness, etc;

- developing your job-related skills and knowledge, and your ability to contribute to the company;

developing your professionalism – your reliability, resourcefulness, integrity, efficiency, etc;

developing workplace skills such as teamwork ability, communication skills, problem-solving skills, leadership and so on.

Q 'What are your greatest strengths?'

You have no experience and your skills are untried in the workplace. How can you say what your strengths with regard to this job are? Turn your lack of experience into a strength and emphasize your potential.

Although you can't offer them experience and expertise as yet, you can bring to the job:

enthusiasm and energy;

an open mind with no ingrained routines to overcome;

your ability to learn – you're still in the habit of doing so;

adaptability – you can be influenced and moulded;

freshness – you haven't seen it all before.

Include these points in your answer along with the personal qualities that will make you good at the job.

Example

'I would say my greatest strengths are [give three of your talents and personal qualities that you feel are genuine strengths and are appropriate for the job]. I believe I've demonstrated these in the past by [give a brief anecdote or example that shows you using your strengths]. Although experience isn't one of my key strengths as yet, I do have [give the experience you have and any theoretical background]. As well as that, though, I believe I can bring to the job [go through the points above – enthusiasm, open mind, etc].'

Q 'What have you done that shows initiative?'

Pick up to three occasions where you've shown this useful quality. Aim to give examples that:

show you acting responsibly;

display your problem-solving abilities;

show independence and self-reliance;

demonstrate good thinking and planned action.

Don't forget to say what the resulting benefits were, especially to others as well as yourself.

Q 'What outside interests do/did you enjoy?'

Aim for a selection that covers the range of desirable qualities. Include:

an example of a team activity;

something requiring self-motivation;

anything that has a community focus;

positions of responsibility you hold/held – team captain, editor, treasurer, etc;

something you are genuinely passionate about.

Beware of anything controversial. If you are a committed hunt supporter or hunt saboteur, for example, this is probably not the best time to argue your case. Otherwise, let your interest and enthusiasm come through in your answer.

Professional knowledge

As well as the above questions, be prepared to answer specific questions relating to:

any courses you've done and the knowledge you've gained, both practical and theoretical;

details about any project work you've done;

details of any work experience you've had – what you did, how you did it, etc;

any extracurricular activities you've been involved with – sports, teams, special-interest groups, etc.

EXPERT QUOTE

Be positive about yourself; know what you have to offer even if your examples aren't from the workplace. Persistence, resilience, motivation, the ability to stick at things and put in extra effort are the same whether you've done them at work, school, college or anywhere else.

David Giles, Resourcing Manager, Westland Helicopters Ltd

EXPERT QUOTE

Practise talking to people about yourself and what you can do. Many of the school leavers I see can say little more than 'Yes' or 'No'. Getting a whole sentence out of them is an effort. Practise with friends, teachers, parents, anyone. It's not just about the interview itself; I worry how they'll get on with the rest of the team if they join the company. A young person who is friendly and articulate will be streets ahead.

HR Manager, insurance and finance company

14
Tackling the difficult questions

Handling questions about perceived areas of weakness

Once the interviewer has asked the structured questions they ask every interviewee, they will move on to the more individual part of the interview – the person-specific questions. Rightly or wrongly, many people feel that this is the most difficult part of the interview.

Having read your CV or application form, the interviewer will almost certainly have queries about the details. They are most likely to want to know more about:

employment gaps;

frequent job changes;

unusual career moves;

reasons for leaving jobs;

being under- or overqualified for the post;

poor matches with the job requirements.

If any of these things apply to you, it will pay to plan your response to the sort of questions that, if you are unprepared, can put you on the spot. You can be sure they'll want to probe these areas more deeply to fill in the details.

Read through your CV carefully with an employer's eye and organize your responses well in advance of the interview. As well as being fully prepared about everything you've put down, ask yourself what questions you would *least* like to be asked, and plan your answers accordingly. If you think the interviewer will worry about something, your task is to allay their anxiety and show them why it's not a problem. Look on the bright side; things can't be that bad or you wouldn't have been asked to the interview.

A useful outline for answering difficult questions is:

agree with the interviewer – don't argue or tell them they've read your CV the wrong way. If the interviewer thinks there's a problem, there's a problem;

appreciate their point of view; then add your 'However...';

give your reasons, explanations and/or mitigating circumstances;

give a brief anecdote underlining your case;

confirm it's not a problem that will affect them.

Example

'Yes, [I have been out of work a long time, I have had some unusual career moves, or I do appear overqualified] and I understand your concern that [I might be out of practice, be uncertain of my career path, get bored and move on, etc]. However, [go through any of the relevant points that apply to you from the more detailed answers below]. For example, [give an anecdote, explanation or example that demonstrates your point]. So, although I understand you bringing the matter up, I can assure you it's [not a problem that's going to arise again, not something that will affect the current situation, very much in the past]. In fact, [if possible, show what strengths, skills or experience you've gained as a result, and how that might benefit the company].'

Q 'You were in your last job a long time. How do you think you'd adjust to a new post?'

You can't just say you'd be fine and leave it at that. You need to reassure the interviewer that you haven't become a fossilized stick-in-the-mud lacking ambition and initiative:

If there are good reasons why you stayed on, give them – you needed to remain in the same town; there was a long in-house training programme; it was the only suitable employment in the area; you were loyal to a small company or family firm; etc.

Explain that, though it might seem a long time, the job was always changing, you worked on several different projects and there were always new challenges.

Explain also that you had to be adaptable and flexible in your old job, and give some examples and anecdotes to support that.

Q 'You were in your last job for x years. Why weren't you promoted in that time?'

Base your answer on the same things as above. Briefly mention a reason for the lack of promotion – it was a small company, there was little expansion, you were top of your field with nowhere to go, etc. Outline what you learnt and what you achieved. Emphasize strongly how your job changed and your responsibilities increased even if you didn't get formal promotion. You could also explain that the lack of opportunity is the reason you're looking for a new job.

Q 'You've been in your current job a rather short time. Why are you changing so soon?'

You aren't changing on a whim and you haven't been sacked. Give your reasons and make your case. Acceptable reasons include:

relocation – yours or the company's;

redundancy or reorganization;

a genuine mistake – the job wasn't what you thought it was going to be;

it was a short contract or temporary job;

it was always intended as a stopgap while you looked for the right job;

an unforeseen change of circumstances – you need full-time work rather than part-time or vice versa, for example;

this new job was too good an opportunity to miss.

Q 'You seem to have changed jobs frequently. Was there a reason for that?'

The interviewer is worried that, if they employ you, you'll be off in a few months. You need to set their mind at rest with an acceptable reason and the assurance that all that is behind you now. Emphasize that you are fully committed and would stay in this job:

If you have had a genuine run of bad luck, tell them. Firms do close down, reorganize and relocate – now more than ever before.

If the posts were short contract or temporary, explain that. It might help in future to change your CV so that all your temp jobs come under one heading and it doesn't look as if you keep job-hopping.

Explain you've been gathering a wide range of experience and are now ready to settle down to your long-term career commitment.

Explain how you made some bad choices through youthful inexperience but have now matured and are ready to apply yourself (give a supporting anecdote to show how and why you've changed).

Show how the experience you gained in all those other jobs will be valuable in this job.

Show how they all contributed to the adaptable, well-rounded, flexible person you are today.

Q 'You've had a wide range of different jobs...'

The unspoken question is *'Have you found the right career yet or are we just another experiment?'* Again, you need to reassure the interviewer and convince them that this time you're on the right track and you intend to stay. Make your case stronger by showing what each of the jobs had in common and how they relate to the job you're applying for. Show a strong, clear thread running through everything. As most people have natural aptitudes and preferences, this isn't as difficult as it might sound. Perhaps they all use your problem-solving skills or your interpersonal skills, for example. Or maybe they all require a high degree of organization, hands-on skills or creativity. Demonstrate how the skills you've learnt will be relevant and useful in this new job.

Q 'I notice that this job is rather different from your current/last one...'

This is a similar question to the last one, just more focused. Again, give sincere reasons for the change and draw parallels between your last job and the one you're applying for.

Q 'It's quite a long time since your last job...'

The unspoken question here is *'Why hasn't anyone employed you yet?'* Your task is to give convincing reasons for your long period out of work. You could:

Explain that you had an offer that fell through – but only if it was the company's fault, not if it failed because of your reference check or something similar.

If this is a rare job that doesn't come up very often, or it demands an unusual skill, or it's a highly competitive job market and jobs are snapped up quickly, then explain how you didn't want to settle for anything less or take a stopgap job and maybe miss a golden opportunity.

Tell them that in the light of the redundancy (or whatever), you've taken the time to think about and consolidate your career plans rather than just take what was going.

Show how you've used the time to update and upgrade your skills through vocational training or study.

Explain that, at this stage in your career, you want to make the best use of your skills and experience and have been very selective about whom you apply to.

Explain how your redundancy package allowed you to fulfil a dream such as travelling or some other activity and that's what you've been doing, but you're ready to settle down again now.

Q 'What have you been doing since your last job?'

The interviewer is worried that you've spent the time watching daytime TV, have become lazy and will find doing a day's work difficult. Make your days sound structured and full of activity. Include:

job hunting itself – emphasize the organized approach you took to research, networking, applying, etc;

updating your skills – any courses of study or training you've done;

outside interests you've become involved with or had more time to develop;

voluntary work you've been involved with.

Q 'There are quite long gaps in your record. Is there a reason for that?'

The interviewer is probing you. They are not only worried about your work record here, but they want to see if the underlying reason could be a long-term liability – drugs, ill health, major family problems, imprisonment, etc. Calm their anxieties:

Explain the gaps in the best light possible, using the examples in previous questions, and emphasize your readiness to settle down and get on with your career now.

If the gaps really are due to a 'liability', either explain that it was in the past and your life has changed dramatically for the better now (give reasons for how and why) or explain that it will in no way affect your ability to work effectively for them.

Give the interviewer an anecdote demonstrating your current commitment and drive.

For real finesse, show how overcoming your problems has strengthened and matured you and how you can use that maturity in the job.

Q 'Your last/current job seems a bit of a step down. Was there a reason for that?'

Q 'Isn't this job a bit of a step backwards/sideways for you?'

Show how the jobs you've had fit in with your overall career plan, even where that means you've had to take a sideways step to consolidate your skills or experience:

If you're still comparatively young, maybe you were promoted ahead of your capabilities and had to take a step back. You've used the time to mature and develop professionally (say how) and you're absolutely ready now.

Your interests have taken you in a direction that involved a sideways step to develop new skills and gain experience.

You've reached the top in one field and want to bring your skills and experience to a different area even if that means retrenching.

You have new skills you wish to use but need to develop experience, which means you can't transfer directly. You could be a manager going into the technical side of the business, for example, or vice versa.

You're simply downshifting – but you need to make a strong case to show how your expertise will benefit this job. Don't on any account make them feel they're just a soft option or the last stop before retirement.

Q 'What are your career plans?'

This question asked of any female between 20 and 50 could mean *'Are you planning to have a baby?'* As this would be an illegal question (see below) you can ignore any subtext and simply answer the question as asked. Outline your career strategy, focus on your immediate plans, show how this job fits in with them and underline what you can bring to the job. There's a time and a place for discussing maternity leave, but this isn't it.

Q 'Do you feel confident you would be able to do the job?'

This is another question that might have a subtext. The interviewer could be concerned that your age, gender or physical ability would influence your capacity to do the job. Again, ignore the subtext and just answer the question in the affirmative. Give a couple of brief anecdotes showing how you have done a similar job or met similar challenges successfully in the past.

Q 'Do you feel you're overqualified/over-experienced for this position?'

The interviewer either is worried that you'll get a more suitable job in a few months and disappear, or they feel you're too senior to take orders from a younger, less-qualified manager. They might also be hinting that they think you're too old for the job. Assure them with appropriate answers from the following:

  You understand their concerns, but you're fully aware of what the job entails and you wouldn't have applied if you didn't think it was right for you.

  Explain what it is about the job that interests you specifically.

  Tell them in detail how the company can benefit from your knowledge.

  Tell them exactly how you could use your experience to the company's advantage.

  Emphasize that you believe you can grow and develop in the job and learn new things.

If, after a bit of gentle probing, you're sure it's your age that's the problem, introduce them to the benefits of older workers:

  You have a track record of career commitment.

  You have a wealth of skills and experience that could benefit them.

  You come with a record of success.

  You are mature – that means reliable, professional, prudent, responsible, etc.

  You're stable – you're not going to shoot off on a tangent at this stage in your career.

  You have realistic expectations of life, work and your colleagues.

  You've seen a bit of the world and, consequently, you're broad-minded and can get on with most people in most situations.

  You've encountered and solved a lot of problems in your time.

  Anyone who survived the technological and employment revolutions of the 1970s, 1980s and 1990s has learnt to be resilient, flexible and adaptable.

Q 'Do you feel your lack of experience could be a problem?'

If they've asked you to the interview, you must have something going for you other than experience. Now is the time to focus in on that:

  Use the experience gained in other areas and apply it to the job in
    question.

  Do the same with your transferable skills – the ones such as problem-solving
    and communication skills that are useful in most jobs.

  Make the most of your theoretical knowledge if you've just left college or
    completed a training course by showing you have a good understanding
    of how it will apply in practice.

  Demonstrate your ability to learn quickly and pick things up fast with a couple
    of anecdotes illustrating this ability in the past.

Q 'Do you feel your lack of qualifications could be a problem?'

As above, they've thought it worth interviewing you, so they should be willing to be convinced. Focus on your practical experience, the skills and expertise this has given you and how it would be of benefit to them. If the job means you'd be managing or instructing people more highly qualified than you, the interviewer might think you'd have difficulty getting their respect. Give a brief anecdote showing how you managed a similar situation successfully in the past.

Inappropriate and illegal questions

The questions asked at interview should not encourage discrimination on grounds of gender, sexual orientation, age, religion, race or disability. However, the laws on discrimination are complex, and there are often exemptions and special considerations allowed for specific jobs. On the whole, though, you shouldn't have to answer questions about your:

  marital status;

  number or ages of children;

  race or ethnicity;

  nationality;

  religion;

gender or sexual orientation;

disabilities or handicaps;

membership of legal organizations;

financial status;

spent convictions;

political affiliation.

You can, however, be asked about anything that does have a direct bearing on your ability to do the job. For example, you shouldn't be asked if you have young children, but you could be asked if you would be able to cover night shifts. You shouldn't be asked outright the extent of a disability, but you can be asked if standing for long periods would be a problem for you.

What do you do if the interviewer asks an inappropriate or illicit question? You have several options. You can:

Answer honestly. Give a straightforward answer if you can do so without feeling intimidated. Assess the situation and the interviewer – the question may have been asked out of genuine interest or sympathy rather than discrimination.

Answer honestly and allay their fears. You don't have to, but you can choose, if you wish, to ignore the inappropriateness of the question and treat it like any other difficult query.

Example

'I understand this job involves a significant amount of [travel, lifting, shift work, etc] and I can assure you that my [family responsibilities, disability, childcare arrangements, marriage plans] would in no way interfere with my ability to do that.'

Give a non-committal answer. Just say what they want to hear. Never, ever lie in an interview, especially about your qualifications or experience. You don't, however, have to tell the whole truth when it comes to your personal life.

Issue a blanket statement.

Example

'I can assure you there is nothing [about my religion, politics, family responsibility, age] that would affect my performance of this job.'

Refer the answer back to them.

Example

'I'm not quite sure how that question relates to my ability to do the job. Could you clarify it for me?'

If the interviewer knows they are fishing in illicit waters, they will move swiftly on to the next question.

Refuse to answer. Politely say that you don't feel the question is appropriate. While this is theoretically the most correct response, in practice it's likely to leave both you and the interviewer feeling embarrassed – never a plus at an interview.

EXPERT QUOTE

Expect to be asked about *anything* you've put on your CV.

Tina M Buchanan, Group HR Director, Hamworthy Combustion Engineering

EXPERT QUOTE

I don't ask people to interview to humiliate them or catch them out, but I do sometimes have to ask awkward questions. If I wasn't willing to listen to the answers, I wouldn't bother interviewing them in the first place.

HR Manager, retail company

15
Dealing with tricky questions

What to say when there's no clear answer

There are some questions that are not so much difficult as simply perplexing; tricky questions that don't seem to have a clear answer. How do you answer questions about your weaknesses, for example? How do you respond to questions about salary without doing yourself a disservice?

In this chapter we'll look at how to deal with these questions, as well as what to do when the interviewer seems to be inviting you to be critical or negative. We'll also consider how to respond to those questions that seem to need only a yes or no answer. Do they really – or is there more to it than meets the eye?

Dealing with critical or negative questions

It's important that you remain positive and upbeat during your interview, showing interest and enthusiasm throughout. So what do you do when the interviewer asks you a question that seems to invite a negative answer? This section looks at how you can deal with these questions without criticizing your job and other people or criticizing yourself.

Invitations to criticize your job and other people

Sometimes interviewers seem to want you to be negative about your job or people you've worked with, asking questions like:

'What do you dislike about your current job?'

'What did you dislike about your last boss?'

'What are the sorts of things colleagues do that really irritate you?'

They're not actually interested in what you disliked; what they really want to know is if you're going to be a moaner or complainer. Are you going to criticize the company outside work? Don't take the bait. Smile, and give a neutral answer. This is the one time you *don't* give examples or anecdotes.

Example

Q 'What do you dislike about your current job?'

Q 'What appeals to you least about this job?'

'I find that [a routine task that everyone dislikes, such as filing or record keeping] is probably the least demanding part of my work. However, it's one of my responsibilities and important to the job as a whole, so I get it done as quickly and efficiently as I can, which allows me to attend to the more rewarding aspects of the job.'

Example

Q 'What do you think your last boss could have done better?'

Q 'What did you dislike about your boss/supervisor?'

'I always found X a very good employer/supervisor. I believe he/she gave me the best guidance possible and the opportunity to develop my career to the point where I'm ready for the challenges this new job presents.'

Invitations to be negative about yourself

Another sort of negative question appears to invite you to criticize yourself:

'What is your greatest weakness?'

'What do you find most difficult to deal with in yourself?'

'What would you change about yourself if you could?'

As before, the interviewer isn't really concerned with your weaknesses as such; what they're more interested in is how you react to implied criticism and your degree of self-awareness. All these factors are keys to how well you will take guidance, or how much trouble you will be to manage, in the future.

The problem is that you are caught between two difficulties. Either you give an answer that reveals damaging flaws in your character, or you claim, improbably, to know of no imperfections in yourself. How do you give an answer that steers a path between the two? You could try one of the following:

a 'flaw' that most people would see as a strength;

a humorous flaw that most people would sympathize with;

a former flaw that you've overcome;

a flaw that will have no impact on the job you're applying for.

A 'flaw' that most people would see as a strength

Example

Q 'What is your greatest weakness?'

'I'm a bit of a perfectionist. I won't rest if I know something isn't right.'

'My family would probably accuse me of being a workaholic because I can't relax while there's something that needs doing.'

A humorous flaw that most people would sympathize with

Example

Q 'What do you find most difficult to deal with in yourself?'

'My passion for chocolate...'

'Still expecting to wake up and find I'm a millionaire/rock star/Booker prize winner.'

A flaw you've overcome

Example

Q 'What sort of things do you find difficult?'

'I would once have said speaking in public and giving presentations was a bit of a problem, but since I went on a course last year to improve my skills I find that it's no longer a challenge.'

'I used to have difficulty keeping up with all the filing the job entails. I've learnt from bitter experience to do it first thing in the morning so that I'm free to concentrate on more demanding responsibilities.'

A flaw that will have no impact on the job you're applying for

---

Example

Q 'What would you change about yourself if you could?'

'I'd find it easier to get down to the gym three evenings a week and stick to a healthier diet.'

'I always wish I'd learnt Italian/the guitar/to play tennis properly. I still intend to get around to it one day.'

Slightly more difficult are those questions that ask you to criticize your performance at work. The best thing to do is to treat them as flaws or problems you've overcome.

Example:

Q 'What do you find most difficult about your current job?'

Q 'What do you think you will find most difficult about this job?'

'I would have said (a difficulty you used to have such as handling spreadsheets or giving presentations) was/might have been a bit of a problem, but since I went on a course last year to improve my skills (or other positive action you've taken) I find that it's no longer an issue.'

> **Example:**
>
> *Q 'What's the biggest mistake you've ever made in your job?'*
>
> The interviewer is asking for an anecdote that exposes one of your weaknesses. Make it a flaw or problem you had in the past that you've learnt your lesson from, along with the steps you took to overcome it:
>
> 'When I first started work, I could never see the point of filing – it was so boring and took up so much time. One day, the managing director himself came in and asked for a particular report sheet. Of course I hadn't bothered to file it and it wasn't in the pile I thought it was in. So I had to go through everything, with the MD getting more and more impatient and me getting more and more embarrassed. I spent the next three lunch breaks getting my filing sorted out and I've never let it slip since. I never want to be that embarrassed again.'

Questions about salary

How do you deal with questions the interviewer may ask about the salary you currently earn or the sort of salary you expect from this new job?

'What sort of salary are you expecting?'

'What do you think you're worth?'

'What is your current salary?'

The problem is, if you name a figure, are you underselling yourself, or are you pricing yourself out of the market?

It's difficult to answer a blunt question evasively, but if you say what your current salary is you could be creating problems for yourself:

They could just make you an offer as close as possible to your current salary, when they might have been prepared to pay more.

If your salary is much lower than that of the job you're applying for, they might think you're trying to jump too far ahead and miss out a career stage.

They might wonder why you had to take a low-paid job in the first place.

The salary for the new job might not be that much more than your current one, in which case would you take the job if they offered it to you?

Your current salary might actually be more than they are offering, especially if you're moving sideways rather than up.

They might wonder why you seem prepared to move into a lower-paid job.

Ideally, you don't want to mention a figure before they do. It helps to do your homework and try to get at least a rough idea of what the job is worth:

Are there similar jobs advertised where the salary is mentioned?

Does the organization have a fixed pay scale?

Are there salary surveys for your profession you could refer to?

Are there perks that would add to the package as a whole?

Can you talk to someone in a similar job? (Don't ask people bluntly what *their* salary is, by the way. Just ask what someone like *you* might be expected to get.)

Politely but firmly dodge any questions about salary until you are actually at the negotiating stage after they have offered you the job. Note that the offer of a job should not depend on the level of salary you are prepared to accept. The job should be offered first and the salary stated. It is up to you then to accept or reject the offer after negotiation.

Example

Q 'What is your current salary?'

'I think it would be misleading if I just gave you a simple figure. My salary is part of a much wider package that takes into consideration [include whatever else you currently receive – overtime pay, bonuses, perks, discounts, pension contributions, company car or staff facilities]. I could prepare an accurate figure if we needed to talk about it in more detail [when they offer you the job, for example].'

Example

Q 'We're offering around £22,000. How does that sound to you?'

'I believe current salaries for this type of job are around that figure, up to £27,000.'

You've done your homework, and you know roughly what the salary range is for the job. You are also aware that they are not saying 'The salary *is* £22,000'; they are just sounding you out. If you reply that it sounds fine, £22,000 is what you'll get, rather than the £25,000 they were prepared to go up to.

Example

Q 'What sort of salary are you expecting?'

Q 'What do you think you're worth?'

'I believe this sort of job attracts a salary of around £22,000 to £27,000. Bearing in mind my qualifications and experience, I would expect to be at the higher rather than the lower end of that range.'

As above, you've done your homework and can make an educated guess at the salary range.

Answering closed questions

An experienced interviewer should ask open questions that allow you to respond with full, example-laden answers. However, interviewers aren't always perfect and sometimes they ask closed questions which invite nothing more than a 'Yes' or 'No' answer. Some, of course, require nothing more than that, but you could be missing opportunities and selling yourself short if you answer all closed questions with a one-word reply.

Treat any closed questions as if they were open ones. Say 'Yes' or 'No' as appropriate, and then follow up with a relevant example or anecdote.

Example

Open questions:

> *'What do you like about your current job?'*
> *'How do you get on with your colleagues?'*
> *'What would you say are the key skills for a manager?'*

Closed questions:

> *'Do you like your current job?'*
> *'Do you get on with your colleagues?'*
> *'Is leadership a key skill for a manager?'*

Example

Q *'Do you think attention to detail is important in this sort of job?'*

'I would say attention to detail is very important in this type of job. If I may give an example, in my last position [say how checking details was part of the job and, how your eye for detail saved time, inconvenience or money for your employer].'

Note how the answer is softened very slightly by saying 'If I may give an example...'

Example

Q *'Do you like your current job?'*

'Yes, I do like my current job. I particularly like [mention something relevant to the new job] and I can use my [skills and abilities relevant to the new job]. However, I believe that the position you are offering would allow me to [use or develop skills and abilities not currently fully employed].'

Here, the applicant has anticipated that the follow-up question to *'Do you like your current job?'* is likely to be *'Then why do you want to leave it?'* Note that, even though they want to change their job, they are still positive about the current one. Interviews are not the place for negative comments, even about past jobs or employers.

Some questions are not just tricky, they can seem downright crazy. How do you deal with the sort of question that's purposely intended to stop you in your tracks? That's what we'll look at in the next chapter.

EXPERT QUOTE

I need to know if someone is going to be difficult to work with. We're a small, high-precision company. Recruiting someone costs time and money that could be used elsewhere and employing the wrong person causes all sorts of problems with the rest of the staff. It could be a disaster.

Managing Director, engineering company

16
Answering off-the-wall questions

What is the interviewer really asking?

It's just possible that the interviewer will ask you a question that seems deliberately designed to throw you. Questions like:

How many cars would it take to completely block the M25?

If you were a vegetable, what type would you be?

What's wrong with the human body and how would you redesign it?

Who would you invite to a dinner party if you could have anybody?

How many cats are there in Aberdeen?

How would you reinvent the wheel?

Faced with a question like any of these, what on earth do you say? Is there even a right answer, and how would you be expected to know it if there is?

Although these questions are often more common in myth than in actual interviews, they do go through phases – going in and out of fashion – and could, unfortunately, be enjoying a period of popularity just when you're going through the job-hunting process. In this chapter you'll see that, however intimidating they appear, there is nothing to fear about these types of questions. Knowing how to set about answering them means you can tackle them coolly and calmly if and when they are thrown at you.

No interviewer asks a question for no reason, so what is the purpose of these seemingly crazy questions?

Off-the-wall questions originated in university interviews in an attempt to sort the wheat from the chaff in a situation where every applicant is more or less equally qualified in the same areas. They were intended to discover which interviewees could think on their feet with flair and originality under pressure, who could use their existing knowledge in novel and unexpected situations, and who would be prepared to extend their thinking skills outside what they comfortably knew and understood. They were designed to dig beneath the surface to find out what was going on inside the applicant's mind and establish what they might potentially achieve rather than what they had already accomplished.

Employers, especially in the newly established IT companies of the time, were quick to adopt the questions as one way of predicting interviewees' future perform- ance where an established track record in such a new industry was rare. They subsequently became popular with creative and typically 'hi-tech' organisations and are now most often used by creative, blue-sky and leading-edge companies whether they are in media, technology, PR, retail or any other line of business.

So how do you answer them?

If you look at the examples above, you'll notice that there are actually two basic types of question:

Questions that ask you to work something out or estimate something you couldn't be expected to know offhand.

More 'psychological' questions asking you to define yourself, your likes and dislikes, or your personal attributes.

Each type of question has its own different approach which we'll look at in detail below. It's important to remember, though, that ALL questions, no matter how they're phrased, are about your suitability for the job. Bring every one of your answers back to that and you won't go far wrong.

Questions asking you to work something out

The point of these questions isn't about knowing the correct answer; you are deliber- ately being asked something you couldn't possibly know the answer to. Nor are they looking for some slick, 'clever' response. The question is genuine and the real point is to see how you go about working it out and whether you stay calm and unflustered while you do so.

Consequently, it's important to think aloud and show how your mind is analysing the problem. The temptation is to take a wild stab at the first answer that comes into your head. Resist it; it's not what's wanted. Instead, you need to explore, consider and evaluate. Gather any facts you do have and/or make educated guesses, giving your reasoning. Consider out loud what information you might need that you don't have and describe how you might go about getting it. Then outline how you would set about arriving at an estimate. Finally, round things off by giving some rough figures.

Example

Q 'How many footballs would it take to fill the lift you came up here in?'

'Let me think about that... The lift was about two metres high by two metres wide and deep, so the volume would be eight cubic metres. I'm not sure how big a football is without measuring but from memory I'd say it was about thirty centimetres. As a rough estimate you'd get three balls along a metre line, so... twenty-seven in a metre cube, and... two hundred and sixteen in an eight-metre cube, plus a bit more because three balls is ninety centimetres, not a full metre, so... very roughly, I'd say it was about two hundred and twenty footballs.'

Whether the lift was two metres wide or two and a half or one metre seventy, the exact size of the lift isn't the issue. What's important is that the interviewee was observant enough of their surroundings to make a guess and then think logically under pressure about the problem presented. It doesn't even matter that much about their mental arithmetic – the ability to round numbers up or down to make calculation easy is a very useful one:

'... twenty-seven in a metre cube, let's say thirty to make it easier... three eights are twenty-four, making two hundred and forty in an eight-metre cube, so... very roughly, I'd say it was about two hundred and twenty footballs.'

'Psychological' questions

These questions are designed to find out aspects of your character that aren't going to be readily apparent from your CV. They are especially popular with companies that have a clearly defined 'company culture' and/or a carefully nurtured brand identity and who need to know if you will fit in with and contribute to that ethos.

Give the question proper consideration and be sincere in your answer. Don't just pick something at random; justify your choice and explain your reasoning. Remember, though, that they're not trying to delve into the deepest recesses of your psyche. They don't need your answers to reveal anything deeply meaningful about your psychology, just how you see yourself on a day-to-day level. They want to know what you're like to work with, so don't confuse what sort of person you are in private with what sort of employee you are.

Your research into the company should have given you an impression of the characteristics that they value, so match your answer to these. If this means giving an answer that is truly unrepresentative of you as a person, consider whether you would really be happy working there.

Example

Q 'If you were a fruit or vegetable, what sort would you be?'

What are your best, most relevant qualities for the job? What fruit or vegetable (or animal, or colour, or car, or whatever the question asks for) sums up those qualities? Your preparation for the interview should have included an assessment of your suitable characteristics, and if the interviewer had asked, 'What makes you a suitable person for this job?' you would be able to give a comprehensive answer. Treat it as essentially the same question:

> 'I think I would say I was an apple, because they are versatile – you can eat them raw or cook all sorts of dishes with them; they stand up well to knocks – unlike, say, peaches or strawberries; they get on well with most other fruits – you can add apple juice to sweeten any other sort; and, well, they're a good, honest, wholesome, dependable, down-to-earth sort of fruit.'

You may never face one of these off-the-wall interview questions, but if you do, understand that the interviewer is asking them for a reason, not just to wind you up. Take a deep breath, relax, and give yourself time to put together a reasonable response. Explain the logic behind your answer, and remember that all questions are ultimately about your suitability for the job.

So, now you can deal confidently with general questions, tricky questions, difficult questions and even off-the-wall questions. But what happens when it's your turn to interogate the interviewer?

EXPERT QUOTE

Everyone here is employed for their unique creative abilities, there's no room for padding. I can't use someone who's just going to plod along in the same old tracks, so the point of the interview for me is to find out exactly who has got that break-out potential.

Creative Director, media company

17
Your questions for the interviewer

What to ask at the end of the interview

The interview isn't over yet. Having asked you everything that they want to know, the interviewer will ask if you have any questions for them. Your questions should convey your interest in the job and the company, so have some ready. No questions can look like you have no interest.

Use the questions suggested in this chapter as a prompt, but try to think of the ones you really want answered. That's something that's going to be different for every job. The more appropriate and relevant the questions, the more it looks like you've done your homework on the position and the company, and the more interested and enthusiastic you look.

Two or three questions should be enough unless there are a lot of things you are genuinely unclear about. More than that, and the interviewer might worry about overrunning and keeping the next candidate waiting.

Try to avoid practical things that can wait until the job offer. Salary, hours and holiday entitlements can all be negotiated once the job is yours. For now, you're still being interviewed, so your task is to demonstrate how keen, intelligent and committed you are.

Areas you might want to ask questions about include:

The job itself – responsibilities, special projects, key goals, performance criteria. Don't ask the sort of thing you should be expected to know from reading the job specification, but you might want clarification.

Performance appraisal – appraisal schemes, review methods, pay and promotion reviews.

Company and/or department organization – whom you report to, who feeds into your department, where you fit in the organization.

Opportunities – travel, training, in-house schemes, qualifications, opportunities to branch out into extra responsibilities.

Career path – promotion opportunities, company expectations, company growth and development.

Here are some sample questions to start you thinking.

Q 'What are the main priorities of this job over the next six months?'

Q 'What are the biggest challenges facing the team/department currently?'

This question gets right to the core of the job and shows you as someone keen to take on and tackle key objectives. Even if the main tasks and responsibilities have been covered in the job description, try to find a way of phrasing the question so that you can find out from the interviewer what they consider the most pressing issues. It then gives you the opportunity briefly to recap any experience you've had dealing with similar situations or any specific skills you have that could be useful. It demonstrates that you are ready to take on responsibility and helps the interviewer to picture you doing so. It could also be useful information if they do offer you the job.

Q 'Why has the job become vacant?'

If this hasn't been answered already, it can be worth finding out why the last person left. If it's because they were promoted, you can then lead into a question about the company's promotion policy (see below). If it's a newly created post, you can ask about further company expansion (see below, again). If the present incumbent is moving on to better things after a long and happy career with the company, you can probably expect to do much the same yourself. If you get the feeling the interviewer is hedging and doesn't want to answer the question, you might want to probe a little deeper – 'Is there anything about their leaving I should be aware of?' Or you might just want to make a mental note to come back to the question should you be offered the job.

Q 'What would my career prospects be with the company?'

Q 'If I were to join the company, where do you see me in five years' time?'

Q 'Do you promote internally?'

It's nice to know what to expect. This question also suggests that, not only are you ambitious and intend to get on, but that you mean to stay with the company and let them benefit from your developing skills, knowledge, and maturity. You're showing not just commitment, but long-term commitment.

Q 'What are the company's current development plans?'

Q 'How does the company see the job/department developing over the next few years?'

This shows an interest in the company, demonstrates a sense of long-term commitment and also tells you what opportunities might arise in the future should you be offered the job.

Q 'I'm very interested in this job and I believe I could do it well. May I ask if you have any reservations about my suitability?'

If you feel confident you can do it, this is a good question to ask. It lets you know almost immediately if you are being seriously considered at this stage. It also, of course, gives you the chance to recap your good points and reassure them about anything that they have doubts or are unclear about. You might even find they have genuinely overlooked or misunderstood something.

Q 'When can I expect to hear from you?'

Q 'How will you inform me of your decision – letter, phone, e-mail?'

For your own peace of mind, find out what the next stage in the process is, and when and how you will hear from them. Not asking makes you look as if you don't care.

EXPERT QUOTE

When the interviewer asks if you have any questions, don't ask about money or holidays; it doesn't make a good impression. I'm interested in people who are keen to develop, so questions about training and development opportunities are always good ones.

Helen Cole, Learning Services Coordinator, South West TUC

EXPERT QUOTE

Ask about the job itself rather than terms and conditions. Show your interest and a sense of involvement. Interviewees can ask open questions as well as the interviewer; make it a two-way communication.

Janet Hembry, Head of Education and Skills Policy,
Government Office for the South West

18
Variations on the theme

Different types of interview and how to deal with them confidently

As well as the straightforward one-to-one interview, there are a number of variations you might come across. These can be either instead of or in addition to the simple interviewer–interviewee set-up and can include:

screening interviews;

telephone interviews;

video interviews;

panel interviews;

serial interviews;

assessment centres;

informal interviews;

second interviews.

Screening interviews

As the name suggests, these interviews actually screen candidates out. They usually take place before the selection interview so that the interviewer doesn't have to interview anybody lacking the basic requirements. Cheaper, quicker and more immediate than an application form, and less effort than reading a CV, screening interviews ask a set of standard questions. If you get the answers right, you automatically go forward to a selection interview. If you get the answers wrong, you may still be able to apply again at a later date, and failure will not necessarily affect any future applications.

The interview rarely takes place face to face; usually it's on the phone or on screen. Questions can range from what your qualifications are to multiple-choice aptitude tests. The interviewer should explain before you start what is involved and how long it will take. If it isn't convenient, you weren't expecting it or you would like some time to prepare, explain politely and call back when you're ready. There's little you can do, though, to prepare for a screening test – the questions are usually fact based and you either have the basic requirements or you don't. There is no point arguing about the result, either, or asking if you can come in to discuss it; the person you're speaking to just doesn't have that authority.

Telephone interviews

It's very rare to have just a telephone interview; you usually have to undergo a formal face-to-face meeting as well. As above, these are mostly screening interviews to see if you meet the basic needs before being passed on to a selection interview. Other reasons why you might have an initial telephone interview are:

because the job is phone based – customer enquiries or telephone sales, for example – and you are demonstrating an important skill required for the post;

because it's a supposedly informal chat (see below for more about formal interviews) designed to find out more about you and see if you could be suitable for the job;

because the employer is in a hurry to fill the post and needs to get up a shortlist quickly.

In all these cases, don't ring until you have the time, concentration and freedom from interruption to give a decent performance. It's a pre-interview interview, so make sure you have all the information you need to hand and are fully briefed and prepared. Have with you:

your CV;

your application letter or form;

the job advertisement, job description and any other information that will be useful;

your diary;

something to make notes on.

If *they* call *you* unexpectedly, stay calm. Remember to make a note of who's calling – name, position and company – and their phone number. If possible, get hold of your CV and other useful information. Keep it to hand in a desk drawer, near the phone or on your organizer for just this eventuality.

When you're on the phone:

Speak clearly – don't drink, chew or smoke while you're talking or even while the other person is talking.

Smile – it alters the muscles in your face and throat and makes your voice sound warmer and more relaxed.

Make notes – they could be useful for the formal interview.

Avoid one-word answers – however unprepared you are, try to say more than just 'Yes' or 'No' in answer to questions.

Don't worry – the person calling you won't expect you to be fully prepared or make the sort of presentation you would at a formal interview, but do make sure you sound enthusiastic.

Video interviews

A cross between a telephone interview and a face-to-face interview, video interviewing via the internet, like video conferencing, is becoming increasingly popular. You could be doing it from home or a recruitment agency office. Whichever, treat it the same as a face-to-face meeting but keep in mind some of the shortcomings of webcam images:

Dress smartly, even if you are doing it from home.

Clear away foreground and background clutter that might intrude into the shot and distract the interviewer.

Prepare as fully as you would for any other interview.

Beware of patterns and stripes on clothing – they can produce interference patterns on screen that can be distracting.

If you are at home, make sure that you won't be disturbed.

Be aware that there is usually a slight time lag between broadcasting and receiving signals. Don't jump in to fill what seem to be gaps in the conversation.

Image and sound are not always perfect, so speak a little more slowly and clearly than normal – you don't need to take it to extremes.

Similarly, keep hand gestures and other movements to a minimum – waving your hands around will look odd on screen.

Remember to smile, just like you would in a face-to-face interview, and make appropriate 'eye contact' by looking into the camera lens.

Panel interviews

These are usually formal selection interviews where several people in turn ask you the usual questions, instead of just one. Where the hiring decision affects several people they can all be included on the interview panel. They typically include:

human resources manager;

technical manager;

department head;

line manager.

You will usually be told beforehand if it's a panel interview. Each member of the panel will have their own questions that address their particular concerns, so don't be unnerved by the thought that they're all going to question you. There probably won't actually be many more questions than there would be at a one-to-one interview. There is usually one person leading the panel who will take charge of the interview, welcome you and introduce you to the others.

The formalities of a panel interview can be a little tricky. Do you shake hands with everyone? Whom do you look at when answering the question?

On the whole, be alert to the situation and be led by the panel itself. If, for example, the leader stands up, shakes your hand and then asks you to take a seat, assume you don't shake hands with everyone else.

Make eye contact and smile as you are introduced to each member.

Try to remember their names and what their particular specialities are.

Always look at the person asking you a question.

When you answer, direct your answer chiefly to your questioner, but include the rest of the panel by glancing round and making eye contact.

Address your own questions to the panel leader, unless it's something clearly more suitable for the technical manager, for example.

At the end of the interview, thank the group as a whole for inviting you. Say how much you enjoyed it, that you found it interesting and that you look forward to hearing from them. Look around, smile and make eye contact as you do so.

Once outside, make a note of everybody's name and job title before you forget.

Serial interviews

Also called a sequential interview, this is similar to a panel interview, except that you have a one-to-one interview with each person in turn instead of all at once. Each interviewer is focusing on their own particular interest, and will ask you questions with a different emphasis. This means that overall you will undergo a very thorough investigation. Keep in mind what each person's concern is likely to be when you answer their questions. For example, though not exclusively:

human resources manager – career pattern and background, work style, training and qualifications, general educational background, training and development needs, salary and benefits;

technical manager – technical experience, specific knowledge, training and qualifications, technical skills, specific job-related problem solving;

department head or senior executive – cultural fit, ability to meet targets, contribution to profitability and growth, career aspirations;

line manager – working style, manageability, team fit, transferable skills, strengths and weaknesses, understanding of the job and ability to perform it.

The point of the serial interview is to get individual, unbiased assessments of you from each interviewer. This means you can start afresh with each person you meet. Even if you feel you failed to make a stunning impression on one interviewer, you have a couple more chances to claw back the situation. After the interview, the interviewers will get together to compare notes and arrive at a consensus decision that satisfies all parties.

Assessment centres

An assessment centre isn't so much a place as a battery of tests used to select employees. The technique was developed to select army officers during the Second World War when there was no time for leaders to emerge naturally and work their way up through the ranks. It uses a range of assessment techniques overseen by trained and qualified observers. Several candidates are observed together working in a group, and discussion and teamwork are expected. Assessment tests can include:

interviews;

tests;

individual exercises;

group exercises;

indoor and outdoor tasks;

informal and social observation.

See Chapter 19 for some ideas for dealing with these sorts of tests and exercises.

Assessment centres for different companies follow their own individual programmes, lasting from half a day to two days and involving from five to 30 people at a time. Some are residential and nearly all involve some social interaction such as coffee, lunch or an evening meal. A typical programme might be:

DAY ONE:

Morning
Induction – meeting fellow candidates and assessors; introduction to the programme
Ice-breaker exercise
Aptitude and personality tests

Afternoon
Group problem-solving activity
Individual interviews

Evening
Group role-play exercise

DAY TWO:

Morning
Group case-discussion exercise
Individual in-tray exercise

Afternoon
Individual presentations
Individual interviews
Conclusion – question-and-answer session; next steps and leave taking

Prepare yourself fully for the interviews just as you would in any other situation. Do your research on the organization, understand the competencies they are looking for and know where, when and how you have demonstrated them. Don't forget, you are still under observation during breaks and meals – be on your best social behaviour.

Informal interviews

There is no such thing as an informal interview. Beware of the offer to 'get together for an informal chat'; it is never an occasion to relax and let your hair down even if it takes place in a bar or over a meal. An interview is an interview. If the person you are talking to has a job to offer, they will be weighing you up very carefully to see if you fit the role, so prepare as thoroughly as you would for any other interview. Let your interviewer take the lead and set the tone of the meeting. Follow their example as to the degree of formality or informality – using first names, for example. Use your social skills and be friendly and pleasant but don't drop your guard and be drawn into discussing anything or relating anecdotes that you wouldn't at a formal interview.

Second interviews

If you're invited back for a second interview, the company is seriously interested in you. Part of your task is to show that you are seriously interested in them, too. Find out more about them and the job, and prepare some intelligent questions about both.

It's a chance for them to find out more about you. That could mean a formal interview by a senior executive about your experience, skills and achievements, or it could be an 'informal' meeting over lunch to see how you get on with your potential colleagues. Remember: there is no such thing as an informal interview. You'll usually be told beforehand what to expect so that you can prepare for it. You'll also be told if the interview involves tests or exercises, presentations, or if you need to take examples of your work or projects you've worked on. If there was anything they seemed unhappy about at the first interview, expect to be closely questioned about it this time and prepare for that. However, if they weren't ready to be reassured they wouldn't have bothered to ask you to a second interview, so be positive.

EXPERT QUOTE

We're not giving you tests and things just to make you jump through hoops. We're genuinely trying to be fair. Why should someone who has genuine potential be overlooked just because they don't have good interview skills? Assessment has made us look more closely at people we might have ignored in the past, with very positive results.

HR Manager, engineering company

19
Interview extras

Tasks and tests they might include and how to approach them

As well as the question-asking part of the interview, there may be additional tasks and tests to go through so that your skills, qualities and specific suitability for the post can be assessed. Although there is no way to rehearse some of them, be as prepared as possible. You should be told when you're invited to the interview about any tests or presentations you'll be expected to go through, but you might like to check to make sure. Suddenly being faced with an unexpected aptitude test can throw even the most confident candidate.

These extras can take place before, during or after the main part of the interview, or they can be held on a different day altogether. They can include:

making a presentation;

showing your portfolio;

technical and attainment tests;

physical tests;

job-replica exercises;

role-play;

group exercises;

psychometric tests.

Making a presentation

You might be asked to make a short, formal presentation – either to the person interviewing you or to a panel or group of people involved in the hiring decision. What they are looking at is your ability to:

stand in front of a group and speak confidently;

arrange information coherently so that others can understand it;

explain key points clearly;

be concise;

think on your feet and respond flexibly to circumstances.

You'll be told beforehand what the presentation will be about and how long you'll have to deliver it. Always assume you will be asked questions afterwards and prepare accordingly even if it's not mentioned specifically. The sort of things you could be asked to do include giving:

a five-minute talk presenting your key qualifications for the role;

a five-minute outline of how you would develop the position given a free hand;

a 10-minute presentation on what you see as the three main priorities for the job;

a 10-minute profile of the key issues currently facing the industry;

a 10-minute presentation on why you believe you are suitable for the job;

a 15-minute analysis of the strengths, weaknesses, opportunities and threats facing the organization.

Plan and rehearse your presentation thoroughly before the interview, and don't forget to check what equipment will be available to you on the day. It's a good idea to make a summary of your presentation, preferably on one sheet of A4 paper. You can not only use it as a prompt yourself, but give it to members of the group as a handout. Plan thoroughly. It's always better to make a few points strongly and clearly than to cram too much in and confuse everybody. Don't run over time, either. If they say five minutes, they mean five minutes. Some companies are ruthless about cutting you off once your time is up and it would be a shame for them not to hear your final point, especially if you saved the best for last.

Showing your portfolio

In creative jobs especially, you can be asked to bring along a portfolio of your work. Don't leave it until the last moment to choose what to take. Pick things that have relevance to the job you're applying for, that you can talk about and that allow you to bring in some valid points and anecdotes. Showing your portfolio can almost be a mini-presentation. Rehearse it beforehand so that you can do it confidently and gracefully. Even if your 'portfolio' is a DVD, CD, PowerPoint presentation or website, you can still polish and edit it for the interview, practise introducing it, and prepare to answer questions about it afterwards.

If you are asked to leave work with a company or drop work in for someone to look at, be a bit wary. If possible, say that you would prefer to bring it in personally so you can discuss it and answer any questions they might have. If that's not possible, give them copies and avoid leaving originals or your one and only copy. Examples of your work are among your most valuable assets. Any loss or damage could hinder your prospects, and accidents do happen, unfortunately, especially to things lying around in offices.

Technical and attainment tests

You may be asked to give a practical demonstration of a skill essential for the job, such as driving, typing, translating and interpreting, or technical skills. Practise beforehand so that you're confident you can give a good performance under pressure on the day.

Physical tests

There are occasionally specific physical requirements for a job and you may be asked to take, for example, a sight test or hearing acuity test, or be tested for manual dexterity, colour blindness, etc. These tests cannot be done without your consent, but you are unlikely to be offered the job unless the tests are completed. It's possible you may also be asked to undergo a general health check for some jobs or by some organizations.

Job-replica exercises

These are practical demonstrations designed to assess how you'll behave in the job. They include things like:

in-tray exercises;

case studies;

role-play.

In-tray exercises

You're given a typical in-tray for the sort of job you want to do, including letters, phone messages, memos, reports, etc. You can also be interrupted by phone calls and e-mails while you work. Your task is to sort through it all and say or mark down how you would deal with each document or letter and what action, if any, you would take. It's designed to assess your management and organization skills as well as your ability to handle pressure and make decisions. One useful tip is to sort everything into three piles first:

urgent;

important but not urgent;

neither urgent nor important.

You can then work through the piles in order of priority. Read up on time-management and prioritization techniques to improve your confidence, and practise on your own in-tray.

Case studies

You may be asked to write a report or give a short presentation based on a briefing or case history about a relevant business matter. You have to assess the information and reach a decision, outlining your approach and reasoning. Brush up your familiarity with decision-making processes if necessary so that you feel confident you can handle the exercise under pressure.

Role-play

You could be asked to role-play a common workplace situation that you'd be expected to handle in the job. If you're told to expect a role-play exercise, think about the job, read the job description and try to anticipate what sort of thing you'll be asked to do. If the job is in retail, for example, it would be reasonable to expect a role-play dealing with customers – a difficult customer or a customer complaint, perhaps. For a management job, you could be asked to deal with a staff problem. The interviewer wants to see how, and how well, you deal not only with the problem, but also with the people involved and the stress of the situation. Stay calm, approach it professionally, and think about the sort of skills the interviewer is looking for.

In all cases the rules and expectations of any exercise should be explained to you clearly before you begin. If you have any doubts or aren't sure about anything, tell the person overseeing the exercise. Tell them, too, if there is anything that would make the test unnecessarily difficult for you – not having the right glasses with you, for example.

Group exercises

If teamwork is a major factor in the job, you could be asked to take part in a group exercise. These tests can last for anything from a couple of hours to a couple of days. They generally involve you interacting with a group to achieve some goal. What the goal is doesn't matter as much as how you work together as a team to achieve it.

The exercise should be assessed by trained observers who are scrutinizing things such as your:

contribution to the success of the team;

communication and interpersonal skills;

natural role within the team;

persuasion and negotiation skills;

judgement and reasoning;

problem-solving skills.

Your main tasks are to participate fully in the exercise and be a good team member. It doesn't matter so much whether you win or lose, but it really does matter how you play the game:

Avoid extremes. Don't take over and boss everyone around, but don't be too reserved, either, or opt out for any reason.

Avoid conflict. Give reasoned opinions when necessary but don't let them degenerate into arguments.

Take responsibility for seeing that everything in the team goes well:

> Include members who seem to be on the fringes.
>
> Find common ground when there is disagreement.
>
> Summarize discussions and agreements so that everybody knows where they are, what they're doing and what the next step is.
>
> Remind the group what their goal is and keep them focused on it.

Psychometric tests

The interview extras you are increasingly likely to encounter are the psychometric tests designed to give the interviewer an independent, unbiased view of your talents, characteristics and abilities. Psychometric tests fall into roughly three different types:

> *Aptitude tests*. These measure your natural abilities and test for specific job-related skills such as verbal or numerical ability; spatial, mechanical or clerical aptitude; or logical thinking or reasoning skills.
>
> *Personality tests*. These assess what sort of person you are and whether you have the personal qualities and characteristics thought right for a particular job. They usually ask what you would do or how you would feel in particular situations, or whether you agree or disagree with a given statement such as 'I enjoy meeting people' or 'I sometimes start things I don't finish.' The results are matched against an existing profile to see how well you fit.
>
> *Motivational and career interest tests*. These are less common in recruitment; aptitude and personality tests are more popular. Motivational tests focus on what motivates and drives you, what you like doing, what stimulates you, where your natural tastes and inclinations lie, which occupations suit you best and so on.

What they have in common is that they are all 'paper-and-pencil' tests – though these days they're often taken on screen – devised by occupational psychologists, that ask you to answer multiple-choice questions rather than give a practical demonstration of a skill.

You'll usually be told when you get invited to the interview whether you'll be facing any psychometric tests. If it's not clear, find out:

whether there will be any tests;

what the aim of the test is: to explore your aptitude or to learn about your personal characteristics, or a combination of the two;

whether they can provide you with examples before the interview;

whether they know what sort of tests there are going to be – a Myers–Briggs personality test, a spatial reasoning or spatial recognition test, etc – so you can look them up and get an idea of what to expect;

how the tests will be taken – on screen, online or using paper and pencil;

whether you can use a calculator for numerical tests;

whether you will get feedback about the result;

when the tests will be taken – before or after the interview.

Knowing when you will take the tests can give you some idea of how important they are to the final decision. If you take them before the interview itself, it's possible they could be used for screening, and the decision will rely heavily on your having the right combination of abilities and characteristics, backed up by your performance at the interview. If you take them after the interview, it's more likely that the interviewer will make the initial decision, using the tests simply to confirm their own impression of you.

There is nothing to be scared of about psychometric tests, as long as you're prepared for them and ready to apply a little common sense.

Aptitude tests

Aptitude tests shouldn't require specialist knowledge or training, nor should they depend on your general knowledge. They are designed to measure specific natural inherent skills such as:

your ability to understand and work with numbers – useful in jobs where numeracy or the ability to handle data is essential;

your ability to use logic to solve problems – widely used to predict your general intelligence and ability to work your way through challenges;

your ability to understand and use words – valuable in jobs where you have to understand written instructions such as manuals, follow verbal instructions, assess information, or prepare information for others;

your ability to visualize in two and three dimensions – mainly used in jobs such as engineering, design and production, surveying and architecture, etc, where a grasp of how things fit together is essential;

your ability to understand and interpret diagrams – an advantage in jobs where the use of diagrams is common, such as engineering, computing, electrical, design and technical jobs;

your understanding of basic mechanical principles – used principally in jobs that entail assembling, running or maintaining machinery.

Only tests that are relevant to the job in question are chosen, and they give a precise score that allows the interviewer to see exactly what your aptitude for that particular skill is. Qualifying scores are set at a reasonable level – you simply have to be able to do the job competently, not be a genius.

Aptitude tests are usually in the form of puzzles where you're asked to do things like select the next number in a sequence, fill in a missing word, say whether a statement is true or false, pick out the missing diagram, and so on. The test is often timed but there's usually a chance for a short rehearsal first, answering a few specimen questions so you can get the hang of it and the tester can make sure you've got the right idea. Here are some examples.

Numerical question

Underline the next number in the sequence

1   5   9   13   17

Answer: (a) 21; (b) 23; (c) 19

Verbal reasoning question

Which is the odd one out?

(a) happy   (b) cheerful   (c) jovial   (d) precise

Abstract reasoning question

O is to o as OO is to:

(a) OOO; (b) oo; (c) Oo

Answers: (a), (d), (b).

Before you start the test, find out:

Whether the test is timed and, if so, how long you'll have to complete it.

Whether the test is negatively marked – meaning that you will actually lose points for wrong answers. This is unusual, but it can happen and will make a difference as to whether you should guess at answers you don't know.

Whether the questions will get more difficult as you go through them.

Whether you can have a practice run before the actual test to make sure you're doing it correctly.

Whether you can use any aids – a calculator for numerical questions, for example.

Although it's difficult to increase your natural aptitude for something without giving it years of practice, there are some useful points for doing aptitude tests that can help you improve your chances and get the best score you are capable of. They include the following:

Practise beforehand if you can. Familiarity will not only increase your confidence, it will help you work more quickly because you'll recognize what the questions are about. It will also alert you to some of the twists and turns questions can take (asking for the next *but one* in a sequence, for example).

Keep going. If you can't answer a question quickly, skip it and come back if there's time at the end.

If you really don't know the answer, make a guess – you have a one in four chance (for example) of being right. Make sure first, though, that you will not have points deducted for wrong answers.

When making a guess, first eliminate any answer that's definitely wrong, then make your choice from what's left.

With numerical questions, you can often avoid careless mistakes by roughly estimating the answer first. Is it likely to be in the tens or the hundreds? Where will the decimal point be? – and so on. This can stop you choosing a similar but wrong answer – 4.54 instead of 45.4, for example.

The questions in aptitude tests often get harder as they go on – ask about that before you start. When you feel you've reached your limit, go back, double-check your existing answers and fill in gaps rather than plough fruitlessly on. If you still have time after that, carry on with the difficult questions until asked to stop.

There are plenty of books and internet sites available that will allow you to run through sample tests. Look them up if you want to see what to expect and get some practice to improve your speed and confidence.

Personality tests

Different jobs suit different personalities. Some require you to be outgoing and involved with people; others need you to be self-reliant and able to work alone. Some jobs require you to analyse facts; others need you to assess feelings and instincts. Increasingly, employers believe that when they pick someone with the right sort of personality for a job, they will be better at it, progress more rapidly, be more enthusiastic about it, be more tolerant of the problems and setbacks associated with it, and be generally happier and more productive. Consequently, many now use personality profiling as part of the employee selection process.

Unlike aptitude tests, there are no right or wrong answers as such in a personality test, and the test is not usually timed. It's designed to predict how you will behave and relate to other people at work and usually involves multiple-choice questions, or questions that ask you to agree or disagree with a statement or to rank various statements in order of preference. These are easy if you have strong preferences, but more difficult if you like or dislike all the options more or less equally.

Example 1
Would you prefer to:

(a) present a lecture to a group of people?
(b) put together an engine from a kit of parts?

Example 2
I am interested in trying new things: YES   NO

Example 3
Friends often tell me their problems.
(strongly agree)   (agree)   (not sure)   (disagree)   (strongly disagree)

There are no right or wrong answers, and as you don't know exactly what profile is required for the job, there is little you can do to prepare specifically for a personality test. There are, however, some general points that can help you show yourself at your best:

Put yourself in a positive, professional frame of mind before you start. Think what you're like when you're at your best and base your answers on that. For example, a question asks if you enjoy meeting new people. Virtually everyone has had times when they would prefer to relax at home rather than have to go out and deal with strangers. The point is how you *usually* react, and how you expect to behave professionally, not what you do occasionally.

The better you know yourself, the easier it will be to answer the questions. Practise doing personality tests and questionnaires, so that you have a chance to think about your preferences, how you behave and how you react in everyday situations.

Think about the job. While it's difficult to skew the results of personality tests, most of us adopt roles for specific jobs and emphasize different sides of our natural personalities accordingly. Think about the role you need to play in the job you're applying for: will you need to wear your empathy hat or your efficiency hat, for example? Weigh your answers accordingly.

Don't overlook the obvious. If the job is in sales or customer services, for example, questions that ask whether you like being with people, get to know them easily, and enjoy social situations clearly need a positive answer.

Try to answer all the questions. The more you leave out, the harder it will be to form an impression of you. If in doubt, trust your gut instinct and go with the answer that first occurs to you.

Be honest, confident and up front about who and what you are. While it's possible to 'invent' the right personality profile for a job, it's virtually impossible to do so consistently throughout an entire questionnaire. You may be mistaken about what they want, anyway. What if you present yourself for a management job as a tough-minded, results-oriented go-getter, when they've decided the post needs a supportive, team-focused people person?

Online tests

Online tests are becoming increasingly popular. Their content is very much the same as that of any other sort of aptitude or personality test, the only difference being that you complete the test on screen rather than using a paper and pencil. They are sometimes used on company websites as a way of screening potential applicants before they even get to the interview stage.

The tests are not designed to check your keyboard skills, so the actual process should be straightforward. You should be provided with full instructions and the opportunity to practise a couple of questions. Complete the tests as you would any others, but make sure you are aware of a few things before you start:

Do you need to enter a code number or password before starting?

Does the format allow you to go back and answer questions you've missed out?

Can you change answers after you've entered them?

Will you get feedback and, if so, how?

To recap, the general tips for doing any form of psychometric test, whether an aptitude test or a personality test, on paper or on screen, are as follows:

Keep calm.

If you have any condition that might make the test more difficult for you – partial sightedness, dyslexia, or even not having your reading glasses – tell the person giving you the test and they can make suitable arrangements.

Read the instructions carefully all the way through.

Take full advantage of any practice questions you can do before the timed part of the test.

If there's anything you don't understand, ask the person giving you the test.

If you have any problems during the test – a broken pencil, missing page, disturbing noise outside or bright light in your eyes, for example – let the person administering the test know immediately.

Future trends

Tests are becoming increasingly popular as an objective means of assessing suitability, rather than relying on the interviewer's gut instinct alone. Employers see them as quick, reliable, impartial and fair, and are keen to add to and refine them. The sorts of tests that could well find their way into the interview process in the future include the following.

Emotional intelligence tests

These are personality tests that predict the likelihood of your success by analysing the possession of life skills such as:

self-awareness – the ability to understand and control your own feelings;

emotional resilience – the ability to adapt to situations and recover from setbacks;

motivation – drive, energy and enthusiasm;

interpersonal sensitivity – empathy and respect for others;

influence and persuasion – the ability to influence others positively;

intuitiveness – the ability to trust your instincts;

conscientiousness and integrity – honesty, commitment and reliability.

Cognitive process profiling

Another type of personality test, one that looks at how you think, how you approach problems and your preferred method of working. It can predict whether you will be more comfortable dealing with concrete tasks, parallel processing or strategic thinking when it comes to problem solving, among other things.

Virtual reality

Already widely used for selection and training in the navy and air force, simulated reality tests could become more widespread, testing your reaction rates, dexterity and ability to think on your feet and respond to emergencies in a variety of situations.

Business learning tests

One stage on from job-replica exercises, business learning tests teach you what you need to know in order to carry out a task and then assess your ability to apply that learning in specific situations. They require no previous knowledge, but they do test your ability to both take in and use information reliably, appropriately and intelligently.

EXPERT QUOTE

Don't make things difficult for the interviewer. For example, we ask people to give a short presentation. We tell them it's 10 minutes, but some people still run over. What do you do? If you allow them 12 minutes, it puts the people who stuck to 10 minutes or under at a disadvantage. I let them run over but I resent it and it puts my back up for the rest of the interview.

Mark Riches, Unit Manager, Health Protection Agency

20
Looking the part
Making a good impression from the start

You've done your research, got all your answers prepared and are ready for any question the interviewer might throw at you. All you need to do now is make sure you look the part.

You need to create the right impression from the very first moment of the interview. By the time you're sitting down answering questions, it may be too late. The interviewer will begin to form their opinion the second you step through the door, so make sure they get the right idea from the start. This chapter focuses on the positive impression you can make with your appearance and your body language – how you look and how you behave – and suggests ways you can put yourself across with confidence and assurance even when you feel nervous.

Your appearance and behaviour should convey the same message that your answers to the interviewer's questions do – that you are intelligent, confident and experienced, and can do the job. Everything about you should support this message, from the clothes you wear to the way you sit.

Appearance

Your general appearance

It hardly needs saying that when you go for an interview you must look clean, groomed and smart. Take a little extra care with your appearance, apply a little extra polish and the results will be worth it. Everything you've been told is true – interviewers do notice things like clean fingernails and nicely polished shoes, so pay attention to the details. Things like that help to make you feel confident about meeting strangers and being judged by them. More importantly, they show that you've made the extra effort. Nothing impresses interviewers more than someone who's made an effort.

How you dress

You have to look as if you belong. Dress like a smarter, more polished version of the staff already employed. The current working environment is all about teamwork, so if you look like part of the team you're already ahead of the game.

> If you're applying for a job in a field you already know well and are a part of, this shouldn't pose too much of a problem. Lawyers and accountants nearly always dress like lawyers and accountants; design and media people dress like design and media people the world over.

> If you're entering a new industry you'll need to do some research to find out what the dress code is.

> Look at the company brochures, newsletters and other material to see what type of image they want to project, as it will help you avoid sticking out like a sore thumb.

> Shots of people all looking formal in suits and ties tell you that nothing less than a smart suit for both men and women will do for the interview.

> If, however, the annual report features pictures of the staff in jeans and T-shirts, then smart casual wear will fit in better.

> If in doubt, ask someone who works in that type of job what they recommend, go and see what employees going in and out of the building are wearing, or simply ring the company, say you have an interview there and ask what the dress code is.

In general, you want to present a highly professional appearance in the manner most appropriate for your chosen field. Whether you're dressed in a three-piece suit or chinos, the way to look like a professional is:

> Be clean, fresh, tidy and well pressed.

> Dress for an important meeting or presentation rather than your average day.

> Avoid extremes – if in doubt, lean towards a neutral style and colour.

> Avoid fussy accessories – it's too tempting to fiddle with them when you're nervous.

> Avoid anything jokey when choosing ties, earrings, bags or briefcases, etc – it will cancel your authority immediately.

Avoid anything too short or too tight, as this will also cancel your professionalism.

Dark colours convey professionalism better than light ones.

Plain colours are less distracting than busy patterns.

Quality shows. Well-cut clothes in natural fibres with a good finish are essential whether you're wearing a suit or business casual wear.

It's tempting to buy a new 'interview outfit' just for the big day. If you do, wear it at least a couple of times before the interview, even if only at home. Make sure that the outfit is comfortable and trouble free and that you can sit comfortably in it without anything riding up, twisting round or creasing, and that you can stand up and shake hands without anything gaping or straining. Having to adjust bits of clothing continually will distract both you and the interviewer.

Posture and bearing

Some people can wear the most expensive clothes and still give the impression they've just borrowed them for the occasion if they carry themselves badly. You have to convey the idea that you're keen and capable, and project your confidence and interest:

Think up and open – stand tall, head up, shoulders back.

Remember to breathe.

Aim to be alert and poised in your manner and gestures.

Avoid clutching bags or folders so hard your knuckles go white.

Look around you rather than at the floor – take in your surroundings.

Meet people's gaze and make eye contact.

Smile.

Behaviour

First impressions

Get off to a good start and not only will the interviewer be impressed, but you'll feel confident too. That confidence will help carry you through the first few questions until you relax and get into your stride. You look good; you're dressed well; now greet the interviewer in a friendly and confident manner:

Before you even enter the room, take a moment to centre yourself. Stand tall, pull your shoulders back and your head up. Take a slow, deep breath and let it go.

Smile as you enter.

Close the door behind you.

Make eye contact with the interviewer – and with anyone else in the room.

Be ready to shake hands when they introduce themselves.

Say 'Hello, very nice to meet you' or 'Pleased to meet you' or any other of the usual greetings.

Sit down when invited to.

If the interviewer forgets, wait for a moment before asking 'May I sit down?' or 'Is it OK if I take a seat?'

Be alert to the interviewer's behaviour and follow their lead. Let the interviewer take the initiative and be ready to respond appropriately.

This is the interviewer's territory, so don't attempt to dominate it – hence the advice to wait before shaking hands and sitting down so that the interviewer can take the lead and remain in control. It's not just politeness; it's essential psychology.

Keeping up the good work

Keep the right impression going throughout the interview. By now, your answers should be doing much of the work for you and all that careful preparation is starting to pay off. Underline your suitability with great body language. You want to come across as confident, enthusiastic, responsive and energetic, as well as interested, alert and intelligent. You also want to appear reliable, so develop a moderate voice, controlled gestures and a calm yet keen disposition:

Sit well back in your chair rather than perching nervously on the edge.

Sit upright with both your feet on the floor and your hands resting in your lap or on the arms of the chair.

This position should help you appear alert yet relaxed and help you to avoid nervous or defensive mannerisms such as folding your arms, crossing your legs, fidgeting, tapping your feet, biting your nails, etc.

Keep your head up and look at the interviewer with an interested expression – lean forward slightly in a listening position.

Let your gaze move easily around the interviewer's face as you talk. This helps you maintain good eye contact while avoiding a fixed stare.

Nod intelligently while your interviewer explains things to you or asks you questions.

As you relax, allow your natural gestures to emphasize points and show more of your character.

If you feel yourself getting bogged down or lethargic, pull yourself upright, breathe in and concentrate on being up and open with your posture, gestures and facial expression. It should make you look and feel alert and energetic again.

If, on the other hand, you start to feel uncontrolled and nervous, glance away, breathe in deeply from your stomach, relax your shoulders and let your hands rest on your lap for a moment. You'll look like you're taking a moment to consider and you can resume your answer with renewed poise.

Remember to smile frequently throughout the interview.

Lasting impressions

Having established a good impression and maintained it throughout the interview, leave a good impression behind you when you go:

Be alert to 'winding up' signals from your interviewer.

They might say something like 'We'll be in touch early next week' and thank you for coming in to see them.

Make eye contact.

Smile.

Shake hands.

Thank them for seeing you.

Add something like 'It's been very nice meeting you; I look forward to hearing from you soon' or 'It's been a very interesting afternoon; I look forward to your decision.'

Leave; don't linger.

The interview isn't over until you're off the premises. Wait until then to loosen your tie, light a cigarette or whatever.

Overcoming nerves

Everyone dreads looking nervous in interviews, but, oddly enough, interviewers are quite tolerant. Believe it or not, they actually want you to do well and will usually try to help you display your best qualities. The interviewer has a vacancy to fill. If they don't, they've got a real problem. You could be exactly the person they need, so they're not going to rule you out just because you seem a bit jittery at the start. Only if nerves persist throughout the whole of the interview (they'll worry about your reactions to stress) or stop you giving coherent answers (they'll never find out what you can do) will they be a major problem.

Don't let fear of nerves prevent you from making a positive impression:

Thorough preparation of the sort outlined in this book will improve your confidence. You will understand what they want, why you are right for the job and how, where and when you have demonstrated that.

Practising interview skills – entering a room, shaking hands, etc – and rehearsing answers to interview questions will make them feel more familiar.

Getting organized before the interview will help you avoid unexpected setbacks:

- Make sure you know exactly where the interview is and how to get there.
- Double-check the date, time and name of the person you're meeting.
- Get everything ready the night before, including a copy of your CV or application form, name, address and phone number of the company, fully charged mobile in case of accidents or delays, car keys or money for fares, and any other documents or equipment you need for the interview.

Arrive at your destination a little early. When you get there, ask for the cloakroom and check your appearance thoroughly – hair, teeth, make-up, all your buttons and zips, and any runs or unravellings. Don't forget the obvious reason for using the cloakroom, either – nerves have a terribly stimulating effect on the bladder.

Avoid tea and coffee for an hour or so before the interview – caffeine can make you jittery and it, too, has a stimulating effect on the bladder. Alcohol is best avoided altogether.

Do this quick relaxation exercise to get your nerves under control. Try it a couple of times on the way to the interview and when you're checking your appearance in the cloakroom. It's very unobtrusive, so you can do it while you're waiting to be called as well:

Relax your shoulders and arms.

Breathe in slowly to the count of three.

Hold your breath for the count of three.

Breathe out slowly to the count of five.

Breathe in to the count of five.

Hold your breath for the count of five.

Breathe out to the count of seven.

Breathe normally.

If you start to feel nervous during the interview, remember that:

A deep breath will relax your chest and release tension.

A smile will help relax rigid face muscles.

Nodding slowly while the interviewer is speaking will release neck tension.

Nerves can make you physically close up – hunched shoulders, folded arms, crossed legs, lowered head. Take a moment every so often to open up consciously – head up, shoulders back, feet on the floor, hands on chair arms or on lap. Breathe in and answer the question.

EXPERT QUOTE

First impressions count. I naturally prefer someone who's made an effort; it means they're interested enough in the position to want to make a good impression on me. I look for someone who is appropriately dressed, confident but not overconfident and with good body language. The first 10 seconds really *are* important – the greeting, the handshake. Get that wrong and you spend the rest of the interview trying to retrieve the situation.

Mike Tredrea, HR Manager, West Pharmaceutical Services

EXPERT QUOTE

It's nice if someone is friendly and confident from the start – it means I can relax, too. I feel if someone is too self-conscious, it could mean they're more interested in themselves than they are in the job.

HR Manager, retail company

21
What happens next?

What to do after the interview

While you're waiting for their decision

Make notes

Immediately after the interview, while it's still fresh in your mind, write down some notes about:

who you saw – name and title;

any useful information they gave you about the job and the company;

how the interview went;

the sort of questions they asked;

what went well;

anything you would do differently next time;

what will happen next – if there will be a second interview, when they'll contact you, etc.

These notes will be useful for your records, and also when you go to your next interview – whether that's a second interview with the company, or with another employer. Recalling what questions they asked can be helpful. Were there unexpected areas of your skills and competencies that were focused on? Were there problems in your previous career or work record the interviewer picked up that you hadn't anticipated? Use the experience to polish and perfect your next performance.

Write a letter

After the interview, that day or the next, send a brief letter or e-mail thanking the person who interviewed you, or the leader of the panel if it was a panel interview. This serves several purposes:

It creates a good impression – it's polite, it looks thorough and it conveys enthusiasm.

It gives you a chance to recap your suitability for the job, your enthusiasm for it and the key benefit of employing you.

You can include anything important you missed out at the interview.

It puts your name and suitability at the forefront of the interviewer's mind.

The letter on the next page gives an example. This letter can also be adapted easily for e-mail, of course.

If they don't make you an offer

Bad luck. You were right for the job or they wouldn't have asked you to the interview. Unfortunately, it was someone else's turn to be picked. Look on the bright side, though: that successful candidate won't be at the next interview you go to.

There are several reasons why you might not have been selected this time:

The interviewer didn't believe you had the skills or experience necessary to do the job.

They weren't convinced you understood sufficiently what the job entailed or required.

They didn't think you had the personal qualities such as energy, stress-hardiness or ambition to be successful in the job.

They didn't feel you fitted in – with the team profile, the company culture or whatever.

Note that the reasons above focus specifically on what the interviewer thinks, feels or believes. They may be right or wrong. Their conclusion might be entirely factual, or based on their own misunderstandings and prejudices. They might, on the other hand, be entirely a result of your own failure to convince them. Your task next time is to be so convincing they can't overlook your suitability. Examine each of those areas carefully before the next interview and try to see where any flaws were. Make sure that:

You know from the job ad and the job description (and any other information you can get hold of) exactly what the job entails.

You have the skills and competencies required.

First line of your address
Second line of your address
Third line of your address
Postcode

Telephone number
E-mail address

Date

Name of interviewer
Position
Company name
Address line one
Address line two
Address line three

Dear [Mr, Mrs, Ms – Name]

Thank you for interviewing me for the post of [whatever you are being interviewed for] yesterday [include the date]. I greatly appreciated the opportunity to meet you and find out more about [the company or organization]. It was very interesting to see/hear about [something that impressed or interested you] and to see/hear/understand/experience [something else that stuck in your mind].

Having heard about the work in more detail, I believe I could make a significant contribution to [the company, organization, department, project]. My current experience in [what you do or the most relevant facet of it] has developed my [specific skill, area of experience or responsibility] and my [another relevant strength] to the high level required by your organization. I should also add that [now is the time to mention anything relevant you didn't get a chance to include in the interview].

May I confirm that I would be very interested in taking this position with your company. It offers the opportunity I am looking for to [develop my career, my skills, professional growth, experience, whatever fits your particular circumstances]. I would welcome the chance to work in/with [your team, for example] and believe [in time] I could contribute substantially to the success of [the company, department, project].

I hope you will consider me favourably. I look forward to hearing from you.

Yours sincerely

Your signed name

Your typed name

You can give examples of how, when and where you've demonstrated these in the past.

You can present these examples confidently and enthusiastically.

You display in your appearance and behaviour the personal qualities they want.

Keep in contact

If you really liked the look of the job and felt the company was a good place for you to work, don't give up at the first hurdle. It's worth keeping in contact with them because there's always a possibility that:

the successful candidate initially accepts the job, but their current employer offers them a better deal to stay on;

the successful candidate only stays in the job a couple of months – maybe they weren't right for the job or they found a better one after accepting, or maybe the job didn't turn out to be what they wanted;

another, similar job comes up in the same company.

Swallow your disappointment and reply to their rejection letter. By doing so, you maintain the good impression you worked so hard to establish and remind them that you are still interested in the job and the company. The letter opposite gives an example.

If you are still interested and haven't found anything better after three to six months or so, contact the person who interviewed you again – by letter or e-mail – to keep you and your interest fresh in their mind. An example of this kind of letter is shown on page 208.

Keep in contact for as long as you're still looking for the right opportunity to come up. Even if a suitable vacancy doesn't open there, your interviewer may hear of something in another department, branch or organization and let you know about it.

Keep applying

Get as much interview experience as you can. The more you do, the better you get, so that when your chance of a lifetime comes up you won't miss out because you are unprepared.

Don't wait for the result of one interview before applying for the next. You need to keep up the momentum. If you get a rejection, it's much easier to shrug and put it down to experience if you have another three or four promising meetings lined up and five or six applications in the post.

First line of your address
Second line of your address
Third line of your address
Postcode

Telephone number
E-mail address

Date

Name of interviewer
Position
Company name
Address line one
Address line two
Address line three

Dear [Mr, Mrs, Ms – Name]

Thank you for your letter of [the date]. Although I am naturally disappointed at not being chosen for the position of [whatever it was], I would like to thank you for taking the time to consider my application.

What I saw of the company at the interview interested me greatly, and I would still like the opportunity to work for you. I would, therefore, like to ask if you would keep my name and details on file for consideration should the situation change or another vacancy arise.

Yours sincerely

Your signed name

Your typed name

First line of your address
Second line of your address
Third line of your address
Postcode

Telephone number
Email address

Date

Name of interviewer
Position
Company name
Address line one
Address line two
Address line three

Dear [Mr, Mrs, Ms – Name]

You may remember interviewing me for the post of [whatever you were being interviewed for] on [the date of the interview]. Unfortunately, I was unsuccessful on that occasion, so I am writing to you again to see if any opportunities have arisen in the meantime. Although I was disappointed at not being chosen for the post, I was very interested in what I saw of the company at the interview and would still like the chance to work for you.

I am [remind them what you do] with a sound background in [remind them what your background is] and many/several/some years' experience of [your experience that would be of benefit to the company]. Since our last meeting, I have [tell them about any skills, qualifications or experience you've gained in the meantime].

I believe I have the skills and abilities that fit well with your need for first-rate staff [for example], and I believe I could make a valuable contribution to [the company, organization, department, team].

I look forward to hearing from you.

Yours sincerely

Your signed name

Your typed name

After every interview and before the next, look over your notes and review your performance. Is there anything you could do better next time? Is there any area you could strengthen or polish?

If they do make you an offer

Congratulations, they want you. You now have to decide if you:

want the job, no question;

want the job subject to negotiation;

might want the job if a better offer doesn't materialize;

don't want the job.

If your answer is no or maybe

If you don't want the job, tell them so immediately: they'll want to offer it to someone else as soon as possible. Be polite, though; you may want to apply to them again in the future.

If you might want the job, contact them immediately, thanking them for their decision. Be enthusiastic and positive, but ask for a day or two to think it over. It's better to do it this way than simply avoid calling them until you've made a decision.

While thinking it over:

Weigh up the pros and cons of the job you're currently in, or your current situation if you're unemployed, and decide if you want to stay or go and at what price.

Weigh up the pros and cons of the job you've been offered and see if it's worth accepting regardless of whether it's the only one on offer or not.

Contact any potential employers who have interviewed you but not yet made an offer. Explain the situation and ask if they are in a position to make a decision. Even if they're not, they should at least let you know if you're definitely out of the running, which should make your choice easier.

If you have interviews to come or promising applications in the system, you have to make an educated guess about their likely outcome.

Weigh up the importance of the offer. Getting an offer on your first interview might be very different from finally getting one after a dozen or so interviews.

Negotiation

Having just been offered the job, you are in a very strong position to bargain. Unless they state categorically that the offer is standard for all employees at that grade and non-negotiable, ask for the best deal you can get. As long as you remain reasonable and polite, there is little chance you'll negotiate yourself out of the job even in the current economy. If they can't meet your requests, they'll just tell you they can't and put the ball back in your court. Accept it gracefully and either carry on bargaining or give in, depending on your skill and confidence as a negotiator.

Before you start negotiating, decide if there are any deal breakers – a salary below which you won't go, hours you can't work and so on.

Know your worth. Reread the job description and requirements. If you have more than they ask for – qualifications, experience, training, extra computer skills or a language, for example – and it's relevant to the job, that could be a useful tool.

Get clued up about all the added extras available – what does the company offer other employees? What do other similar companies offer? Can you negotiate childcare contributions, car or travel allowance, expenses, a laptop, mobile phone or pocket PC and so on?

Are you prepared to offer any concessions – cover extra duties in exchange for a higher salary, for example?

Be prepared to compromise. If they can't offer a higher basic salary, are you willing to accept other benefits such as higher commission, increased overtime, bonuses, or the promise of a pay review in six months, for example, to make up the difference?

Your working conditions might be negotiable as well – location, type of office, starting and finishing hours, for example.

Once you've finished negotiating and agreed a deal that you're both happy with, you should receive a formal offer letter along with your starting date. Make sure you know exactly what the job entails and what you are being offered in return before you formally and bindingly accept the offer in writing. Give your notice to your current employer only when you have everything in black and white, not before – accidents can always happen. Notify anyone else who might need to know, such as companies that have just interviewed you or are about to do so – don't just leave them in the lurch.

All that's left to say is: good luck in your new job.

EXPERT QUOTE

My decision to employ somebody is not necessarily based on their availability. If they're the right person, I'd rather wait three or four months while they work out their notice rather than lose them. I hope they're going to be with us for some years, so what are a few more months? I also hope they're going to be loyal, so why penalize them for showing loyalty to their previous employer?

Tina M Buchanan, Group HR Director, Hamworthy Combustion Engineering

INDEX TO THE QUESTIONS

The interviewers' questions

Your questions for the interviewer

INDEX

THE ENERGY-EFFICIENT HOME

PAUL WAGLAND
LAURA COOK

GUILD OF MASTER
CRAFTSMAN PUBLICATIONS

First published 2009 by
Guild of Master Craftsman Publications Ltd
Castle Place, 166 High Street, Lewes,
East Sussex BN7 1XU

ISBN 978-1-86108-648-8

Associate Publisher Jonathan Bailey
Production Manager Jim Bulley
Managing Editor Gerrie Purcell
Senior Project Editor Dominique Page
Editor Naomi Waters
Managing Art Editor Gilda Pacitti
Design Chloë Alexander

Set in Helvetica Neue and Nofret
Colour origination by GMC Reprographics
Printed and bound by Hung Hing Printing Co. Ltd.

Image credits
All photographs by Paul Wagland and Laura Cook, with the
following exceptions:

Baufritz.co.uk: 3; 12TR; 26T, 38, 39

Bellapierre.com: 146

Bumblebeeconservation.org: 109TR: Penny Frith; 109BR,
110TR, 110TL: Dave Goulson

Chloë Alexander: 89

Dreamstime.com: 12: Stuartkey; 13BL: Rkudasik; 14T:
Einbog; 15TR: Baloncici; 16L: Mishoo; 17T: Alphaspirit; 18TL:
Iwan-drago; BL: Jogough; 20T: Pheby; 20B: Wayfarer; 21B:
Andreyg80; 24: Tinabelle; 25T: Plumdesign; 25B: Coppit1606;
26B: Copit1606; 28: Douglas_freer; 30T: Lagom; 30BR: Sergo;
34T: Hpphoto; 34B: Lugers; 35: Baburkina567; 36: Socrates;
37: Noonie; 48: Anthonyata; 51: Roberto222; 55: krzyssagit;
59TL: Zygomaticus; 59TR: Gabilungu; 60B: Donkeyhotay; 61T:
Sebcz; 62R: Spe; 63: Terex; 64BL: Jakich; 70L: Peter.wey;
71TL: Bradcalkins; 71TR: Monkeybusinessimages; 72: Kayella;
73T: Leifstiller; 73B: Chepe; 76: Thinkomatic; 77T: Westbury;
77B: Photodesign; 78: MariaUK; 79: Ca2hill; 86: Mashe; 95:
Dusanjankovic; 96BR: Andorapro; 97TL: Elenathewise; 97BR:
Andystjohn; 99: Aaneela; 108TR: Igordutina;108B: Stevebyland;
109TL: Graemo; 110BL: Chloetru; 111TR: Davidmartyn;
111B: Artandphoto; 112TR: Paolo-Frangiolli; 116: Asist; 117T:
Easyshoot; 120: Johnnychaos; 121: Darrinb1; 130BL: Dmitry
Maslov; 131: Jack Schiffer; 134T: Darkop; 134BR: Elenamiv; 138;
Inavanhateren; 139T: Evgenyb; 139B: Kshishtof; 143B: Jms; 147:
148TR: Looby; 148BL: Molka; 149: Polusvet; 152BL: Edisaacs;
152TR: Teamarbeit; 153: Pinkcandy; 154: Blumenfan; 158: Tiero;
159TL: Armonn 159TR: Sleiselei; 160R: Perkmeup; 164: Bsenic;
165TL: Johnnychaos; 165BR: Diego.cervo; 166: Innocent; 167T:
Sugarfoot; 169: Geoffp99; 170: Alexshalomov; 171: Swimnews

Ecocentric.co.uk: 157

Ecofreak.co.uk: 46

Ethicalsuperstore.com: 60TR

Flikr.com: 16, 17: Bryn Pinzgauer; 29: onemananhisdogs; 31:
buildingdiy; 32: Bryn Pinzgauer; 42: Shazari; 52 dominic's pics;
74: gluemoon; 75: chegs; 84 nicolasnova; 88: mlinksva; 96:
sheilaellen; 98: timparkinson; 100 nationalrural; 101: Kai Hendry;
118: David Spender; 119: ciamabue; 122: KirrilyRobert; 132:
John-Morgan; 133: net_efekt; 133: jawcey; 155: OiMax; 155:
.Martijn; 161: SharonaGott; 163: timparkinson; 163: dumbledad;
168: Frankh

iStockphoto.com: 14BL: Jill Kyle; 15TL: Bmcent1; 15B:
Gmnicholas; 19: iofoto; 27: Shelly Perry; 32: Melhi; 33:
Greenpimp; 41: Miklav; 47T: Jitalia17; 50: Eliandric; 52: Tacrafts;
54B: Keithpix; 54T: AndreasWeber; 59B: Diane39; 123: Peter
Eckhardt 135: Robin702; 140L: Tacojim; 162: Parema

Mygreenerhome.com: 22L; 23TL; 23BL; 58; 61B, 62L

Pinsandribbons.co.uk: 21T

Recyclenow.com: 80; 81; 82; 83; 84; 85; 126; 127TL; 128; 129;
156; 160L

Thomson-Morgan.com: 104; 118TL

Totsbots.com: 156

UKJuicers.com: 105TL; 105TR

Yes-reedbeds.co.uk: 64BR; 65; 66; 67

Contents

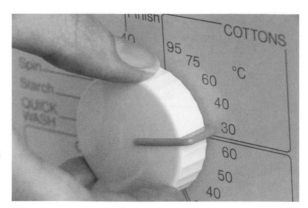

1 Building Fabric

2 Energy

4 The Green Kitchen

3 The Green Bathroom

5 The Green Garden

6 Shopping and Lifestyle

The concept of 'peak oil' has become familiar to anyone who reads the papers or watches TV. It describes the point when the growing demand for global energy will outstrip the rate of new discoveries of oil. In other words, more people are using more energy, but we're finding less and less oil to generate that energy. With the number of people on the planet rising steadily, there will inevitably be power shortages, leading to breakdowns in transport, communications and the global economy.

The most obvious solution to this problem is to use other ways of generating energy, besides burning oil (or natural gas, coal or other finite fossil fuels). While it is theoretically possible to meet the global energy demand using entirely sustainable technologies (including solar, wind and wave power), the logistical challenges of doing this are huge. Furthermore, there is immense social and political inertia to be overcome before we can even begin to perform this giant switchover in any meaningful way. The sad truth is that it is unlikely to happen before we reach crisis point.

But this does not mean that there is nothing we, as individuals, can do to alleviate the situation or to prepare ourselves for life in the very different world after the end of the oil age. Reducing our dependence on cheap, almost limitless energy is an easy way to achieve both of these goals. Take a look at your lifestyle and you will find some areas where you waste energy. Perhaps you travel by car to a place of work that is well-served by public transport; doubtless there is imported food in your weekly shop; maybe you like the central heating turned up high but have yet to properly insulate your home. We are almost all guilty, to a lesser or greater extent, of this sort of waste. Partly the reason for this wastage is that up until now we have never had to worry much about the consequences. It is often surprisingly easy to reduce our consumption, and there are often other secondary benefits to a change in our energy-consumption habits. These include avoiding the stress of rush-hour driving by taking the bus, buying better-quality local food, and so on.

There is little doubt that all our lives will need to change dramatically over the next decade or two; what remains to be seen is whether we make that a change for the better. Through often simple and straightforward measures and practices, this book will help you to transform all aspects of your home and lifestyle for a greener future, today.

Building Fabric

Housing in the UK is embarrassingly outdated compared with that in much of Europe. Poor-quality postwar construction, a lack of government investment, inefficient technology and a mass-production approach to recent housing demands have combined to leave the UK with little to be proud of in this regard. While an integrated, far-sighted approach to construction is not unfeasible, we also need to look at what we can do to improve the housing we already have.

Heating

KEEPING WARM consumes by far the largest amount of energy in the home but much of what we use is wasted simply because of bad housing design. Perhaps as much as 75 per cent of the energy we use to heat our living space is expended unnecessarily, so there's clearly plenty of room for improvement here.

Central heating options

MOST MODERN houses have some form of central heating. This is normally serviced by a boiler of some description, which is a heat-centralized generator that feeds the radiators around the house. The boiler and the design of the system needs to be energy efficient, but the type of fuel that feeds the system also needs to be taken into consideration. See also the section on solar gain (pages 37–8) for a further space-heating option.

Wood-burning and biomass boilers

The idea of burning wood to generate heat has been around ever since man discovered fire. Happily, the technology has moved on since then but the appeal of sitting in front of a real

▼ **Keeping an eye on the heating is the first step to saving energy in the home.**

▲ A real fire can create a focal point in a room, but is not without disadvantages.

▼ When choosing a wood-burning stove, first consider where you will source the fuel.

flame has probably not. It is a pleasant, sociable appliance that can transform the atmosphere of a home. One downside is that wood produces ash that requires disposal. Another is that you have to move the wood from the point where you had it delivered (your drive or garage, for example) to the woodshed every month when it arrives. You have to move it again to the stove every morning and evening. If you can get used to the job of going out and collecting your firewood (and there's no reason you shouldn't even enjoy it) then fitting a wood–burning boiler could be a very positive step.

In fact, wood burned in a modern, properly maintained stove will produce less carbon dioxide than the same wood left to rot on the forest floor. That's right – a wood–burning stove can make your heating system carbon–negative! Add to this the fact that a commercial firewood–producing venture would need to plant and manage many acres of deciduous woodland

(along with its concomitant plants and wildlife) and you have the blueprint for an eco-friendly system. Unfortunately, not every country on the planet has the land necessary to grow the wood to heat all of our homes, but that's not to say nobody should be doing it.

▼ **Fuel for biomass boilers is available in chipped or pelleted form.**

▲ **Wood-burning can be an energy-efficient method of heating the home.**

If the idea of burning wood appeals to you, but you want something a little more convenient and low–maintenance, a biomass boiler could be the answer. They look a bit like industrial machinery so are generally less attractive than straightforward stoves. They can include a self-feeding mechanism that pulls the fuel (often wood chips or pellets) into the burn chamber at the desired rate. Extremely efficient, they have the two–fold drawback of a hefty initial price tag and usually the need for some kind of boiler room or outbuilding.

Mains gas

The most common form of heating fuel in the UK is gas, available in all large urban areas and piped directly into 18 million UK homes. As a primary fuel, gas is pumped directly to your home. Unlike electricity, it does not need to be converted outside your home before it can be used. Compared with all–electric heating, this

▲ While gas boilers are efficient, they ultimately rely on an unsustainable fuel source.

cuts down on one area of wastage. This is because when a primary fuel (gas, coal, oil, etc.) is burned to create electricity, much of the energy in the fuel escapes as waste heat.

Although it is a fossil fuel (and therefore the supply is ultimately limited) it is the most efficient member of the fossil–fuel family. Unless you are in a position to generate your own heat from a renewable source, to make use of passive solar heating (see pages 37–8) or to run your heating on electricity from a 100 per cent–renewables supplier, then gas is the best option available to you.

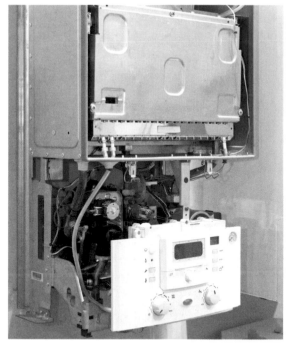

▲ Boilers require regular servicing to ensure they are energy efficient.

Heating oil

Oil is a similar proposal to gas because they both rely on a fossil fuel to provide energy via a conventional boiler. Many boiler designs can easily be converted from one fuel to the other. On the downside, it's a limited resource and prices are on the rise. Furthermore, because oil heating

▼ Oil is an efficient source of heat, although inconvenient to store.

▲ **Although intended to save money, storage heaters can actually prove very expensive.**

requires regular deliveries from a supplier and a large, outdoor storage tank, it is by no means as convenient as a mains supply of natural gas.

Electric heating

In places where mains gas is unavailable, and oil or wood–burning boilers are not fitted, an alternative is to have electric radiators. Sometimes these are storage heaters, which use a cheap, late–night electricity supply to warm up then slowly release this heat through the day. Invariably these are inefficient and, as a result, are expensive. For one thing they make use of a secondary energy source (electricity) that has been converted from a primary one (coal or gas) at the power station, and this conversion itself involves a considerable energy loss. What's more, storage heaters tend to be cold by evening, so they get used on a 'boost' setting which is rather defeating the point. That's not to say electric heating doesn't have a place – it is easy to install, even in small or remote properties, and can feasibly be run using a renewable supply of electricity, which makes it very sustainable. See chapter two for more on this subject.

Ground-source heat pumps

Although they may be beyond the resources and budgets of many people, it's worth mentioning heat pumps here as they are slowly becoming more affordable (around £5,000 to £10,000 at the

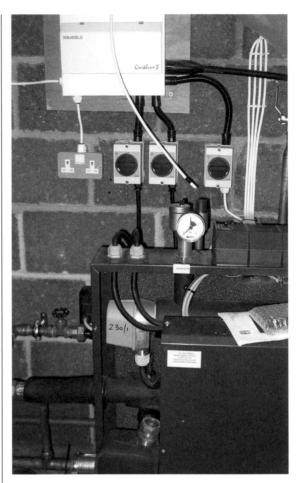

▲ **If you can afford the initial outlay, a heat pump will reduce your CO_2 emissions.**

time of writing, for a typical house). They work by circulating a mixture of water and antifreeze through a system of pipes buried below the surface of the ground. These pipes often run horizontally at a depth of 2m (6½ft) or so, but can also be installed vertically down as far as 100m (328ft). Because the temperature of the ground remains constant throughout the year, the circulating fluid absorbs warmth even when it's below zero above ground. This warmth can be transferred to radiators in the house, and even used to preheat hot water. In addition to the installation costs there will also be running costs (perhaps £500 per year), as the system requires an electric pump. All the same, compared to electric heating, a ground–source heat pump could save you £1,000 (and 7t of CO_2) every year.

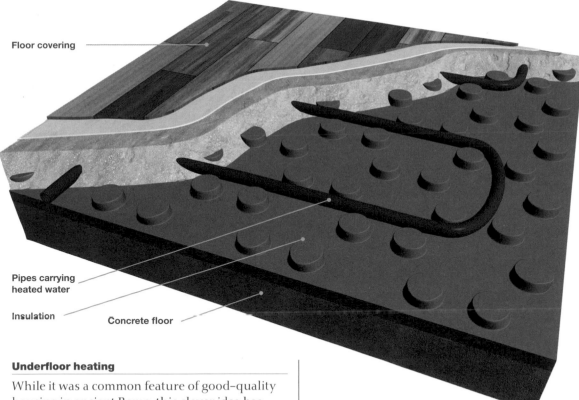

Floor covering

Pipes carrying
heated water

Insulation

Concrete floor

Underfloor heating

While it was a common feature of good–quality housing in ancient Rome, this clever idea has yet to properly catch on in modern building design. The principal of a modern system is straightforward: simply heat water using a conventional boiler and pump it around a system of pipes just under the surface of the floor. The water will lose heat as it travels, warming the room above in the process. Underfloor heating can be used in conjunction with a combination boiler or even a wood–burning stove.

▼ **Underfloor circuits ensure that the heat source is felt rather than seen.**

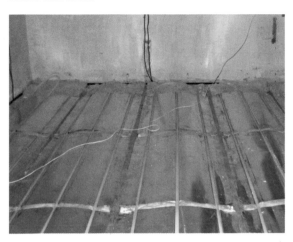

▲ **Underfloor heating is an ancient concept, yet is relevant to the modern, energy-efficient home.**

There are many advantages to this technology; perhaps the most important of these for us end–users is that the heat provided is even, with no hot or cold spots and variation across the room. This comfortable environment means you won't feel a chill as you would when sitting a long way from the radiator, and thus won't be tempted to crank–up the boiler to compensate (over–heating the rest of the house in the process). Furthermore, localized sources of heat such as radiators and open fires are prone to causing convection currents in the air, which may contribute to draughts as cold air is pulled in from outside.

Improving efficiency

Whatever source of energy you use to supply your household heating, you can cut down on your demand by making sure the system is as efficient as possible. Boilers have to function almost every day and combine electricity, water and naked flames in close proximity. Quite apart from the safety requirement to

▲ **Air vents are an important safety feature of boilers, and keeping them clear improves efficiency.**

have them serviced regularly, central heating systems will work more efficiently if they are given a little attention now and then. Much of the work involved here is strictly the preserve of a professional tradesman, but there are things you can do to help. If your boiler is in a cupboard or storeroom, make sure it doesn't get covered up by other things stored with it. Air intakes and vents need to be uncovered in order to work properly and this means giving them a good clean every few months. There's no point in heating the water for your radiators and taps if half the heat is lost before it gets to its intended destination. Make sure all pipework (especially any that goes outside) is well insulated with special lagging tubes.

▼ **Many of us use heating to compensate for lack of adequate clothing. Instead, turn down the heat and put on a jumper!**

▲ **Pipe insulation is an easy and cost-effective way to reduce heat loss.**

Other improvements to efficiency depend as much on adjustments to the way you use the system as they do to the physical equipment. Using a heating system efficiently is often a question of habit. For example, if there is a part of the house that is rarely used (perhaps a hobby room or spare bedroom), then turn down the radiators in these rooms and get into the habit of closing the doors between them and other parts of the house. Room thermostats cost very little and can easily be fitted by anyone without even the most basic DIY knowledge. It won't take long to turn up the radiators and warm up the rooms again when they're needed. Another simple change is to dress warmly with extra layers when the weather is cold. This simple resolution will enable you to turn your heating down by several degrees with no great loss of comfort. Lying around in your underwear in the middle of winter with the boiler blazing away is obviously not a sensible or responsible use of energy.

▲ **When heating your home, concentrate on the areas that are in constant use.**

How you run a heating system should depend firstly on how you use the house. If your home is occupied all day long then the heating demand will reflect this. If the whole family is out from 9am to 5.30pm, there is really no need to have all the radiators pumping out heat between these times. It's also unnecessary to heat the house to more than 15°C (59°F) when all the occupants are in bed. If you find you are cold at night then a thicker duvet or an extra blanket will save you a great deal of money compared to heating unused or empty rooms. While you could turn the heat on or off manually every day, you would be better advised to install some decent heating controls that include an automatic timer. This will allow you to tailor the heat supply to your regular demand. The heat can be programmed to come on an hour before you get up in the morning or 30 minutes before you get home from work – so

there is no time lag between your arrival and the house warming up. Take professional advice when choosing heating controls – they will need to be matched carefully to your house and boiler. Look for a seven–day timer that will allow you to run different programmes each day and thus take into account the weekend when you may be at home all day. A 24–hour timer only allows you to repeat the same on and off times every day of

Did you know ?

If your heating system is more than 10 years old, you could probably save a third of your heating bills by replacing the old boiler.

▲ **Thermostatic radiator valves allow you to control heat distribution in each room.**

the week. These timers vary in complexity from a simple device that fits between a plug and a socket (ideal for a simple electric heater) to a fully programmable, wall–mounted control panel that runs every aspect of your household heating. Some can even be activated by mobile phone, in case of an unexpected early return home.

Dealing with draughts

Pressure differences between the inside and outside of a house will encourage air to move in or out. This might not be too noticeable on a warm summer's day, but in a chilly winter it is both uncomfortable and an expensive waste of warm air. Draughts are often caused by the wind, but could also be the result of an open fire

sucking fresh air in to feed itself, or simply by the upward motion of warm air within the house, which draws cold air in behind it (sometimes called the stack effect). Whatever the cause, it is a very good idea to draught–proof your house early on in your energy–saving programme. It's a low–cost, high–impact improvement.

Your draft–exclusion strategy should initially focus on areas of 'high infiltration', i.e., those where the draughts are strongest. This is most likely around windows and doors (particularly old sash windows or badly fitted doors), which may well benefit from the addition of draught–proofing strips, threshold brushes or letterbox excluders. Even a cover for the keyhole can make quite a difference over a long winter. Don't forget to check chimneys (which can be sealed or capped) and loft hatches (which can have draught–excluding strips added). Lastly, any bare floorboards may allow air to seep between them. Consider filling the cracks between them and below skirting boards with a flexible sealant.

Ventilation

While it might seem wise from a heat–retaining point of view to completely seal a house, this would allow a build–up of stale air, bad smells and humidity. Older houses, especially, need to 'breathe' in order to avoid becoming damp.

▼ **The obvious areas of heat loss, such as letterboxes and doors, are extremely easy to insulate.**

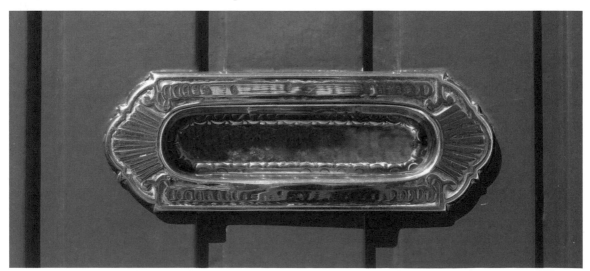

Did you know ?

While most of us would act quickly to repair a leaking tap, a leak of warm air through a draughty window is a far more costly problem. It's probably easier to fix, too.

You want to avoid draughts but need to be able to control the amount ventilation you have in different parts of your home. The amount required will vary from room to room – in many cases a simple trickle vent in a window will be enough. In a humid area, such as a bathroom or kitchen, you may well need to install mechanical ventilation; for example, an extractor fan.

▼ **Controlled ventilation will prevent your house from becoming damp and stale.**

▲ **Badly fitted doors lead to high levels of heat loss. As a temporary measure, try a fabric draught excluder.**

Insulation

ONCE YOU'VE expended all that energy generating the heat you need, the next step is to keep the warm air where you want it. The way to do this is to create a well–insulated barrier between your home and the outside world. While this will not entirely prevent the heat being lost, it will substantially slow the rate of loss, so that you have the benefit of the heat for longer.

U-values explained

IN ORDER to compare the insulating properties of different materials, people in the construction industry use something called u–values. In essence, every wall, ceiling, window and door has a u–value that reflects how good it is at reducing heat loss. The lower the u–value, the better the insulating properties; for instance, a roof or external wall with 200mm (8in) of rockwool insulation might have a u–value of 0.2, while a window might be around 1.0. This allows you to compare different products (for example, triple glazing vs secondary glazing) and to rate materials by their effectiveness.

Improving loft insulation

AS WE all know, heat rises. This means the air that you've just spent good money on heating will have a tendency to move upwards. As a result, one of the biggest energy–efficiency improvements for a typical house is to upgrade

▼ **Modern loft insulation is simple to install, and easier on the lungs than traditional fibreglass.**

▲ **Roll-out insulation is the most common solution to preventing heat loss through the ceiling.**

the thermal insulation in the roof space. As our attics are generally quite accessible but rarely on display (so don't require a smart finish), this is also one of the easiest improvements you can make.

Most of us have at least some type of loft insulation in place, but this is often just 50mm (2in) of tired, tatty fibreglass that may have

▼ **Crushed and ancient fibreglass is inefficient. It is best replaced with a thicker layer of insulating material.**

been squashed and displaced by stored boxes of Christmas decorations, old toys and broken TVs. The current UK building regulations (which must be applied in all new–build properties) state that the minimum insulation thickness should be 270mm (10½in). Many environmental campaigners say even this is nowhere near enough to be effective.

It's worth remembering that heat will search for the easiest way to seep out of a building; there's no point installing 1m (3¼ft) of loft insulation if you have badly fitted single–glazed windows.

External walls

AFTER THE roof, the outside walls of the house are the next most important target for insulation. As a matter of fact, most houses lose more heat through their four walls than they do through their roof, but the job of reducing this loss is harder and more expensive. The type of work you can have done will depend on the construction of your house. Cavity walls present an obvious opportunity for placing insulation within the cavity itself.

▼ **Cavity wall insulation is installed by pumping expandable foam into the gap between masonry layers.**

▲ **Insulation can cause lung irritation, so protective breathing apparatus should be worn during installation.**

The installation is very quick and simple – it can often be done in just one day and entails little mess or disruption. The process involves drilling small holes in the outer wall, then injecting the insulating material through these holes.

If you have solid walls, your best option may be external surface insulation, which involves fixing rigid insulating panels to the walls, and usually rendering over the top. This is a job for a professional and can be expensive, as there are a number of difficult design considerations, such as what to do around doors and windows, and how the insulation will join the overhang of the roof.

In some situations (such as in a conservation area) it may not be possible to treat the problem externally, in which case internal surface

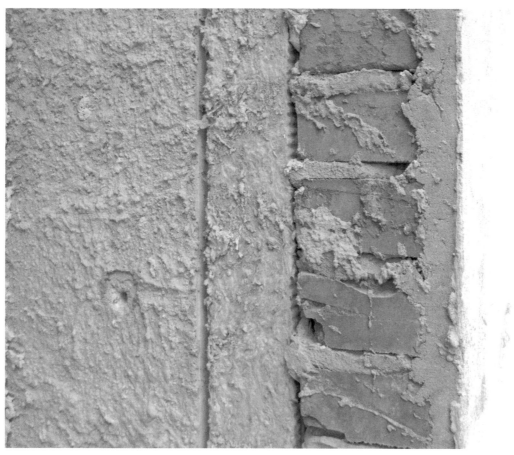

▲ A layer of insulation can be covered with plasterboard to conserve heat.

insulation is the answer. This is sometimes known as insulating dry–lining, and can be done in one of two ways. The first way is to fix rigid insulating panels to the interior walls and cover with plasterboard. You may find some plasterboard has the insulation already attached. The second way is to build new timber studwork against the walls, and insert mineral wool or a similar insulating material between the gaps between the timbers. The drawback to this method is the disruption involved, and the obvious loss of internal space. It would be cheaper to do the whole house in one go, but may be more convenient to do one room at a time, perhaps as you redecorate.

If you are in the process of building a new house, make sure it is constructed with well–insulated walls.

◄ Building a layer of studwork allows extra insulation to be accommodated, but can reduce room size.

▲ A well-designed house should include insulation as an integral component.

Under the floor

HEAT CAN also travel downwards, especially if you have wooden floorboards with gaps between them. A suspended timber floor (that is, one that has boards on top of joists with a void underneath) can be insulated simply by filling the gaps between the joists with insulation. In theory, this is much like insulating a roof space but, of course, you will need to lift the floorboards in order to put the insulation in place. If you carry out this improvement, make sure you don't obstruct any vents or airbricks that were originally installed to allow underfloor ventilation.

A solid concrete floor can also be insulated, either underneath it or on top. Obviously, if you put the insulation underneath it's rather easier to do so before the concrete is poured. As an improvement to an existing property, insulation above a concrete floor is only feasible as part of a major refurbishment. You will need to be careful not to raise the floor level to the point at which it would interfere with power sockets and other fittings.

◄ If you are replacing a floor, it is a good idea to add insulating underlay at the same time.

▲ **Adding a layer of thick lining fabric to existing curtains will reduce heat loss through the windows.**

Curtains

WHILST THEIR most obvious functions are to provide privacy and to exclude light, curtains can also be very effective insulators. If you are replacing them, use thick material with a thermal lining. Existing curtains can also be taken down and lined. It is worth considering fitting an additional blind within the window recess to provide yet another barrier against heat loss.

Glazing

AN UNINSULATED house will lose about 10 per cent of its heat through its windows, which is a lot, considering they make up such a small proportion of the surface area. Modern houses are all built with double glazing, but there is quite a range of quality, and some budget products can prove to be a false economy.

▼ **With careful planning, traditional windows can retain their charm when renovated to improve efficiency.**

Restore or replace?

THIS IS the big question when it comes to windows: should you repair old, single-glazed windows, filling holes in the wood and repainting as necessary, or should you rip them out and put in modern, perhaps double-glazed replacements? In terms of energy-efficiency, new

▲ **Whilst double glazing will improve the energy-efficiency of a house, it can result in a mismatched exterior, so choose with care.**

windows are a much better option. There is little doubt that they will be better at keeping heat in (and draughts out). But of course there are other things to consider: architectural conservationists point out that old buildings need plenty of air movement to stay dry, and replacing beautiful four–over–four sash windows with plastic–framed double glazing is not a clever move. If you need to improve the performance of old windows, first look into having them professionally restored. This will reduce draughts and extend their life. Next, investigate installing secondary glazing, which is very efficient and relatively inexpensive. If you decide old windows are beyond saving, it is possible to have timber double–glazed units made to match an existing design.

▲ **Double glazing traps layers of air between glass. This slows, although doesn't prevent, heat loss.**

▼ **Large areas of glass, such as these doors, can be made far more energy-efficient with double glazing.**

Double and triple glazing

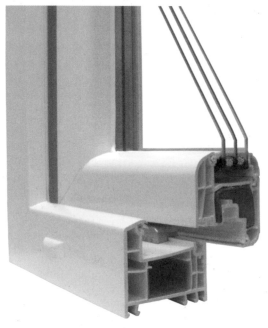

▲ **The larger quantity of trapped air makes triple-glazing an even better choice for slowing heat transfer.**

A DDING EXTRA panes of glass, one inside the other, has the effect of creating a more effective barrier to heat loss through a window. This has little to do with the extra thickness of glass, but is more a result of the layers of air between the panes acting like a blanket to slow down the transfer of heat. Generally speaking, higher–quality windows feature a bigger air gap between the panes, and are better at insulating as a result. Some products also feature special low–emissivity glass that blocks radiant heat transfer, while others replace the trapped air with inert gases such as xenon, which have even greater insulating properties. While triple glazing is not common in the UK, it is widely used in Scandinavia and has great potential.

Replacement windows often come in sealed units, with the frames constructed of PVC–u, aluminium or timber. The choice of material has important ecological consequences; aluminium is the least effective in terms of keeping the heat in, so should be avoided. PVC–u is a good insulator and is often the cheapest option, but the manufacture of the plastic components is quite an unsound process, involving a number of harmful pollutants. Timber, then, is the best choice on ecological grounds, but do check that the timber comes from a sustainable source. Windows with a softwood frame have been proven to last just as long as PVC–u (given the proper maintenance) and hardwood frames last even longer. While they do require repainting from time to time, wooden units are also easier to repair. Search the internet or ask in timber yards and builders' merchants for suppliers of timber windows.

Secondary glazing

IF YOU have single–glazed windows in good condition, or you are keen to retain them as an original feature of the house, you can improve their insulating properties by adding secondary glazing. This is simply an extra layer of glass fitted in a frame inside the existing window. While they are not as elegant or convenient as a self–contained double–glazed unit, they are often considerably more efficient in terms of heat retention. The reason for this is that the air gap is so large. For a really well–insulated window, there's no reason why you shouldn't install secondary glazing inside double–glazed units.

Another option is to use stick–on plastic film, which adheres to the inside of a window (often using the heat from a hair dryer) to improve the thermal qualities of the glass. This material doesn't last very long (some are designed to be replaced every year) but it does offer a cheaper, quicker alternative to secondary glazing that may suit people living in rented accommodation.

▼ **Old buildings are often draughty and need re-glazing to improve heat retention.**

Lighting

WHILE INDIVIDUAL lights don't use as much energy as, say, an electric heater, they tend to be used for long periods of time. A number of lights can be on at the same time in different parts of the house, which can contribute quite a bit to the overall energy footprint of a house – anything from 25 to 60 per cent of the total once electrical heating has been discounted.

▼ **Clean windows and plenty of natural light can have a positive impact on your well-being.**

Natural light

THIS IS the first thing to consider when looking for a low–energy lighting solution; natural light is free, plentiful and very good for your mental health and sense of well–being. Sunlight is a good source of vitamin D. The fact that we go without it for so long over winter is the sole cause of Seasonal Affective Disorder

▲ **A skylight will brighten up even the darkest, smallest corner and is easier on the eye than spotlights.**

(SAD). If you're looking at a new–build home then, of course, you can include plenty of south–facing windows and even a courtyard or light well to flood the interior with natural light.

But what can you do in an existing house to maximize this natural resource? The first thing is to keep your windows clean. You might not think this makes much difference, but a dirty window really does block out quite a bit of light and make a room much darker. The next step is to assess the furnishings inside the room; dark walls, carpets and furniture will all absorb light, while light ones will reflect it. Lastly, make sure that the windowsill is free of unnecessary clutter and cut back any plants that grow under or around the window, as both these will shade the interior.

Skylights

IN ROOMS where natural light doesn't reach far enough into the interior, it can sometimes be possible to create light from above via a skylight. This has the advantages of providing a pleasant, well–lit environment without sacrificing any wall space. Of course, the feasibility of this depends on what is located above the ceiling. If the roof is only just above the room then installation should be simple, but even if there is a large roof void (or even an entire storey) then light can be directed through a reflective 'sun pipe', topped by a plastic dome.

Low-energy light bulbs

WHILE CONVENTIONAL incandescent light bulbs have been in use for many years, they are, in fact, very inefficient. They transform as much as 95 per cent of the energy they use into heat, with just 5 per cent being used for light. Fluorescent lights are four or five times more efficient, but it's only recently that they have improved to the point at which they have become a realistic alternative. Fluorescent lights are now very compact, and can give a warm, pleasant glow rather than the harsh light with which they are most often associated.

Where fluorescent lights are not suitable, consider low–voltage quartz halogen bulbs. These still have a filament design but require much less energy to run than conventional light bulbs and will last longer as well.

▲ LED lights are becoming increasingly popular, and require minimal energy to run.

▼ Energy-efficient bulbs are now commonplace, and great value for money compared with traditional bulbs.

▲ **As well as being useful for close work, a lamp also creates a cosy, relaxed and homely atmosphere.**

Task lighting

A PART FROM the fittings themselves, what else can you do to make lights more efficient? The answer is to use them only when and where they are needed. Get into the habit of turning off the light every time you leave a room. Other examples of good practice might include using a table lamp to top–up the illumination offered by a softer overhead light. However, you should turn one or both off when you turn on the TV to watch a film. A desk lamp will give you the localized light you need when you're working, so that you do not need to have all the main overhead lights on as well.

Did you know ?

So-called 'long-life bulbs' may last longer but still use the same filament technology as conventional incandescents. They have a thicker filament, which means they actually use more energy to produce the same amount of light. So don't be taken in!

Intelligent building design

A ROOT CAUSE of much of our energy wastage is the way our homes have been designed. Many houses were built to make use of cheap and plentiful fossil fuels, such as coal. Today, we still mimic those traditional designs. One example of this is building a chimney in houses that will never have an open fire. With developing technology and the intelligent design of new housing, it is increasingly possible to build homes

▼ Intelligent design considers available fuel sources, local environment and the lifestyle of the occupants.

▲ **Making use of natural heat from the sun is an important part of low-energy building design.**

that will have the potential to generate their own power and have such low-energy demands that they will, in fact, *contribute* to the national grid rather than draw from it. If you are fortunate enough to be building your own house then you have the opportunity to contribute to the intelligent-housing revolution. There are also some measures that can be taken during renovations to an existing property.

Solar gain

SOLAR GAIN is a greatly under-used resource that refers to the simple process of heat from the sun creating a greenhouse effect inside a building. This occurs when the sun shines through a window and becomes trapped in the room. While any window can potentially admit heat in this way, the way we build often fails to make use of its full potential. Sometimes called passive solar heating, a house designed around this idea can have its artificial heating requirements reduced to almost nothing, even in a cold winter. While this might be a little too demanding for most self-builders, the principle works on a smaller scale, too. Even as part of an eco–renovation of an existing house, it is perfectly possible to make use of solar gain simply by adding a conservatory to the exterior, creating a heat reservoir that will insulate and gently warm the rest of the house.

Heat stores and thermal mass

A 'THERMAL MASS' is a very happy partner to solar gain. It absorbs heat when the sun is shining and then releases it when the air around it is colder. This not only helps a house remain warm through the night, but

▼ **An intelligently-glazed building can trap a lot of heat, the effects of which will last well into the evening.**

also lessens the risk of a building over–heating in hot weather. As a general rule of thumb, the heavier and darker a material is, the better it will be at absorbing heat. A black slate floor in a conservatory is a great thermal collector and should stay warm underfoot late into the evening. You can recreate this effect on a smaller scale simply by placing water butts (that save rainwater for the garden) against house walls or under windows. Inside a greenhouse a dark–coloured water butt left in full sunshine can often keep a sharp night–time frost at bay.

Planning and the use of space

THIS VERY basic aspect of building design has far–reaching effects in terms of energy. Are the busiest areas of the home close together so that they can benefit from each other's heat? Or are they separated by less frequented rooms that might not require any heating at all? Are the

bedrooms – which are generally only used after dark – taking the best natural light? Could the inhabitants sleep on the north side of the house or even downstairs, to allow better views from an upstairs lounge? These considerations may affect how you choose to use your house and should certainly be a factor in new–build projects.

▼ **Before building begins, ensure that you have grouped rooms together according to heat requirements. Heat flowing into unoccupied or spare rooms is wasted.**

Combined servicing

A NOTHER IDEA that is easy to incorporate into a new–build is to place services, such as water pipes, air ducts and electric cables, in close proximity to one another. An example would be to fit an upstairs bathroom directly above a kitchen, so that the water supply can be shared without much extra pipework.

Painting and decorating

MANY MODERN decorating products contain volatile organic compounds (VOCs). These artificial chemicals are thought to be bad for your health. This alone is a good reason to use a natural alternative. A general rule of thumb is that the more processing a product requires, the more energy it has consumed to produce it.

▼ **Since paints can emit VOCs over many years, natural paints are a safer option.**

Lime renders and plaster

LIME HAS been an important resource in the building trade for more than 10,000 years, but the introduction of cement in the nineteenth century led to its virtual disappearance by the mid–twentieth century. It wasn't until the 1970s, when it first became clear that the use of modern mortars and plasters on historic buildings was causing significant damage, that the use of lime was revived. Lime also requires much less energy in its manufacture than cement. It is worth considering for this reason alone.

Traditional building techniques relied on the porosity of materials such as stone, brick, timber and earth in order to 'breathe' effectively and thus help to keep structures free from damp. Lime–based products share this permeability, and thus can be used to protect the integrity of a building without hindering its ability to breathe. Moreover, lime mortars are softer than stone or brick, and are therefore better able to accommodate slight movements caused by settlement or temperature changes. Non–hydraulic lime is often used for conservation work, usually in its saturated form as 'lime putty'. It's ideal for making fine plasterwork and as a base for limewash, but it's also widely used for pointing masonry and making render.

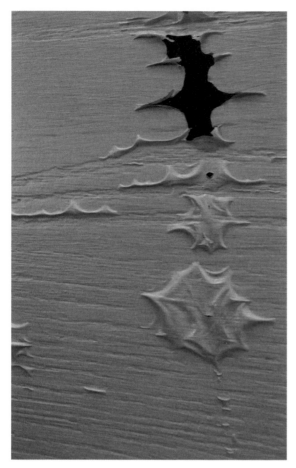

▲ As lime-based paint is more breathable than those containing solvents, it is less likely to bubble and crack.

▲ Linseed, milk, clay or lime-based paints emit fewer fumes, making decorating a far more pleasant experience.

Natural paints and finishes

LIME WAS also an important component of traditional paints. The high porosity of limewashes and distempers made them the ideal partner for breathable building materials. Limewash is a traditional choice for external walls, as it is easy to use and fairly inexpensive. In the past, a lime–tallow wash, which incorporates animal fat, was popular for this purpose, as it was the least porous option. It was also sometimes used to treat the exposed beams of timber–framed houses in order to neutralize infections in the wood and repair minor cracks.

Modern paints can contain high levels of VOCs. These potentially harmful chemicals can continue to evaporate into the air for months,

even years, after the wall surface has dried. The manufacture of any decorating product will have a certain impact on the environment, but by steering clear of conventional, mass–produced wall coverings you can significantly reduce air pollution inside your home and go some way to ensuring that important natural resources are protected.

Eco–friendly paints offer an excellent alternative, avoiding the issues associated with their solvent–based counterparts. Their principal ingredient is most often linseed oil, though clay, lime and milk also make suitable bases. As a result, natural alternatives are a great solution for those who suffer from allergies or respiratory conditions that may be triggered by the hazardous substances in modern paints.

Just as paints can release harmful fumes into your home, so too can conventional wallpapers. Vinyl alternatives, which have been widely recommended for use in bathrooms and kitchens, usually contain solvents and are best avoided wherever possible. Instead, finish these areas with a coat of water–based acrylic paint. Truly eco–friendly wallpaper is still some way from becoming a reality, but you can be sure you're doing your bit by checking that the paper you choose is either recycled or sourced from trees taken from managed forests.

▼ **Water-based acrylic paints offer a solvent-free finish for bathrooms and kitchens.**

▲ **Non-solvent paints mean less brush cleaning and a quicker tidy-up after decorating.**

Energy

This chapter looks at other choices and changes you can make around the house to make your home as energy efficient as possible.

Small changes make a big difference when it comes to saving energy at home. Do you fill the kettle to maximum capacity each time it is used, or run a half load of washing? If so, there's certainly room for improvement.

According to the Energy Saving Trust, the average household could reduce carbon emissions by up to one and a half tonnes per annum, simply by addressing habits such as these. It's good news for your bank balance too, as increased energy efficiency can represent a saving of around £300 per year.

choosing and using fuels

As we discovered in chapter one, the energy we use in our homes can come from a number of sources. The fuel you choose to use to provide your energy will depend to some extent on your budget, convenience and accessibility. Not all people have the budget to switch to a green electricity tariff, or the time to load–up a wood–burning stove twice a day. And not all houses have access to mains gas. When you've decided which options are realistic for your circumstances you can compare these for energy efficiency (see table, right).

Fuel	Approx. Kg of CO_2 emitted per GJ of energy delivered
Wood	0
Natural gas	54
Domestic oil	79
Domestic coal	81
Electricity generated from fossil fuels	142

Note: Figures for electricity produced from renewable resources vary widely.

Embodied energy

Energy use can take many forms, but one we commonly overlook is known as embodied energy. This describes the energy used to create a product or service, and can be thought of as a form of energy debt that will be repaid through the life of the product. In order to reduce your use of this hidden resource you need to look at your lifestyle as a whole (see chapter six).

Cutting back on your general consumption is crucial. This simply means not buying stuff you don't need. It also means making the most of whatever you buy. The mantra is: reduce, reuse, recycle!

▼ **This gadget helps to save energy by putting your computer into eco mode at the press of a button.**

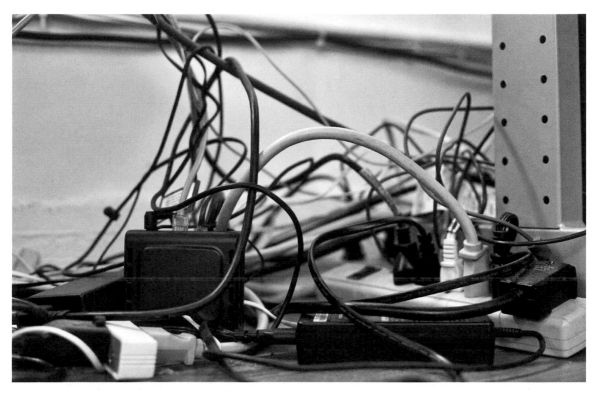

▲ Avoid having a number of unnecessary appliances on standby at any given time – it is greener and safer.

▼ A home-energy meter will allow you to keep track of your energy consumption.

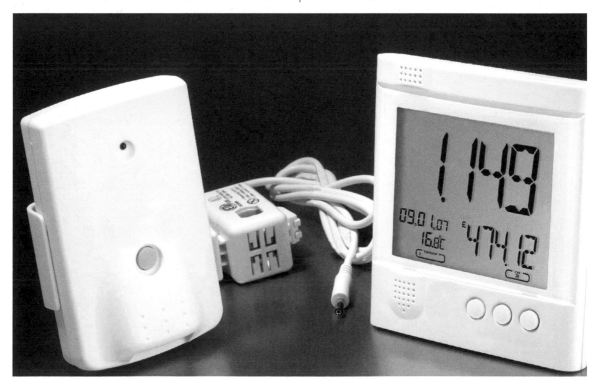

▲ **Wind power is one of the cleanest forms of renewable energy, yet installations are often opposed by residents.**

Buying 'green' electricity

I'S A sad fact that most existing homes are so inefficient that even with extensive eco-renovations they are never likely to reduce their energy requirements to anything even close to zero. In other words, we will have to continue with our current system of mains-supplied electricity for a long time. If we have to accept this as a fait accompli, then the next best thing we can do is turn our attention to *how* this power is generated for us.

The generation of electricity is responsible for producing more greenhouse gases than any other activity, and this has an impact on climate change. The UK produces 2.3 per cent of the world's CO_2, yet has just 1 per cent of the world's population. This is because most power (more than 70 per cent) in the UK is generated by the combustion of fossil fuels, a process that releases CO_2. A further 20 per cent of power in the UK comes from nuclear generation (possibly even less sound in terms of safety) and only 3 per cent is generated from renewable sources. This is despite the fact that the UK benefits from the single greatest renewable energy resource in Europe – the power of the winds in and around the British Isles.

Write a letter

While an energy-efficient home is our goal, we obviously can't reduce our energy requirements to zero, so what can we do to ensure that the energy we really do need is produced responsibly? One positive step is to write a letter (a real one has more impact than an e-mail) to each of your utility suppliers (and, while you're at it, any supermarket and department store you use) asking the directors what steps they are taking to reduce their company's energy footprint. Being called to account by just a few paying customers is often enough to cause corporate policy makers to give serious thought to the issues involved.

Renewable energy has several benefits: it has the potential to reduce pollution; it is very safe, unlike nuclear power; and will never run out, unlike coal, oil or gas. If there is any doubt as to the practicality of the technology we need only look at what other countries are doing. Wind energy is the fastest growing power source in the world, averaging 20 to 30 per cent annual growth in recent years. At present, nearly 20 per cent of European electricity is generated from hydroelectric power; Norway is almost entirely run on hydroelectric power.

The British government has introduced a system of Renewable Obligations. This means that a percentage of the electricity that each supplier sells must come from renewable sources. This obligation is currently set at less than 10 per cent but this figure is set to rise every year until it reaches 15.4 per cent in 2015/16. Confusingly, each unit of energy from renewable sources is accompanied by a Renewable Obligation Certificate (ROC), which does not have to be sold with the electricity itself. This means that power companies that are not involved in any renewable generation can buy ROCs from elsewhere to meet the government demands. There is also a Climate Change Levy, essentially a tax on the power consumed by business users, who can only claim exemption from this levy if they switch to a certified renewable producer.

But what can we do as domestic consumers to change the way our power is generated? Since the British government's deregulation of the energy market in 1998, home owners have been able to choose the supplier of their electricity. In response to an increase in public demand, there are a number of power companies that now offer a domestic 'green tariff' with some environmental benefits attached. Switching to one of these tariffs is the easiest and simplest step that people can take towards reducing their homes' carbon footprint. It has the added benefit of showing the power companies what you think about fossil fuels – make sure you tell them why you are switching! This is a market that cannot afford to ignore public opinion; if people vote with their money, the industry will have to change.

Due to the demand for green electricity from business customers looking for tax breaks, there is a significant reduction in the amount of green electricity available for domestic use. So, by giving your custom to a green supplier you are actively encouraging the construction of new renewable energy installations to meet this demand.

There are more than a dozen suppliers of green energy in the UK at present, so how can UK residents find out which one is the best? Obviously, the price of the electricity will have some bearing here, and this is often subject to local differences (indeed around half of the suppliers in the UK are regional rather than nationwide). Further to this, there are two basic types of tariff available, and some schemes offer a combination of these.

Green sources

Green source schemes supply energy that is generated from renewable sources. Of course, nobody can be sure where the electrons that power their homes originally came from, but with green sourcing you are essentially guaranteed that for every unit of power you use and for which pay the supplier, they will generate a corresponding unit from renewable sources.

Green funds

Green fund schemes supply electricity that is generated from non-renewable sources, but donate a portion of the profit they make to the development of renewable technologies, or another related programme. This is obviously a good thing but is a less direct solution than a green source.

Did you know?

You can find out which of the many tariffs is best for you. You can find them rated independently at www.greenelectricity.org.

▼ **Check the eco-credentials of your energy supplier. If less than satisfactory, go elsewhere for power.**

Self-sufficient energy

IF YOU want to go a step further down the road towards total energy efficiency, you may well have considered generating your own heat and electricity for your home. Until quite recently this was very much a project for the tinkering engineer with too much time on his hands, but there is now a rapidly increasing number of products and systems available for just this purpose. The initial cash investment is still quite considerable, but most such projects will more than repay the outlay during their lifetime, assuming you remain in that house for long enough. In the short term, however, they should only be considered after other energy-saving methods have been implemented.

Solar hot water

THE EASIEST way to reduce your reliance on bought-in energy is to use a vast, free resource: the sun. This may well make you think of photo-electricity – and we'll come to that later – but an easier and more direct method is to use the sun to heat your domestic hot water. There are around 50,000 solar water heating panels in use in the UK, and they are now so efficient that a good system should provide most

▼ **Solar water-heating systems are becoming more feasible for domestic residences.**

▲ **A domestic solar panel could provide you with over half the energy needed to heat water for baths, showers and washing over the course of a year.**

of the hot water you need in summer, and a good proportion in winter, between 40 and 60 per cent of the total demand through the year. The price of a professionally installed system is likely to be between £2,000 and £5,000 if you shop around, and will save perhaps £100 or more in fuel costs each year. This represents a long pay–back period, it's true, but still offers a better return than keeping the same money in the bank.

How they work

In simple terms, a mixture of water and antifreeze is pumped slowly through a roof– or wall-mounted panel that is exposed to the sun. The fluid absorbs heat on the way, and is then piped to a hot–water tank, usually located in the loft. The water, which is mixed with anti–freeze, doesn't empty into the tank but circulates inside a heat–exchanging coil to warm the clean water in the tank around it. If necessary, the temperature in the tank can be topped–up with an electric heater or a conventional hot–water system from a boiler.

Photovoltaics (solar panels)

THE FAMOUS 'solar panel' produces electricity from the rays of the sun. The science is not as complicated as it might seem; nonetheless, the efficiency of photovoltaics has only just reached a level at which they are a realistic proposal for domestic use. The system is simple to install, involving an array of panels mounted on a south–facing roof or wall and wired to storage batteries that release the power when it is needed.

Did you know?

In three to five years, solar panels produce enough electricity to repay the energy that it takes to build them. They have a life expectancy of up to 40 years.

▲ If you have the money to invest, you can install enough panels to greatly reduce your heating bills.

▼ To ensure that your panels are efficient as possible, have them fitted by a professional.

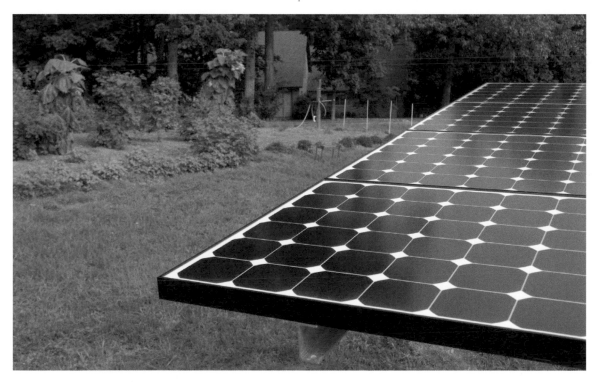

▲ As this set-up illustrates, photovoltaic panels need not be unattractive.

The main drawback is the expense. The panels and batteries, plus associated monitoring and control circuitry, will probably cost more money to install than they will save – at current energy prices, at least. Photovoltaics have not yet come of age, but with fossil fuels running out and the efficiency and affordability of the panels increasing, this is likely to be an important technology in future years.

Wind turbines

For the UK and other countries that frequently have breezy conditions, the simplicity and low cost of the technology and the ease of installation and maintenance should really be making wind power the number–one energy source in such countries. Unfortunately, political maneuvering and public confusion in the UK have combined to scupper many large–scale generation projects. On a domestic scale the viability depends very

▲ **Large-scale wind turbines are usually found in rural or off-shore locations.**

much on the local geography – wind turbines are not very effective in built–up areas where houses and other obstacles disrupt the flow of air. The precise positioning and specification of a turbine is a matter for quite serious engineering, so it's best to consult a professional if you think this technology is for you.

Planning issues

One thing that still restricts the use of wind power in the UK is planning law. Most householders will need to apply for planning permission to install a wind turbine of any size, and this is much less likely to be granted in urban areas (where the power demand is greatest). Contact your local planning authority to find out more about the issues involved before you make any other commitments to this type of project.

The Green Bathroom

Some of the energy used in the bathroom – just as in other rooms around the house – is for heating and lighting. Then, of course, there's a fair amount that goes into running a hot shower or bath.

Lighting, heating and hot water have already been covered in the previous two chapters, so what else is there to say specifically about energy in the bathroom? The answer is water itself. Water is a natural resource – just like any other – that we should not waste. More importantly, it is the energy that is consumed transporting and processing the water at various stages along the cycle that should concern us.

This chapter will show some very easy ways in which we can quite dramatically cut down on the amount of water we use.

Daily ablutions

WATER USAGE is an important environmental issue because of the polluting chemicals used to clean water, and the habitat–destroying reservoirs we need to build in order to contain that water. Perhaps even more critical, however, is the 'embodied energy' in the water we use (see box on page 46). Each person in the UK uses around 135l (30gals) of water a day. That's nearly 1,000l (220gals) a week, and 1,000l weighs 1t. While some water is moved around by means of gravity, much of it has to be pumped to its destination and this uses a lot of energy; so much so, in fact, that water companies are some of the biggest energy consumers in the UK. Cutting your water use and thus reducing the demand on the national system, is a very important way of shrinking your energy footprint.

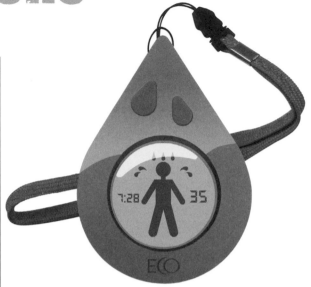

▲ It's easy to spend too long in the shower, so a timer will not only save water but get you to work on time!

▼ This shower timer is simply a digital clock, sealed in a waterproof chamber.

▼ A diffuser spray creates a slower, finer mist, which feels like a stronger spray while using less water.

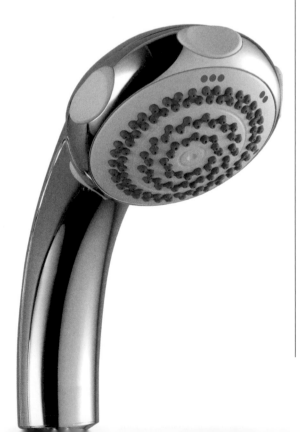

▲ Help children to save water by setting up a race: first out of the shower wins!

▶ Every little helps, so turn off the tap when you're brushing your teeth.

The first step you should take in your bid to save water is to examine your current usage. The way we perform a number of simple daily tasks can greatly affect the amount of water we use. Start off in the morning, for example, by turning the tap on to wet your toothbrush is pretty much a necessity, but leaving the tap running while you brush for just 90 seconds will waste no less than 12l (under 3gals) of water.

Having a wash is also not something we can happily live without, but many of us are guilty of spending far too long in the shower or over-filling the bath. Personal hygiene as a whole accounts for around 25 per cent of domestic water use in the UK. A short shower will generally use much less water than a bath, but can still use as much as 30l (7gals) per minute. Shortening your shower by just a minute or two is easy enough to get used to; you can buy a shower timer to remind you when your time's up. Nor will sharing bath water do you any harm either. By these measures alone you might already have saved 70–100l (15–22gals) per day, and you haven't even had breakfast yet.

▼ Bathing can actually use less water than a prolonged shower, especially if you share the bath.

Low-flow taps and showers

WHILE NOBODY likes a weak flow from a tap or enjoys a miserly trickle of a shower, it is possible to make the water running through such fittings go further. A low–flow design will be one of two types. The first squeezes the water through tiny holes so that it comes out at high pressure and feels like a much more substantial stream of water than it really is. This can have the added benefit of giving a massaging effect, especially in a shower. The second type of fitting aerates the water, giving a lush, bubbly flow that again appears to contain much more water than it really does. Some of these taps and showerheads claim as much as a 50 per cent saving, which is not to be sniffed at.

▲ This cartridge can be retrofitted onto most styles of taps, and reduces water flow by up to 70 per cent.

▼ Simply taking note of how much water is wasted in the home can be a real eye-opener.

▲ **A reduced-flow showerhead can offer a saving of up to 50 per cent on conventional models.**

Grey-water recycling

THE TERM 'grey water' refers to water that has already been used but is not heavily polluted; for example, it might be the waste water from a washing machine, dishwasher, shower or bath. If you can collect and reuse this water, you will be getting double the value from its embodied energy.

The simplest water recycling system is to use a siphon to drain the water from your bath instead of just pulling the plug. Attached to a length of garden hose this siphon could direct the water out into the garden to water your plants, or perhaps to wash the car. Whilst this has the benefit of simplicity, it is perhaps not the most convenient arrangement. It would be better in the long term to invest in a more complex system that stores the grey water and pumps it to where it is needed; flushing toilets, for instance. In this case you need have no concerns over hygiene: any soap or shampoo residue in the water will

do no harm, and you will be reducing your household water consumption dramatically. Such systems are becoming more common, but they are relatively expensive and will take time to repay your investment.

▼ **A siphon system allows you to divert grey water from your bath to a water butt.**

Toilets

A TOILET CISTERN may hold as much as 13l (3gals) of water, yet until quite recently there has been no means of controlling the amount of water released with each flush. This means you empty the whole cistern every time you use the toilet – and, don't forget, that's purified water good enough for drinking that is being used. Small wonder that toilets are responsible for 30 per cent of household water use. What can be done to reduce this waste?

Cistern displacement

ONE SIMPLE idea that is often recommended for older–style toilets is to fit a special displacement device (such as a 'save–a–flush' or Hippo). The device sits inside the cistern and takes up some of the space that would otherwise be filled with water, thereby leaving less water to come out when you flush. The same effect can be achieved using a plastic bottle filled with water, or even an ordinary house brick placed inside your toilet cistern. While this may offer some saving, particularly if you have a particularly antiquated toilet with an over–sized cistern, most toilets are calibrated so that a 'full flush' is no more than is required to clear a fully loaded pan. You are then limiting the maximum effectiveness of the flush when, in fact, that full effect may genuinely be required. The result is that you will sometimes need to flush a second time, thus entirely negating the original saving.

▼ The 'Hippo' reduces flush volume by up to 3l (5pt).

Dual-flush toilets

NEWER TOILET designs are invariably fitted with a dual–flush system, which at least allows you to moderate the amount of water used to a very basic degree. An efficient model might use 4l (1gal) for a full flush, and 2l (3½pt) for a half flush, although 6l (1¼gals) and 4l (1gal) respectively is more common. These reduced cistern sizes, combined with better–designed pans and drainage, do have the potential to offer a saving. There is a serious drawback, however. These systems generally have a push–button

▼ Dual-flush toilets can save water, but are not without disadvantages.

▲ Siphon toilets are less prone to leaking than valve designs.

flush, which might have consumer appeal, but means they use a valve rather than an old–fashioned siphon. And the fact is, valves leak, siphons don't. In fact, siphon toilets (in use in the UK since the 1880s) were specifically invented to replace leak–prone valve designs. As a result, we now have a situation where all the UK's siphon toilets are slowly being superseded by wasteful valve models (albeit with a smaller flush). To put this into perspective, US water agencies estimate that valve toilets leak 15–30l (3¼–6½gals) of water per person, per day.

Variable-flush siphon toilets

THE BEST option when it comes to saving water is to stick with a traditional siphon design (if you can still find such a thing in a plumbing store) but to fit it with a device that regulates the flow. An Interflush is a good example of this. They are available from around £15 and give much more control than the two–stage valve designs that only offer half or full flushes. The toilet still looks just like any other, but instead of emptying the cistern when you work the handle, it flushes for as long as the handle is held down. This means you can use exactly the right amount of water every time you flush.

Waste not, want not

QUITE APART from the supply of water, every household needs some form of sewage system. Just as for water supply, dealing with sewage is an energy-intensive process requiring pumping, processing and maintenance. Cutting the amount of water that you use will have a considerable effect on the energy cost of dealing with your correspondingly reduced waste water, but is there anything else you can realistically do to help?

Composting toilets

THESE ARE not connected to the mains sewage system, but instead collect and treat waste 'on-site' using biological processes that transform human excrement into harmless compost. Some designs allow the processed matter to be

▼ **Composting toilets are useful on allotments and camp sites.**

collected and used as agricultural fertilizer (where local laws allow), while others may feed into a battery of hungry plants (often willow or nettles) that can then be harvested for fuel, building materials and so on. It is certainly possible (in fact, very simple) to build your own composting toilet, but this is perhaps better suited to an allotment or camp site than a family home. However, there are a number of commercial designs available, some of them very high-tech, which are more in keeping with a modern sanitary bathroom.

Reed-bed sewage systems

FAR FROM being an unsanitary or inefficient choice, opting-out of mains sewerage and treating your own waste water with a reed bed is a very effective solution. Of course, it doesn't suit urban properties with small gardens, but on a farm or smallholding it is a realistic proposition. A correctly designed and installed reed bed allows effluents to be treated to a high standard.

1 ALTHOUGH small reed beds can be installed in a garden, they work best in a larger space.

2 WHERE space is available, a single reed bed can process sewage for a number of homes.

3 REEDS can become very tall, so provide a secluded environment for wildlife.

4 ONCE established, reed beds will blend into the surrounding landscape.

5 THIS well-manicured reed bed is attractive as well as productive.

The cleaning process relies on naturally occurring bacteria feeding upon the harmful materials in the effluents as it slowly filters through the reed bed. This method can be used to treat all kinds of waste water, including farmyard run–off, landfill leachate and, of course, domestic effluents. The

▲ **Installing a reed bed sewage system is an option for larger, rural domestic properties.**

reed beds remove organic materials, reduce nitrates and phosphates in the water and, most importantly, remove pathogens and pollutants such as heavy metals.

▲ Clean water can be collected and re-used, although quality must be carefully monitored.

▼ A small reed bed can still be surprisingly efficient, making it suitable for a domestic setting.

▲ Reed beds remove plant-matter, heavy metals and other pollutants to create surprisingly pure water.

The Green Kitchen

For many of us the kitchen is our first port of call in the morning. We put the kettle on, make toast or treat ourselves to a cooked breakfast. Even if we're not home for lunch, most of us prepare a cooked dinner, wash dishes or run a load of laundry on a regular basis. In terms of energy consumption, the kitchen is a key spot to consider when greening your home.

There is an abundance of eco-appliances available on the market, but don't assume that you have to replace all of your existing gadgets in one go – changing the way you go about your daily chores is equally effective. If you do decide to replace your oven or washing machine, it is important to check that your chosen model is really as green as it claims to be.

Give a little thought to your washing, cooking and recycling methods, and you can make a big difference to both your electricity and water bill.

Energy-efficient appliances

MOST OF us spend a great deal of time in our kitchen preparing food, entertaining or dining. From electric can-openers to toasters, there is now an array of appliances aimed to make our lives easier. Most of us wouldn't be without our time-saving gadgets, but it is still possible to save energy and resources by choosing such appliances carefully.

Washing dishes

USING A modern dishwasher can actually be more eco-friendly than washing dishes by hand. However, this is only the case if the machine is run on an eco setting and not used until full. If you live alone or

◀ **Attention to little details, such as using energy-efficient bulbs, can result in big savings.**

EU energy labels

All new appliances in the EU are now rated according to EU energy standards; an initiative that takes some of the guesswork out of choosing a new kettle, cooker or microwave. Products that demonstrate exceptional efficiency are labelled as 'recommended' by the Energy Saving Trust, but all are rated on a sliding scale. The awards run from A to G, with A indicating the lowest use of energy through to G, the most inefficient.

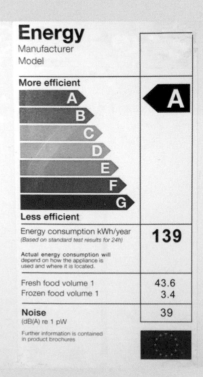

▲ **Washing machines are among the best of the modern labour-saving devices, but consume a great deal of water and electricity.**

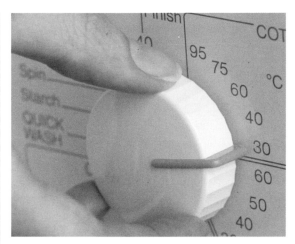

▲ **Unless heavily soiled, most laundry can be washed at the lower temperature of 30°C (86°F).**

with just one other person, you may struggle to fill up a large dishwasher before the dirty plates inside begin to smell, so hand–washing may remain the best use of resources.

Washing clothes

WASHING MACHINES used to be notorious energy–guzzlers, but over recent years they have improved their eco credentials. Many can be set to wash at 30°C (86°F) or on an economy setting, which saves both water and the energy used to heat it. Some detergents on the market claim effectiveness from temperatures as low as 15°C (59°F). It is worth checking the ingredients of these products, however, as you may be adding concentrated enzymes and pollutants to the water in order to save energy.

When buying a washing machine it is best to avoid some of the cheaper models, as these have a limited lifespan. When they break down, sourcing the individual parts can be more expensive than buying an entirely new machine. Stick to well–known brands with an extended warranty – German–built washing machines have a particularly good reputation for durability. If this proves prohibitively expensive, it may be worth considering a reconditioned machine. While older models may not be as aesthetically pleasing, they are often less prone to faults than their cheaper, newer counterparts. Since they have fewer electronic components in the control panel, there is quite simply less to go wrong.

Drying clothes

TUMBLE DRYERS are undoubtedly convenient, but require huge amounts of energy for each cycle when compared with other domestic appliances. Where possible, spin clothes then hang them outdoors to dry. If this isn't an option, a boiler or airing cupboard is ideal. Radiators are extremely efficient for drying clothes but they should not be placed directly upon the hot metal. Radiator racks are extremely cheap to buy and will allow you to dry safely a number of garments – you could manage at least 20 items on a basic £2 rack! For maximum effectiveness,

▲ **Filling the drum for each cycle is a far better use of resources than washing a number of small loads.**

try a radiator heat reflector. As the name suggests, these are simply shiny adhesive sheets that reflect heat outwards to where it is needed. Cheap to buy, these are a wise investment that will prevent you from unnecessarily losing heat through the wall. If all else fails, an old-fashioned airing rack is a simple and practical solution and many of these can be folded away when not in use. Wall-mounted pulley drying racks also make a striking feature in the right setting, and garments can be suspended above head-level to save space. Since heat rises, a high drying system will allow you to capitalize on warmth that would otherwise be wasted.

Boiling water

ACCORDING TO DEFRA (the UK Department for the Environment, Food and Rural Affairs) if each of us only boiled the amount of water we truly required (rather than filling up the kettle each time) our combined efforts would save 1.27 billion kWh of energy – enough to provide all of the street lighting in the UK! The average eco-kettle offers a 30 per cent energy-saving on conventional models. The initial investment can be fairly high but will usually pay for itself, reducing your energy bill over time. Failing this, there are some very obvious but effective ways to reduce water wastage as you will see. When combined, will allow you to save as much energy as you would using an eco-kettle.

If you're buying a standard kettle, choose one with a volume gauge. Note how much you need for two cups, for example, and fill only to that level. This small change will pay dividends for long-term energy conservation.

Keeping the pot warm

If you are a serial tea or coffee drinker then use a teapot or coffee pot. Having fallen out of fashion for years, the traditional teapot is

▲ Allow clothes to dry naturally. Tumble driers are extremely costly in terms of energy consumption.

▼ Before you make a brew, consider how much water is actually required.

now experiencing something of a renaissance. Using a thick cosy will enable you to get four to six cups from one boiled kettle. You'll also use fewer teabags or tea leaves, and the resulting tea usually has a more mellow, smooth flavour.

To boil or not to boil ...

Ask yourself whether you really need to re–boil the kettle; often the water is hot enough for a cup of tea or coffee up to half an hour later, especially if you choose a thick–walled kettle to retain heat.

Choosing an eco-kettle

WHEN CONSIDERING where to save money in the home, many people start with insulation but put appliances near the top of their priorities. For this reason the 'eco–kettle' business is booming. However, as with any 'green' product, it is well worth checking the credentials of the item before purchase in order to check that the savings are going to justify the initial investment. There are various features to look out for when choosing an eco–kettle:

Instant boil

Some eco–kettles claim to produce instant hot water. As you only boil the exact amount needed to fill a cup, this does save energy. There are, however, a number of disadvantages. First, the technology hasn't quite caught up with the concept – many models are actually quite slow, and dispense water at a slow dribble rather than in a continuous stream. This can make serving a number of people rather a time–consuming job. Secondly, although the water is hot it isn't actually at boiling point. Again, this is fine for an instant cup of tea, but can be false economy when filling a whole teapot – the contents will quickly become cold if the water is only tepid to start with.

Rapid boil

Rapid-boil kettles have been around for a long time, although their marketing emphasis has changed. Initially conceived for convenience, they are now sold on the basis of their eco-credentials. Most models do offer an energy saving, but it is wise to check their energy efficiency rating before purchase. It can also be tempting to flick the switch and quickly re-boil water unnecessarily; we've all done it at some point.

▼ **Rather than re-boiling the kettle each time, consider whether it is still hot enough for your purposes.**

Flat element

Most kettles used to have a large heating element situated at the bottom of the jug. Without regular de–scaling, these quickly become inefficient and also occupy a fair amount of space in the appliance. Newer models often boast a flat element, which is easier to clean and is said to conduct heat more efficiently.

Cup gauge

Since the majority of wasted energy is due to boiling a larger volume of water than is actually necessary, a cup gauge can be a useful tool. Of course, there is nothing to stop you marking

▲ **A cup gauge is useful, as it can prevent you from boiling a greater volume of water than is necessary.**

your existing standard kettle in this way. Some eco–models allow you to fill the kettle to full capacity, and then select how many cups you would like to boil by pressing a button. The chosen amount is then released into the boiling chamber; the idea being to save countless trips to refill the kettle each time. A good idea in theory, but a convenience that is well worth weighing against the extra financial outlay! Again, if your kettle's main purpose is to boil water for tea or coffee, you might just as well boil a little more to begin with and keep it warm in a teapot.

Cooking

SINCE IT is an appliance that is used everyday, your choice of cooker will have a direct bearing upon your energy consumption.

Choosing a cooker

IN A number of tests, gas ovens have proved to be more efficient than their electric counterparts, although there is, as yet, no agreed scale upon which gas cookers are rated. If you choose the electric route, opt for a fan–assisted oven, and be sure to check the energy–efficiency rating of your favoured model before purchase. If you decide upon a gas oven, ensure that it has been fitted by a Gas Safe Registered operative (in the UK) and has an auto cut–out function. Whichever type of cooker you choose, there are a number of ways to conserve heat.

▲ **Steaming is a rapid, not to mention healthy, method of cooking.**

▼ **Flash-cooking techniques can prove more energy efficient than baking or roasting.**

On the hob

● AVOID oversized, thick saucepans where possible – don't waste energy heating the pan!

● USE stackable pots on the hob. Many oven-top steamers allow at least four tiers of vegetables to be cooked using the heat from one ring.

● 'HOT spot' cookware can be useful – the coloured circle changes from grey to red as soon as the pan is hot enough to start cooking.

● FLASH-COOKING techniques (such as stir-frying and searing) save energy and are usually better for your health.

● THE heat from the hob often warms the oven and/or grill. Use this residual heat to keep food warm until you are ready to serve.

● IF your cooker doesn't already have a built-in timer, a simple clockwork timer to have by the side of your cooker is a wise investment. Most of us have put a pan on to boil for longer than necessary, or forgotten about something simmering in the oven.

● WHEN buying new cookware it is worth investing in pans with close-fitting lids. This will reduce heat loss and shorten cooking time.

Pressure cookers and slow cookers

LARGE OVENS can require a lot of energy to heat, particularly if you are only cooking a small casserole. Pressure and slow cookers went

▼ **Choosing a thin pan allows for quick, efficient heat transfer.**

▲ **Large ovens and ranges look attractive, but require a great deal of energy to heat.**

out of fashion in recent years but are beginning to enjoy a revival. They are invaluable appliances when it comes to convenience and saving energy.

A thick stew can take hours to cook in the oven, even if it is started on the hob. A pressure cooker can shave up to a third off cooking time and can be turned down to 'low' once it has achieved sufficient pressure – ideal if you want a hearty meal cooked quickly and efficiently. Slow–cookers, or 'crock pots' as they are also

sometimes known, use energy at around the same rate as a standard light bulb. They are ideal for dishes that require slow, gentle heat to release their flavours, and can usually be set on a timer. They are also convenient for those working late: simply add the ingredients to the pot in the morning and return home to a cooked meal.

▲ **With a little experimentation, a number of healthy soups and stews can be made in the microwave.**

Microwaves

MICROWAVES HAVE been much maligned over the last few years, as they have become synonymous with fat–laden convenience food and TV dinners. It is, however, perfectly possible to use your microwave to produce healthy, tasty dishes. A jacket potato, which can take an hour or more in a conventional oven can be cooked in a matter of minutes ina microwave, saving energy and offering a quick, nutritious meal.

Tips for efficient microwaving

- Avoid using the standby and clock function on your microwave oven, since this can use as much energy over the course of a day as cooking a whole meal.

- Convenient needn't mean 'junk'. Experiment with healthy foods, such as canned pulses, potatoes and vegetable soups in the microwave.

- Don't be put off if you don't succeed; it can take a while to master complete dishes in the microwave. Most models have a 'half-power' function that will allow you to cook foods more gently.

Recycling

IN THE UK, over a quarter of our methane emissions are produced by landfill sites. These sites are simply pits in the ground where our rubbish is buried. As well as storing up chemicals and toxins for future generations, we are now simply running out of land, so recycling is the only way forward. It is estimated that household recycling in the UK saves up to 18 million tonnes of CO_2 per year, which is roughly equivalent to taking approximately five million cars off the road! Aside from the more obvious candidates, such as glass, paper and aluminium, there are a number of other materials suitable for recycling. Home composting (see pages 128–31), for example, is a great way to recycle vegetable scraps to produce rich compost for use in the garden. Bokashi compost (see pages 90–4) is a new recycling technique that allows you to recycle a wider range of food waste; although, it must be said, the best policy is to avoid waste in the first place.

▼ **Landfill sites are a growing problem, leaving an uncertain legacy for future generations.**

▲ There are recycling facilities for magazines, junk mail and newspapers all over the country.

▲ All local authorities in the UK offer some form of collection service for recyclable items.

Bins and storage

MOST LOCAL authorities in the UK offer recycling collections from the home for paper, glass and aluminium cans. Some authorities will also collect plastic, although this is by no means widespread. It is usually possible, however, to find a local recycling bank for bottles and plastic packaging – the best policy is to save up a large amount and deposit the load in one go (thus reducing car usage and keeping your carbon footprint as low as possible). In small apartments and houses, however, finding the space to store recyclable items can pose something of a problem, particularly if collections are bi–weekly or monthly.

Whilst most areas will provide a wheelie bin or box for storage, these quickly fill up. It is, of course, much more convenient to have a container in the kitchen for recyclables. There are many space–saving solutions on the market, including bins with separate sections for cans, paper and glass.

Unfortunately, many recycling plants have to discard huge batches of collected waste if it is improperly sorted, as they simply do not have the manpower to hand–pick suitable items.

Get into the habit of sorting your items carefully (see Recycling Guidelines on page 82); it need only take five to ten minutes a week. Perhaps it is an activity you can give your older kids to perform

▼ A storage system makes separating and sorting waste much easier.

▲ **Choosing products with less packaging and avoiding plastic bags means that you will have less to recycle.**

to help them to learn about green issues. If in doubt about what you can and cannot recycle, check with your local authority. Many people are not aware that they will also remove white goods (such as fridges or washing machines) for a small fee. While recycling is vital, it is worth bearing in mind that the process does use a great deal of energy. It is therefore advisable to re–use items where possible first and avoid purchasing products that are excessively packaged.

Recycling guidelines

THERE IS a bit of a knack to recycling. Do check with your local authority first to find out exactly what they can and cannot recycle. For example, many conscientious people leave the caps on their plastic bottles, little realizing that, because these are made from a different type of plastic, they cannot be recycled and could thus cause an entire collection of plastic bottles to be discarded.

Paper

Many recycling systems are unable to process envelopes (particularly those with transparent windows, so remove these first if you can find the time), wrapping paper, laminated or glossy items.

Re-use before recycling

While recycling is good, re-using first is even better. It can save you quite a bit of money, too. Much of this just represents common sense, the sort that seemed to come as second nature to our parents and grandparents during the thrifty war years and before our consumer, throw-away society took hold.

- Old clothes can be torn up for use as cleaning rags.

- Used toothbrushes are ideal for intricate cleaning jobs.

- The reverse of computer-printed paper and the backs of envelopes can be used for shopping lists.

- Ink cartridges for your printer can be professionally re-filled.

- Old ice-cream tubs can be used as all-purpose food containers.

- Jars can be used to store nails, screws or trinkets in the garage, workshop or sewing basket.

- Envelopes and packaging can be re-used; simply cover the old address with a new label.

- Plastic bottles can be used to provide protection for garden plants (see chapter five).

Be imaginative!

▲ Items saved for recycling should be washed and squashed before they are collected.

▲ A can-crusher will free up space in your recycling box, and will help to get kids interested.

Plastic

Unfortunately, not all packaging and bottles are suitable for recycling; many plastic food trays are not, for example. Most conscientious manufacturers mark the bottom of their products with the recycling symbol (see page 85). Clean and crush the bottles and remove the lids before adding to the recycling box.

Cans and tins

Make sure that cans and tins are thoroughly washed. It is also a good idea to crush drinks cans, otherwise they take up lots of space.

Glass

Light bulbs, glass ovenware and glazing glass are not suitable for recycling and should never be added to your doorstep collection. Remove corks and lids from bottles before recycling and give them a good rinse. If using a community bottle bank, be sure to sort your bottles correctly by colour (blue bottles can be added to the green section). If the bottle bank is situated in a residential area, only use it during the day – the

sound of smashing glass will aggravate your neighbours. Don't litter around the bank and take any plastic bags home with you. This advice may sound obvious, but you don't want to give the local authority any excuse to remove the bank!

▶ If your local authority doesn't offer frequent collections, take glass to your local bottle bank.

Larger items

Furniture

If you lack transport, local charities will often visit you to collect old furniture. These items are then sold in their shops or donated to housing schemes. Your local authority will be able to provide information on the schemes running in your area. Alternatively, unwanted items can be disposed of via internet sites such as Freecycle, where members request or donate items to local residents. It is important, however, to observe the etiquette of these schemes – the item must be given to the collector for free, and must be in a reasonable condition. It is unfair to expect your trading partner to travel to you to collect poor-quality, unusable items.

Fridges and white goods

Freezers and fridges contain chlorofluorocarbons (CFCs), which cause damage to the ozone layer. For this reason, it is illegal to dispose of them in landfill sites. If it is impossible to find a new home for your fridge, it must be taken to a local-authority site where it will be degassed and the coolants recycled. If you are replacing your old fridge with a new appliance, you may be able to part-exchange your old model. When hiring an independent waste-removal company to dispose of your white goods, be sure to check their credentials. It is not unheard of for collected items to be fly-tipped by unscrupulous traders who will then pocket the de-gassing fee!

Electrical appliances

Some charity shops are unable to accept electrical goods because second-hand items must be certified as safe before they are re-sold. Since this can prove expensive, it may be better to take your appliances to the local-authority waste site where they will be disposed of properly.

Clothes

While charity shops are for ever in need of donations, it is good practice to ensure that the items are laundered and in wearable condition. If they are dirty then they will cost the charity money to process them, and may well end up at

▼ **White goods may contain hazardous chemicals, and should be disposed of at a specialist site.**

Recycling labels and symbols

The packaging on many food and household items may carry various recycling symbols. Here is a guide to help you to decipher them.

◀ **Indicates that an object is capable of being recycled, not that the object has been recycled.**

▶ **Shows the percentage of recycled material contained in the product.**

◀ **This means that you should dispose of the object carefully and thoughtfully.**

▶ **Indicates recyclable glass to be disposed of in a bottle bank.**

◀ **This does not necessarily mean that the packaging can be recycled. The symbol signifies that the producer has made a contribution towards the recycling of packaging.**

▶ **A reminder to recycle whenever possible.**

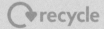

◀ **Identifies the type of plastic: PET and HDPE bottles are recycled by the majority of local authorities.**

PET

▶ **Recyclable aluminium.**

◀ **Recyclable steel.**

---

the landfill site. It is also important to donate to the shop during opening hours – bags of clothes left outside can aggravate local residents and retailers, encourage scavengers (human and animal!), It also puts the organization under pressure. If you are unable to deliver your items during working hours, try donating them via a clothes bank – the Salvation Army has many large containers that can be used all hours of the day. Some charities will also post plastic sacks which can be filled and left out for doorstep collection. Your local–authority recycling site may also have a bin for recycling unwanted clothes and textiles.

Garden waste

If you do not have a garden or lack the space to have your own compost heap (see pages 128–31) or have a large amount of ground to clear, it is worth researching community composting sites. Trees and heavier prunings can be taken to a civic–amenity site where they will be composted and re-used in the local area. Many local authorities will collect green waste from your home during the spring and summer at no charge.

▼ **Clothes placed in a recycling bank should be wearable and clean.**

Worm Composters

IF YOU lack sufficient space for a compost heap, a wormery is a great way to recycle kitchen scraps. The compost will be finer and more nutrient–rich than that produced by an ordinary compost heap. The wormery can be used as a sowing medium and a top–dressing for houseplants.

We are all familiar with the common earthworm. This small creature plays a central role in the decomposition of fallen leaves and plant matter. Kitchen waste creates a medium that is too rich for the humble earthworm, however, so you'll need to use the red, brandling variety. Sometimes called tiger worms, they can be purchased from commercial wormery suppliers.

▼ **Worms are an essential part of our ecosystem, turning organic matter into rich humus.**

You will need

- A small dustbin, bucket or large weatherproof container with a lid

- A drill with a small bit

- A small amount of ready-made compost

- Worms

- A few old bricks

- A garden sieve

1 DRILL DRAINAGE holes in the base of the container, and then a few in the lid for ventilation; use the smallest drill bit available so the worms cannot escape through the holes.

2 RAISE THE container above the ground, as this will allow it to drain freely – a few old bricks are ideal. Place a small bowl between the bricks. Any liquid that seeps through the drainage holes can then be collected and used as a high–nutrient plant feed.

3 ADD A 4cm (1½in) layer of compost to the bottom of the container. This will provide initial bedding for the worms until they become established, at which point they will be able to generate their own earth.

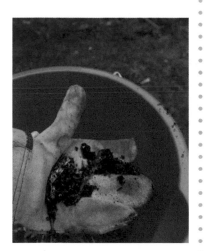

4 RELEASE THE worms into the container, gently placing them upon the compost layer. A further sprinkling of compost on top will help to settle them in.

5 PLACE A handful of composting materials (kitchen scraps) on top of the worms. Only add more once the first amount has been processed, as uneaten food will spoil and pollute the wormery.

6 COLLECT THE compost once the container is full. Use a large sieve to separate the worms from the compost, as they will need to be replaced to make the next batch. Retain a small amount of compost and repeat from step three.

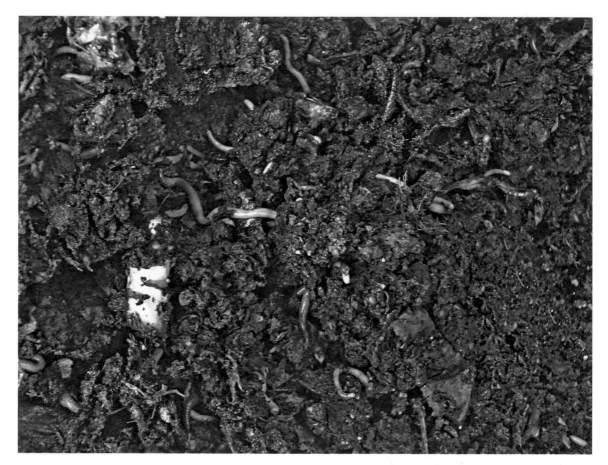

▲ If the wormery becomes overly wet, as the example here, add layers of thinly shredded newspaper.

Materials for the wormery

Suitable Vegetable scraps, peelings and cores. Shredded paper, pet hair, tea bags, torn up cardboard (non-glossy), flower heads.

Unsuitable Citrus fruit, cooked food, cat or dog faeces, garlic and onions.

Troubleshooting

Worms inside the lid

Worms are avid explorers and are often to be found crawling up the sides of their container or inside the lid, particularly if your container has ledges. If, however, *all* of the worms seem to be making a bid for freedom, then they probably don't like the environment you have provided. If the mixture has become too damp or waterlogged, they cannot obtain oxygen and will climb out in an attempt to breathe.

Prevention Place the wormery in a sheltered spot, where rain will not pour straight through the ventilation holes.

Solution Add layers of dry material, such as shredded newspaper, to absorb the water and provide a safe haven for the worms.

Inactive worms

During the cold winter months, worms will begin to slow down. They become dormant and may die if the temperature drops below freezing.

Prevention Worms will stop feeding when the temperature drops below 10°C (50°F),. To keep the wormery ticking over, insulate it with bubble wrap or old sacking. Alternatively, bring the container indoors (a shed or garage is ideal). Since any abrupt changes in temperature can prove fatal, avoid moving the wormery to an artificially heated environment that may be too warm.

▼ **There are currently a number of different readymade wormeries available on the market.**

Odour

The composting environment should smell fresh and earthy. If the wormery contains flies or has a fetid odour, this is an indication that conditions have become unbalanced.

Prevention Avoid adding new scraps to your compost until the previous ones have been at least partly processed.

Solution Remove the bulk of the rotting material and add a layer of dry newspaper. If the wormery has become badly polluted, the conditions will be very acidic. Special lime tablets are available to correct this, and are available from many wormery and worm providers.

Very dry compost

During the summer, the wormery can overheat, causing the worms to die and the compost to dry out.

Prevention Move the wormery into a shaded part of the garden. It should never be in direct sun during the warmer months.

Solution Add cool, damp paper scraps before moving out of the sun.

Commercial alternatives

IF YOU lack the inclination to make your own wormery or find the sieving laborious, there are many ready–made alternatives available on the market. Some have a tray system that allows fresh compost to be harvested from the bottom without disturbing the worms on top. These models are also fitted with a tap to prevent the contents from becoming waterlogged. After a heavy rainfall, the liquid run–off can be collected and used as an all–purpose fertilizer. For use on young plants, dilute the liquid in a little rainwater.

The Bokashi system

THE BOKASHI system recycles items that cannot be composted through conventional means. These include cooked food, meat and citrus fruits, in addition to all the more usual materials that can be put in a conventional composting system. Bokashi, which is the Japanese word for 'fermented organic matter', uses beneficial micro-organisms to accelerate the decomposition of household waste. As a result, a bin-sized container of waste can be garden-ready in as little as two weeks. The final product will not be recognizable as compost, but will look as if it has been pickled. Despite its strange appearance, the Bokashi mixture can be dug straight into the garden where it will decompose further. However, unlike genuine compost, it is not an instantly usable growing medium and requires further processing if it is to be used for this purpose.

How it works

HOME-COMPOSTING SYSTEMS like the Bokashi utilize effective micro-organisms (EMs). These EMs are supplied to the user inoculated into a material such as bran. Since the Bokashi system uses beneficial bacteria such as lactobacilli and

The advantages of Bokashi

- Unlike a normal composting system or wormery, cooked food, meat and dairy products can be composted.

- The turnaround is quick – a wormery can take up to nine months to produce the first batch of compost, whereas Bokashi can be dug into the soil after a couple of weeks.

- Bokashi material can be conveniently stored in the kitchen to receive scraps, unlike the wormery or compost heap.

- Since the Bokashi process is anaerobic (i.e., doesn't require oxygen) it can be kept in an air-tight container to reduce odour. It also produces almost no CO_2 emissions.

The disadvantages of Bokashi

- Unlike a wormery, the Bokashi system does not produce a growing medium suitable for instant use. The fermented waste must be allowed to decompose further (either in the wormery, compost heap or ground).

- The quick turnaround necessitates more frequent trips to the garden to dig in the waste.

- The fermenting Bokashi mixture needs draining every couple of days.

- Since the Bokashi must be left to decompose outside, it can be unsuitable for people living in apartments with no garden. Although the waste will rot down more quickly in a landfill when mixed with Bokashi bran, this is a rather labour-intensive process for something that is destined to go out with the rubbish. Another option is to take the Bokashi waste to a community composting site but, again, the CO_2 emissions involved in transporting it there may well outweigh the benefits.

yeasts, it works in a similar way to the popular health yoghurts that suppress pathogens to aid digestion. Just as yoghurts reduce bloating caused by gas in the human gut, Bokashi prevents the formation of gases during the fermentation process – this means that in a well-maintained system there is virtually no odour.

Part of a home recycling system

SINCE THE Bokashi process will not produce a usable growing medium immediately, it is best used in tandem with other, traditional composting methods. If used as the sole method of recycling, it can be tedious to dig into the ground each time a container is full. However, using Bokashi to prime kitchen waste gives you the best of both worlds – a quicker turnaround in your compost heap and the opportunity to recycle meats and cooked food – without the

tedious bi–weekly digging in of the Bokashi waste. Normally, cooked foods and meat would putrefy in the compost heap and wormery, encouraging vermin and odour. However, when prepared with the Bokashi bran, these items can be safely added to the compost and even the wormery, when restricted to small amounts.

Getting started

ALMOST ANY container can be used to house Bokashi, provided it has an airtight lid. To allow for processing time, two separate containers are required. Two 20l (4½gals) containers should be sufficient to process the kitchen waste of a large family. Since it is important to drain the Bokashi, a container with a tap is the most convenient solution (most commercial containers have this feature as standard). For recycling on a large scale, a large water butt would be suitable, as the tap could be utilized for drainage.

1 ADD A thin layer of the Bokashi bran to cover the bottom of the first container. Make sure that you don't omit this step, as the waste needs to be sandwiched between the layers of bran to process effectively.

2 ENSURE ALL waste is chopped into small pieces, as it will decompose more evenly if there are no large lumps. Pour your waste products over the bottom layer of bran. Avoid adding a layer more than 4cm (1½in) deep.

3 SPRINKLE MORE Bokashi on top. Apply a thin layer, enough to cover the surface of the waste – one handful should suffice.

4 BECAUSE THIS is an anaerobic process, the goal is to remove as much air as possible. Press the mixture down firmly to reduce air pockets – some pre-manufactured kits come with a plunger for this purpose. Close the lid, ensuring that the container is firmly sealed.

5 REPEAT STEPS three and four until the container is full. For an ongoing system you can repeat the process with a second container.

6 LEAVE THE first container to stand for around 14 days. During this time, draw off excess moisture by opening the tap every two days. (don't discard the liquid, as it can be used as an all-purpose fertilizer) and continue to fill the second container with waste and Bokashi bran.

7 AFTER IT has been allowed to stand for two weeks, open the first container. The mixture should smell pickled, rather like cider vinegar. If it smells of putrefaction, it is likely that the mixture has been allowed to become too moist or that the container is not sufficiently airtight.

8 ADD THE mixture to your garden compost heap, or dig into the ground in vegetable or flower beds.

9 YOUR SECOND container should now be full, and should be allowed to stand (repeat step seven). At the same time, the first container can be filled (repeat step one). You should always have one container being filled and one processing.

Buying Bokashi bran

Order Bokashi bran in advance. You'll need to purchase approximately 600g (21oz) every couple of months. Some suppliers can organize regular Bokashi deliveries to your door.

Materials for the Bokashi system

Suitable All raw and cooked foods, fruit, fish, meat and vegetables.

Unsuitable Liquids, bones, plastic, paper and cat/dog faeces.

◀ **If your kitchen scraps begin to emit a foul smell, the balance of your Bokashi system requires adjustment.**

Troubleshooting

Y OU MAY need to experiment a little before you get the process right. If it all goes wrong, the mixture can still be dug into the ground but must be mixed with plenty of bran first.

If the bin emits a rancid smell, the Bokashi mixture has not decomposed properly. This is usually due to one (or a combination) of the following factors:

Too much liquid

If it is not drained every few days, the mixture will putrefy. A little excess moisture can be corrected by adding very small amounts of shredded paper.

Not enough bran

If the layers are not covered in Bokashi, the exposed areas may begin to rot.

Too much air

Oxygen, light and heat should be eliminated as far as possible. Always ensure the lid is airtight and firmly closed. Pressing the layers down firmly will also help to eliminate air pockets.

Green, black or blue mould

If mould begins to grow in the mixture then it is contaminated. Small amounts of mould can be tackled with copious layering of bran. If the mould is widespread, the mixture will need to be discarded.

White mould

If a downy white mould has developed, don't worry! This is a perfectly normal occurrence and part of the natural decomposition process.

Uses for Bokashi

Soil enrichment

Dig a trench 25cm (10in) deep. Fill it with the fermented mixture and cover with soil. After two weeks the ground can be planted with vegetables and ornamental plants.

Liquid feed

The drained–off liquid, or 'Bokashi tea' can be used to feed both house and garden plants. Dilute in water at a ratio of 1:100.

Drain cleaner

Undiluted Bokashi liquid can be poured down drains and sewers to eliminate odour–causing pathogens.

Composting accelerant

Add the fermented waste to your compost bin and the wormery.

> ### Adding Bokashi to a wormery
>
> The pickled Bokashi waste is quite acidic, so be sure to add lime pellets if it is added to the wormery.

Food

From field to plate

THE CONCEPT of 'food miles' was first introduced in the 1990s, and is now a term widely used amongst those seeking a greener lifestyle. Simply put, it is the distance that food is transported, measured from its place of production (the field) to its final destination (our plate). For example, a bag of salad may well have started its journey at the farm before being driven to a packaging plant. Once washed and packed, it will be loaded into trucks and delivered to supermarkets all over the country. The customer then drives to an out-of-town supermarket to purchase his weekly shopping. The bag of salad is then bought, packed and driven home. By this point, it has

▼ **Our food is often transported a considerable distance from the field where it was grown.**

▲ **Markets are a great source of locally produced food, and are often to be found in towns and cities.**

often travelled a considerable distance, which represents increased carbon emissions. Ready-made products that use a number of ingredients may rack up an even higher amount of food miles. The packaging itself will also have to be produced (often using petrochemicals) and transported to where it is needed. All of this mounts up to a considerable carbon footprint.

Cutting out the middle man

To REDUCE the pressure your food requirements place on the environment, try to avoid the lure of the supermarket chain. While these large stores offer convenient one-stop shopping,

they are often located out of town (thereby necessitating a journey in the car) and rack up food miles in obtaining their stock.

▼ **When shopping at the supermarket, opt for products which use less packaging.**

◀ **Unless you grow your own, you'll be hard-pressed to beat a local farmer's market in terms of freshness!**

imported huge distances to reach countries in more temperate climates. It can also be argued, however, that importing such produce supports some of the world's poorer economies.

The real problem lies in foods that *can* be locally produced but aren't, or foods that are imported because they are unavailable at certain times of year in your country. If you can purchase tomatoes in the depth of winter, it is likely they have been imported from sunnier climes.

What to do

When buying and preparing produce, follow the seasons. Many of us have lost touch with them, so eating the produce that is only currently available not only re-connects us with our environment, but also saves food miles, too. Food really does taste better when it is in season!

▼ **Many of the foods we take for granted actually travel thousands of miles to reach our plate.**

What to do

Food can be purchased directly from farmers' markets, farm shops and independent green grocers (if you're lucky enough to have one near you). Unfortunately the latter are becoming scarce, as they are unable to compete with the bulk-buying supermarkets on price. If you are unable to access local food at source, opt for supermarket items that are labelled as locally sourced.

Seasonal grocery shopping

THESE DAYS it may seem odd to regard the banana as an exotic fruit, but, depending on where you live, it has probably undergone a very long journey to reach your supermarket shelf. Many heat-loving fruits have to be

Seasonal food chart

January
Winter squash, cabbage, celeriac, parsnip, shallots, leeks, rosemary, Brussels sprout, Jerusalem artichoke.

February
As January, plus chicory and beetroot.

March
Carrot, parsley, rhubarb, sprouting broccoli, spring onion.

April
As March, plus radish, kale, watercress, spinach, parsley.

May
New potatoes, broad beans, raspberries, cherries, cauliflower, mint.

June
Peas, asparagus, redcurrants, strawberries, elderflower, turnip, mange tout, broccoli.

July
Tomatoes, cucumber, onions, peas, kohlrabi, rocket, salad leaves, French beans, courgette.

August
Lettuce, peppers, fennel, runner beans, celery, sweetcorn.

September
Butternut squash, walnuts, plum, apples, marrow, courgette, blackberries.

October
Pumpkin, swede, squash, artichoke, carrots, elderberries, apples, quince.

November
Garlic, onions, chestnut, passion fruit, leeks, kale, pumpkin, pears.

December
Pears, parsnip, Brussels sprout, winter greens, cabbage.

▲ **Stay in tune with the seasons, and you'll always be eating the freshest, tastiest vegetables.**

Growing your own

GROWING VEGETABLES and fruit is an excellent way to cut down on your food miles. If you save seed, rather than always buying afresh, your food miles may be reduced to zero! Read much more on pages 132–9.

Going organic

THE SIGHT of large fields full of just one type of crop ripening in the sun may now be a quintessential part of our view of the countryside, but this mass–production method of cultivating a single species has long been known to cause problems.

Firstly, large groups of the same crop make an easy target for pests. For this reason, growers are compelled to spray the whole area with pesticides. After a while, the pests become resistant to these pesticides, and the chemicals find their way into the food chain.

Secondly, soil nutrients are depleted when the ground is occupied by a large number of the same type of plant. This problem is

▲ **When shopping at the supermarket, look for items that are locally produced.**

compounded if the ground is used for the same crop season after season – often the soil becomes so impoverished that artificial fertilizer has to be applied up to three times a year.

What to do

Due to consumer pressure, supermarkets are required to meet strict standards when labelling a product as organic. Some organic fruit and vegetables may initially appear somewhat unappetizing. Non–organic fruit and vegetables are often artificially large due to the application of chemical fertilizer so, while they may appear smaller, organically grown produce often has much more flavour and nutritional value.

Fair trade

A CUP OF tea relies on leaves imported from India or China. Similarly, a hot latte or espresso is made from beans grown in Brazil or Ethiopia. Unfortunately, farmers are only paid a fraction of the final sale price. Once the harvest has been collected, it is commonplace for an agent to arrive and offer a negligible price. The farmer can accept, or leave his crop to rot. It is this stark choice which forces many growers into a state of abject poverty. Similar cases of exploitation occur in the cocoa and banana trades. Thankfully, there are now other options on the market that pay a fair wage to producers. Look for the fair trade label on tea, coffee, chocolate and bananas.

Free-range hens and eggs

THE APPALLING fate of battery hens has been well publicized, and it is now easy to select free–range eggs in the shops. Apart from the animal–cruelty issues, factory farming methods produce animal waste on a large scale. With less intensive methods, this waste can be broken down naturally, but excessive amounts can leach into waterways.

What to do

Battery hens are usually slaughtered at around 18 months of age, when they are no longer fit for intensive laying. The natural life of a hen is in fact eight to ten years, and it will continue to lay eggs for most of its life. Many rescue centres have ex–battery hens available for adoption, and they make pleasant (and productive) pets. A group of four hens will keep a family supplied with eggs all year round.

▲ A free-range life allows hens to stretch, scratch the soil and exhibit other natural behaviours.

▼ Free-range eggs are laid in a nest, as opposed to a cage-floor.

▲ **Hens make friendly and productive pets, and their care requires very little specialist knowledge.**

While it may be easy to buy free-range eggs, many pre-prepared cakes, biscuits and sweets contain the factory-farmed variety. Sometimes these products are labelled as containing free-range eggs, but if not it is usually wise to assume the worst. Unfortunately battery eggs are a cheaper option for manufacturers.

◀ **Free-range eggs are available from both supermarkets and farmer's markets.**

Sprouting

Home-grown vitamins

PLANTS CONTAIN the highest concentrations of vitamins and nutrients when they are young and still growing. For this reason, sprouted seeds and pulses are an excellent way to boost your vitamin intake. The seed or bean contains food to see the developing plant through germination, and is therefore a rich source of amino acids, phytochemicals, minerals and proteins – all of which are essential to human health. Upon germination, a number of complex chemical reactions begin to take place in order to produce an initial energy boost for the seedling. At this point, the sprout is easily digested and can be sprinkled on salads or added to sandwiches. Since no soil is required, sprouting is extremely easy – the most basic set-up requires no more equipment than a few squares of damp kitchen towel and some seeds.

The most commonly sprouted varieties are mung beans, chick peas and alfalfa. Since they are easy to sprout they are a good choice for the beginner. Many health-food shops sell alfalfa bagged and pre-sprouted, but this is an extremely expensive (and energy inefficient) way to obtain it, given the minimal effort and expense involved in home sprouting. It is, however, worth doing your research if you intend to sprout weird and wonderful beans (aside from the varieties suggested above). Some types, such as the kidney bean, are mildly toxic and are therefore unsuitable for sprouting.

Suitable varieties for sprouting

Mung bean, chickpea, alfalfa, green lentil (not split), mizuna, peas, barley, celery, cabbage, kale, celery, gungo pea, radish, quinoa, watercress, soy bean, butter bean, brown rice, coriander, mustard, garlic, leek, onion, almonds, pumpkin.

Starting with sprouts

1 DRIED SEEDS are dormant, and need moisture to come to life. Many varieties benefit from soaking, particularly if they have tough shells. Most seeds/beans can be soaked in cold water overnight (8 to 12 hours) while small seeds may only require a 20-minute soak.

2 GIVE THE seeds a quick rinse to remove any dust, dirt or other foreign matter.

3 DAMPEN A piece of paper towel so that it is moist but not dripping. Use to line a container – this can be anything from an old ice–cream tub to a plate. A lid will prevent dust and debris landing on the sprouts, but it must have ventilation holes.

4 SPRINKLE THE soaked seeds onto the surface of the paper towel.

5 LEAVE TO sprout. Depending on the variety this can take anything from one to five days. Contrary to popular belief, sprouts do not have to be started in the dark. Add a spritz of water if the seeds begin to dry out.

How to use sprouts

Eat them raw

Sprouts can be eaten as soon as the green shoot is visible. Alfalfa sprouts make a tasty sandwich–filler, while chickpeas add a nutty flavour to salads.

Stir-fry

When added at the last moment of cooking, sprouts make a crunchy addition to stir–fries. Garlic and onion shoots are particularly tasty.

▼ **Plastic sprouters are easy to clean between crops, and are a cost-effective option.**

More advanced sprouting systems

SHOULD YOU find yourself addicted to sprouting, there are many useful growing systems available on the market. Choose a tiered-version that can house both germinating and ready–to–eat sprouts; this will ensure a regular supply. Many systems are self–watering and have a temperature control, allowing you to grow a wider variety of sprouts. Some varieties of seed, such as basil, cress, mustard and flax, are mucilaginous, which means that they develop a gel–like coating when soaked. To sprout these

▲ A tiered sprouter allows you to have seeds germinating, sprouting and ready to harvest simultaneously.

successfully you will need to use a growing medium (such as an old piece of cloth) to house the roots. Seeds that do not produce shoots are referred to as 'soaks'. Almonds and pumpkin seeds fall into this category, and will develop a noticeable bulge when they are ready to eat.

▼ Sprouts should be rinsed everyday until they are eaten to ensure freshness.

▲ Some seeds need light to develop their characteristic flavour, while others can be sprouted in the dark.

Troubleshooting

Unpleasant odour

If the sprouts begin to smell, they have probably begun to rot and must be discarded. Certain varieties, such as broccoli and cabbage, will naturally have a more pungent aroma, but when this becomes unpleasant something has gone wrong.

Mould

If your sprouts develop a downy coating they must not be eaten. To avoid the formation of mould, wash the sprouts every 12 hours and always before eating. It is also important to sterilize sprouting equipment before adding a new batch. If you are sprouting broccoli, cabbage or grains, the 'mould' may in fact be tiny root hairs.

Failure to sprout

This can be attributed to a number of factors, but excessive moisture levels are usually to blame. Be sure to drain your seeds/beans thoroughly before adding to the sprouting container.

The Green Garden

Most of us don't have acres of land to play with, making self-sufficiency an impossible dream. However, it is still possible for most urban-dwellers to grow some of their own fruit and veg. With careful planning, even the smallest inner-city garden can produce a surprising amount of fresh food, while an allotment presents an even wider range of possibilities – you may even be able to keep your own chickens! If allotment waiting lists are lengthy or you have no garden to speak of, don't despair. Ornamental window boxes and containers can be transformed into mini vegetable plots with a careful choice of plants. Even if you can't grow your own root vegetables, a well-lit windowsill can still house herbs and salad leaves.

Aside from growing to eat, gardens serve another important environmental purpose: encouraging wildlife. On large housing estates there may be little green space available, making your back garden a magnet for hedgehogs, butterflies and also bees. Growing native plants and creating microclimates within your garden can help to save these once common species from extinction.

Gardening for wildlife

By SETTING aside a small part of your garden as a dedicated wildlife area you will be providing a home for a wide variety of birds, insects, amphibians and mammals that will help to control pests and create a healthy, balanced environment.

Once a variety of attractive habitats has been created you'll be amazed at how quickly they are colonized by beneficial species. Frogs, ladybirds, hedgehogs, ground beetles and many others will see your garden as a haven and will happily feast

▶ **With careful planting, you'll have the pleasure of seeing a wide variety of wildlife in your garden.**

▼ **Birds will feast on pests that would otherwise devour your plants.**

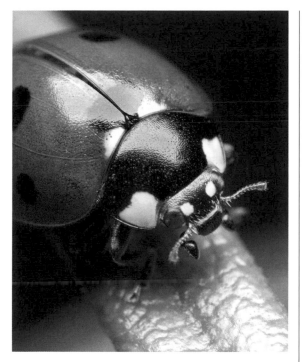

◀ **Ladybirds will quickly reduce the aphid population in your garden.**

▼ **Bees are vital for pollinating vegetables and ornamental plants.**

upon the slugs and aphids that threaten your vegetables. There is really very little to do once the habitats are in place except sit back and watch your guests do their work.

Choosing the spot

To ENCOURAGE wildlife, you don't have to let the garden become a wilderness; a few carefully chosen plants and hiding places will attract a surprising variety of insects, birds and amphibians. Below are some tips to get you started:

• WHEN choosing a spot for your wildlife area, consider how often you will need to disturb the site. Like us, wildlife often look for a quiet corner in which to make their homes.

• HABITAT diversity is important if you wish to attract as many species as possible. Try to include at least a log pile, a stack of rough stones and an area of dense vegetation or long grass.

▶ **Viper's bugloss: its pollen is a favourite food of the bumblebee.**

▲ **Choose native plants to encourage local wildlife into your garden.**

● To make things comfortable for your guests try to shelter the area from strong winds. Use planting or a simple fence made of pallets where appropriate.

● ALL creatures are attracted by water, so a small pond is a great idea. If this isn't feasible you could use a bird-bath or even an old washing-up bowl.

● THE wildlife area doesn't have to look untidy. You could even use it as an excuse to grow some wild flowers or native, berry-producing shrubs.

▼ **Many of the plants that are loved by wildlife are also ornamental in their own right.**

Top tips for a wildlife pond

● Think carefully about where you want your pond. It may seem obvious, but because water runs downhill a natural depression is the perfect place to start.

● When you've decided where to site your pond, mark out the boundaries with a length of hosepipe or a line of sand, so you know where to dig.

● While a pond liner might not seem natural, it is the best way to ensure your pond stays full. Providing wildlife with water in hot dry spells is important.

● Remove the sharp stones that might pierce the liner from the bed of the pond. Consider using a protective layer of sand or plastic under the liner.

● Try to create varied habitats within your pond. Deep water is fine, but gently sloping shallows are more important for many birds, mammals and amphibians.

● Don't be tempted to keep fish in your pond; they are likely to feed on some of the wildlife you hope to attract!

▼ **Even the smallest of ponds will invite a wealth of wildlife into your garden.**

Just add water

WHETHER YOU garden organically or not, you won't fail to notice the damage a few frogs can do to the slug population in your garden, not to mention the hungry thrushes and hedgehogs who will be drawn to your plot by the presence of water.

The planting in and around a natural pond should ideally be composed of native species, as it is these that will attract the insects. There should even be room for a few edibles – you could try your hand at growing a cranberry bush (a bog plant needing acid soil) or even horseradish (be careful, it can be invasive). Quite apart from the practical reasons for including a pond in your plans, there's nothing more relaxing than watching water – the perfect end to a hard day's digging.

▲ **Water-line or marginal plants offer wildlife places to hide from predators (such as the domestic cat).**

▼ **A pond provides a restful environment for both wildlife and humans.**

Building a hedgehog box

Hedgehogs are among a gardener's most valuable allies, munching their way through slugs and snails during spring, summer and autumn. They live in burrows, where they can also hibernate in the winter. However you can really return their hard work by building a simple hedgehog box as a home. It costs very little to make and should take you less than two hours.

▶ **Hedgehogs are natural foragers, and will quickly reduce your slug and snail population.**

▼ **Since hedgehog populations are falling rapidly, any help you give will contribute towards conserving them.**

1 USING MARINE (or exterior grade) plywood and pressure–treated batten (to resist the weather) make a box measuring 54cm long by 29cm wide and 31cm deep (21 x 11½ x 12in). More batten helps to hold the lid loosely in place. The door is 20cm wide by 17cm high (8 x 7in) and the ventilation hole is 30mm (1in) diameter. Two pieces of batten hold the box off the ground.

2 NEXT MAKE the entrance tunnel from more marine ply fixed with wood glue. It should be 20cm by 17cm (8 x 7in) to fit snugly into the door (no glue required here) and 32cm (12½in) long. A single short piece of batten, fixed to the underside of the entrance to the tunnel, helps lift the entrance off the ground and away from the damp soil.

3 HEDGEHOG NESTS are usually well ventilated but this artificial one is much less so. Compensate for this by adding a length of plastic tubing (water conduit is ideal, as is a washing–machine waste pipe) to allow air to reach the interior of the nest. The pipe should be 20cm (8in) long and angled downwards to keep out the rain.

4 PUT THE box in place somewhere out of the way, and add the lid and entrance tunnel. Cover the whole thing with an off–cut of pond liner, roofing felt or thick plastic sheeting. Lastly, camouflage the box with dry grass and twigs, leaves or even a mound of soil, leaving only the entrance and vent clear.

Building a bird box

A SIMPLE BIRD box is an easy project for even the least confident DIY–er, requiring just a few basic tools and a plank of untreated timber. The best size commonly available is 144mm wide by 18mm thick (5½ x ¾in) and you'll need about 1m (3¼ft) in length. Your feathered friends will happily make a feast of slugs and insect pests. When choosing a site for your box, don't worry too much about the direction it faces.

More important is shelter from strong winds, rain and direct sunlight, and inaccessibility to predators such as the neighbourhood cats. Don't be tempted to hang two boxes of the same type close together as you will be promoting aggressive behaviour between birds. Also, keep boxes and feeders in separate parts of the garden, as feeding birds can be noisy and will disturb the inhabitants of your box.

	200mm (8in)	300mm (4¼in)	175mm (11¾in)	175mm (7in)	200mm (7in)	108mm (8in)
144mm (5½in)	Roof	Back	Front	Side	Side	Base

▲ This template shows how to mark and cut your timber, providing the necessary parts from just one plank.

▼ The finished bird box is easy to hang, and can be taken down for cleaning simply by undoing two screws.

1 ON YOUR timber plank mark out in this order from left to right: the roof (200mm/8in); the back (300mm/11¾in); the front (175mm/7in); the sides (one edge 175mm/7in; the other 200mm/8in); and the base (108mm/4¼in) of your box.

2 USING A jigsaw with a fine blade, cut the plank into the constituent pieces. Use a piece of coarse sandpaper to remove any rough edges and splinters. Drill two small holes in the base to allow any rainwater to drain away.

3 USE A hole–cutting drill bit to make a 32mm (1¼in) diameter hole in the front panel, then screw all the pieces together. You will probably need to pre-drill the holes to avoid splitting the wood with the screws.

4 THE ROOF is the last piece to be added and, because you are using screws, it is easily removed when you wish to clean out the old nest in winter. The box can be hung by screwing through the back panel.

Growing native plants

WHILE IT can be tempting to fill the garden with exotic and unusual plants, growing native varieties will benefit local wildlife. It is not necessary to turn your whole garden into a meadow or wildlife haven; a few carefully chosen plants will provide food and an ideal habitat for some of the UK's most endangered species. Since indigenous plants are uniquely adapted to the local environment they are often extremely easy to grow. This can come as something of a relief, particularly if you have had experience in growing fussy exotic ornamentals! While native varieties are often overlooked, many are as attractive as those borne of sunnier climes.

Local plant life

A BRISK WALK around your neighbourhood will hopefully show you an array of garden-planting styles. Looking for the healthier specimens in you neighbour's gardens will give you some clues as to what will flourish on your own plot. If you live in a more rural area, make a note of the wild flowers growing in the hedgerows. Some of these are colourful and easily grown at home. If, however, you are

▼ **Elderflower is an attractive plant, native to the UK, that can be used to make cordials, tea and wine.**

▲ **If you have sufficient space, a meadow of mixed native flowers makes a stunning focal point.**

attracted to the plants in your local woodland, remember you will have to recreate similar conditions in order for these varieties to thrive at home.

Sandy, dry soil

If you live near the coast, you will have seen a number of interesting (and often edible) plants growing in the salty, breezy atmosphere.

Sea kale is an odd-looking plant that is native to northern European and Irish coastal areas. It is resistant to wind as the leaves have a protective waxy coating that reduces evaporation. It thrives in sandy, well-drained soil and will last for years

◀ **Wildflowers are often smaller than their cultivated counterparts and therefore tend to appear more delicate.**

▲ Sea kale is a coastal plant and can be blanched to improve texture and taste.

once planted. When allowed to grow unchecked, the leaves will be bitter and unpleasant, should you wish to eat them. When blanched (covered with a container to exclude light), however, sea kale produces tender and tasty shoots that can be eaten as a vegetable. Seeds can be purchased from companies such as Marshalls in the UK.

Sea milkwort is common in most coastal areas; this salt–loving plant bears small white and pink flowers. It is actually a relative of the primrose, although it looks quite dissimilar.

Plants for a shady spot

Many people have a dark and shady area in their garden where plants struggle to thrive. Often this is caused by an overhanging tree or the shadow cast by a neighbouring building. Rather than removing the tree (and its wildlife) try to work with what you've got – woodland plants may flourish in these conditions.

Bluebells and colombine have beautiful flowers, but their population is in decline. Consider growing them in your shady spot; seeds are available from specialist nurseries. It is illegal to remove them from the wild, and this would also defeat the purpose!

Dog violet is another woodland native with stunning purple flowers that are a rich source of food for fritillary butterflies.

Wild strawberry will provide ground cover and produces very small, edible fruits when planted in dry semi–shade.

Lily of the valley is an elegant and sweet–smelling plant and another dry–shade variety.

Primrose loves damper conditions, and its stunning yellow blooms provide food for moths.

By the pond

If you have added a wildlife pond to your garden (see pages 110–11), choosing native marginal plants will provide an ideal habitat for visiting frogs, toads and newts.

▼ Once a common sight in our hedgerows, the wild primrose is now in decline.

An important note

Plants and seeds should never be taken from the wild. For many species this is illegal and causes further depletion of rare varieties. Always obtain bulbs, seeds and plants from a reputable supplier.

Angelica has attractive pink and white flowers, whilst bistort provides food for the copper butterfly.

Marsh marigold is another good choice, as it boasts stunning yellow flowers that are a rich source of nectar for butterflies and bees.

Shrubs

Shrubs are the backbone of the garden, providing a framework for other planting. Dogwood is an ideal choice, as its red branches provide winter interest. During the spring it produces white flowers favoured by the emperor moth.

▲ **Dogwood adds a splash of colour to the garden during the depths of winter.**

In a pinch

If you aren't an avid gardener or lack the time to research native species, there are many wild-flower seed mixes available on the market. These can be woven through other ornamental plants or sown wherever space is available. To provide food for the bees and butterflies, choose wildlife-attractant mixes.

▼ **A weed is just a plant thought to be in the wrong place. These daises are pretty enough to be left where they are.**

Organic principles and practices

ORGANIC GARDENING is gaining popularity amongst both ornamental gardeners and vegetable growers. Whether you are a strict eco-gardener or choose to adopt just a few organic principles, there is no doubt that it will benefit your plants, the environment and your health. The species of wildlife and plants in your garden are interdependent – tomatoes would not be pollinated without bees transporting the nectar for food, and the soil would be barren were it not for the humble earthworm, which also provides food for birds. Adding chemicals into this complex environment can therefore have far-reaching effects. Slug pellets may poison hedgehogs when they ingest their prey. Artificial fertilizers can cause plants to become unnaturally lush, which in turn causes an explosion in the pest population. Organic gardening is all about balance. Aim to find a happy medium between your needs and those of nature.

Organic alternatives

Pest control

Slugs and snails are amongst the most unpopular visitors to the garden, closely followed by aphids, vine weevils and chafer grubs. These creatures will quickly eat their way through both vegetables and ornamentals unless stopped in their tracks. Methods of organic control are based on prevention rather than cure and aim to reduce the risk of infestation. The goal of organic gardening is not to eradicate any species, but simply to reduce pests to a manageable level.

Companion planting

When planted alongside each other, many species are mutually beneficial. Some will deter insects from their neighbours, while others will accentuate the flavour of edible crops. There are a number of varieties, however, that should not be grown together as they attract the same pests. The table opposite shows you both good and bad plant companions.

Crop rotation

You may see the productivity of your favourite vegetables decreasing if they have been grown in the same spot for a few years. Sometimes this is the result of soil–borne disease (such as club root

◀ **Snails are a common sight in the garden, particularly after heavy rain.**

▲ **These newly hatched caterpillars will quickly destroy a vegetable patch unless they are eaten by birds or controlled biologically.**

Companion planting at a glance

Runner bean

Companions: aubergine, carrot, calendula, sweetcorn, cucumber, potato
Adversaries: cabbage, radish, beetroot, basil, onion, garlic

Broccoli and cabbage

Companions: celery, onion, garlic, mint, tomato, lettuce, kale, geranium, dill
Adversaries: bean, strawberry

Carrot

Companions: bean, cabbage, calendula, sage, tomato, pea, pepper, onion
Adversaries: celery, parsnip

Potato

Companions: cabbage, calendula, pea, sweetcorn
Adversaries: tomato, turnip, raspberry, cucumber

Tomato

Companions: basil, cabbage, carrot, nasturtium, pepper, oregano
Adversaries: potato, runner bean, dill

Brussels sprout

Companions: beetroot, tomato, spinach, pea
Adversaries: kohlrabi, strawberry, bean

Onion and garlic

Companions: cabbage, carrot, leek, pepper, strawberry
Adversaries: sage, pea, bean, parsley

Pea

Companions: aubergine, radish, spinach, strawberry, cucumber
Adversaries: gladiolus, onion, garlic

Kohlrabi

Companions: lettuce, onion, nasturtium
Adversaries: runner bean

among brassicas), or is due to a lack of nutrients (causing discolouration and distortion of growth). To reduce the build-up of soil-borne pathogens, avoid growing any one variety of vegetable in the same spot more often than one year in three.

▼ **Apart from attracting beneficial insects and deterring or distracting pests, filling bare ground with companion plants will help to suppress weed growth.**

Biological control

F̲OR AN infestation already in full swing, it can be tempting to reach for the pesticides. There are, however, effective biological methods that can be employed. It is now possible to buy nematodes that destroy pests, targeting only

▲ **Many ornamental plants can be grown alongside vegetables to ward off pests.**

your chosen species. If, for instance, you wish to eradicate slugs, buy nematodes that are parasitic upon slugs only – this means that the ecosystem is not unduly disturbed. This method of pest control is non-toxic, so will not poison cats, dogs, frogs, birds, toads or hedgehogs. Nematodes are available for each individual species you may wish to control, such as vine weevils and chafer grubs. It is worth noting, however, that this method should not be used in place of good husbandry i.e. crop rotation, companion planting, etc. Remember, even slugs are an essential part of the food chain in your garden, so reduction rather than eradication should be your goal.

Weed control

Even the most manicured garden will become a wilderness if left for a few weeks over the growing season. The best way to manage weeds without chemicals is regular hoeing. If this becomes a routine rather than occasional task, it will take a matter of minutes. Little and often is the key. To reduce the work required, weed-suppressing membrane can be purchased and can be laid under paths and on top of unused ground. The best way to avoid weeds in the flowerbed is to plant your ornamentals densely – open ground is bound to be colonized by weeds.

Fertilizer

Home-made compost, distilled comfrey, leaf mould and seaweed all make excellent soil conditioners and fertilizers without the need for chemical feeds.

Making a leaf mould bin

WHILE SOME people complain about the mess caused by falling leaves, keen gardeners know a good thing when they see one. Many of the nutrients stored by the trees remain in the leaves. They are locked up until time, the elements and a few million bacteria join forces to set them free. Some people like to add leaves to their normal compost heap, where they will certainly do a great job of improving the structure. Try to keep them separate, though, letting them rot down on their own to create a truly wonderful growing medium reserved for your favourite and most treasured plants.

▼ **Fallen leaves are rich in nutrients and should be saved rather than thrown away.**

Collecting leaves is easy enough in most gardens, although they always seem to come from a neighbour's tree! Rather than complaining about this, try to be grateful, and you may even get a buzz out of seeing the piles build up against the fence. If you don't have a garden and your allotment is tree-free, you should be able to find a leafy street where you can fill the back of your car with leaves. Avoid taking anything from natural woodland, though.

Some people are satisfied with stuffing bin bags full of leaves and leaving them behind the shed to rot down, but a simple leaf bin will get the bacterial processes started much quicker.

1 A LEAF bin is a simple structure, easily moved, but it doesn't hurt to put it in the right place to start with. It should be out of the way, but accessible with a wheelbarrow. Take a little time to clear the area of weeds, as you don't want them growing through your compost, and rake it roughly flat.

2 THIS DOESN'T have to be a permanent structure, so use cheap timber posts for the four corners of your bin. Bang them at least 45cm (18in) into the ground so they are sturdy enough to withstand the odd knock. A lump hammer should do the job, but on some soils you may need a sledgehammer.

3 STARTING AT one of the front posts, tack the end of a roll of chicken wire to the wood using wire staples. Unroll the wire around the other three posts, tacking it in place as you go. After the last leg, cut the wire off leaving a couple of extra inches. Don't tack this end to the starting post.

4 CUT OFF or fold back any sharp ends, then tie the loose end of the cage in place using garden wire to form the last side of the square. This 'door' will allow you access to the rich leaf mould within, but first you need to collect up the fallen leaves. Suddenly it doesn't seem like a chore any more!

Sustainability

ALTHOUGH SUSTAINABILITY isn't synonymous with organic gardening, the latter is most commonly taken to include recycling and waste prevention. As well as conserving resources, sustainable gardening will save a great deal of money. In time, it is possible to make your garden completely self-sufficient.

Water

ARGUABLY, WATER is the most important commodity in the garden and is often in short supply. A summer drought compounded by a hosepipe ban will spell death for your lovingly tended vegetables and ornamentals. Rather than filling the watering can with tap water (hard on the wallet as well as the environment), save rainfall in water butts earlier in the year. If you have the space, don't limit yourself to just one – the water saved in three or more water butts

▲ Plastic bottles can be used as cloches to prevent evaporation and protect seedlings from cold and pests.

▼ With its base removed, a plastic drinks bottle provides a clever way to deliver water straight to the roots of the plant.

will keep most gardens ticking over during a dry spell. Connecting each butt with a hose will ensure that the second and third will fill when the first has reached capacity.

A great deal of water is lost through the process of evaporation, particularly when the surface of the soil is watered during summer. A drip hose may prove a more effective solution, as it can be sunk below ground level closer to the roots.

Mulching is another way to reduce moisture loss and involves copious application of organic matter to the surface of the soil. This method works particularly well when the mulch is applied after the soil has been soaked – the extra layer prevents surface evaporation and is itself beneficial when incorporated into the soil by worms. Almost anything can be used as a mulch – bark chips, paper shreddings, straw, compost, grass clippings and leaf-mould are all suitable.

▲ Water is the most precious commodity in the garden, so it is worth re-evaluating when and how it is used.

▲ Sprinkler hoses can be an efficient method of irrigation, but only if used with care.

Heat

MANY YOUNG plants need heat in order to thrive, and the avid gardener often has a greenhouse for this purpose. The temperature can drop dramatically over the winter period, however, even under glass. For this reason, many gardeners heat their greenhouse with electric or paraffin heaters. But since so many of these heaters are fuelled by unsustainable energy, it is worth considering other options. A filled water butt will act like a storage heater, absorbing heat during the day and releasing it at night as the ambient temperature drops. When situated in or next to a greenhouse, it can provide enough warmth to ensure tender plants are not damaged during freezing winter nights.

Heirloom varieties

MONOCULTURAL METHODS of food production have led to the loss of several types of vegetable. Only a fraction of the available varieties are grown on a large scale, and not necessarily the tastiest are chosen, as suitability for mass production is the overriding consideration in modern agriculture. For this reason, many smallholders and gardeners have opted to grow heirloom varieties in order to preserve rare yet tasty crops for future generations. More than just a 'worthy' enterprise, growing rare crops is a satisfying and enjoyable hobby, allowing the gardener to try foods that are simply unavailable elsewhere. In the UK, seeds can be obtained from the Heritage Seed Library. This organization also offers advice and the opportunity to become a 'guardian' of a particular cultivar.

Compost

YOUNG, DELICATE plants appreciate the nutrient boost provided by compost. Many vegetables also require a rich growing medium to produce a sufficient yield. For this reason, compost is an essential ingredient for growing plants. It is, of course, available to buy from garden centres and supermarkets, but it is far more cost–effective to make your own from scratch. Generally speaking, it is only necessary to purchase compost if your own heap isn't yet up and running. Producing your own compost performs two essential tasks. First, it provides soil conditioner for all kinds of gardening jobs. Secondly (and of equal importance) is the recycling of garden and kitchen waste. Without composting, the average garden would produce bags and bags of organic waste that would have to collected or taken to a local waste site.

Making compost

HOME COMPOSTING is an excellent method of recycling, as it requires no specialist equipment or knowledge. The purpose of home composting is to convert kitchen and garden waste that would otherwise end up in landfill sites into a rich growing medium for garden plants. If you grow your own vegetables, you can compost old plants and peelings to create a growing medium for future use, thus creating a completely sustainable system.

▼ **Kitchen scraps needn't end up in a landfill site when they can be turned into garden compost.**

Getting started

AS A general rule, anything green and growing is suitable for composting. Meat, fish and cooked foods are unsuitable for the compost heap, as they will attract vermin. Such items are best recycled by using the Bokashi system (see pages 90–4). Since the resulting compost will be used to enrich the soil in your garden, it is best to avoid adding perennial or seeding weeds to the heap, as there is a danger that these will be spread when the compost is

▲ **Composting your garden waste will provide you with a nutrient-rich growing medium.**

used. Some materials, such as grass clippings, have a high water content and will quickly disintegrate into a sludgy mess if added in large quantities. However, if well combined with drier ingredients, moist green items can act as an accelerant. Larger items of garden waste, such as pruned branches, are best omitted from the heap. While they can be composted, they will take much longer to decompose than the other items in the bin, thus dramatically slowing your rate of production. Take tree cuttings to a community composting site, or shred them if you have access to the equipment – the resulting chips can be used as a moisture–conserving mulch. If the wood matter is very finely shredded, sandwich a thin layer of bark chippings between layers of grass clippings – the moisture provided will speed the decomposition of the drier bark.

It is best to start the compost heap with easily degradable waste, such as vegetable peelings, as this will help establish the bacteria it needs for

decomposition. If starting from scratch, your first lot of compost will be ready in six months to a year. This depends upon your climate, the size of your composting bin and the type and quantity of kitchen waste used.

Siting and containing

WHILE IT is perfectly possible to make compost without a container, it is far more convenient and effective to use a large, purpose–built bin. As well as making the heap easier to turn, this will also retain heat and speed up the composting process. In theory, an old dustbin will suffice for compost, although a larger, open–necked container will make it easier to maintain the heap. If you lack the time or inclination

▲ **Compost bins are quick and inexpensive to construct.**

to make your own container, there are many composters available on the market. Although only suitable for small gardens or homes, a 'tumbler' bin is a convenient solution; the barrel can be rotated to ensure even decomposition. Most local authorities now offer subsidized compost bins for purchase, which can provide

▼ **Although they can be composted, leaves are better saved and used to make leaf mould.**

a massive saving on shop prices. It is well worth contacting them to find out what is on offer for local residents.

Although it may be tempting to hide the composter in a dark, shady spot, it will be far more productive when placed in full sun or partial shade where it is warmer. If, however, you are not in a hurry for your compost it can be placed in a cooler area, but decomposition will take a year or more.

Items for composting

- Vegetable peelings, skins and tops
- Tea bags and coffee grounds
- Young weeds (avoid if gone to seed)
- Soft plant trimmings or prunings
- Soiled bedding from vegetarian pets such as hamsters, gerbils, rabbits and Guinea pigs
- Sawdust
- Eggshells

IN SMALL AMOUNTS

- Grass clippings
- Shredded paper
- Cardboard
- Citrus fruit

NOT FOR COMPOSTING

- Meat and fish
- Cooked food
- Wood
- Glossy paper
- Diseased plants
- Invasive or perennial weeds
- Cat or dog faeces

Maintaining your compost heap

Moisture

If the heap becomes too damp, the waste will putrefy rather than create usable compost. For this reason it needs rain protection. Most commercial composters have a lid but if you have made your own, cover the heap with waterproof material to protect against waterlogging.

Turning

If left totally undisturbed, the compost heap will decay slowly and unevenly. It will therefore benefit from a thorough turning every few months. Use a large garden fork so as to get the mixture moving, and aim to combine the fresher waste with the decomposing items. There is no hard and fast rule as to how often this task should be completed, but it is worth bearing in mind that the more the heap is turned, the quicker you get your compost.

Temperature

Since heat is a by-product of decomposition, the centre of the compost heap can reach temperatures of 60°C (140°F). To keep the heap ticking over during the colder months, insulate the bin with straw, bubble wrap or an old blanket.

Using compost

Your compost is ready to use when it appears earthy and has a fresh, loamy smell. There may be a few pieces of eggshell or twig still visible, but this won't affect the quality of the compost. Use the compost in containers, pots or dig into the soil to add nutrients.

▼ **Homemade compost should smell sweet and earthy once it is ready for use.**

Growing your own

WHETHER YOU choose to supplement your shopping with home-grown items or become totally self-sufficient in fresh produce, there is no doubt that growing to eat is extremely rewarding. Garden produce not only tastes better, but dramatically reduces your food miles (see page 96). Choose to grow your own and you'll always know where your food has come from and what chemicals have been used to grow it. If you practice organic gardening (see pages 120–3) you can be sure that your vegetables and fruit are as fresh and pesticide-free as possible.

▼ **Growing your own vegetables is an easy hobby to get into; you'll be surprised by the amount you can produce.**

Confined spaces

No garden

Many urban-dwellers have no garden beyond an unpromising square of concrete around the front door. Of course, your growing space will be extremely limited, but it is possible to grow a number of small vegetables, salads and sprouted seed or pulses (see pages 102–5).

A windowsill

A warm and sunny windowsill will provide a suitable environment for a few containers. Basil, parsley and mixed salad leaves are frequently

▲ You can squeeze a surprising number of containers onto a small balcony. Choose climbing varieties to capitalize on vertical space.

▲ Where sufficient natural light is available, it is possible to grow fruit and vegetables indoors.

▼ Flat-dwellers can grow small vegetables on the windowsill, as well as herbs and salad leaves.

used in the kitchen, making them an ideal choice for windowsill cultivation. Salad leaves can also be grown in a confined space as cut-and-come-again plants. Rather than reaching maturity (adult size) the leaves are harvested when they are still young and are sown closely together. It is usually possible to get two or three harvests from a single sowing.

A balcony

Depending on its orientation (whether it faces south or east, etc.), a balcony can be used to grow all kinds of vegetables. Use climbing vegetables such as beans to maximize the vertical space.

A concrete yard

Many city-dwellers have a space around the front or back door that is covered in concrete. A few large containers will provide plenty of room for tomato plants. Choose dwarf varieties to save space – some cherry tomatoes can even be grown in hanging baskets.

A small garden

IF YOU have a small garden, there are many varieties of vegetables you can grow. Choose quick–growing crops, such as radish, salads and runner beans to maximize productivity.

Raised beds provide an effective growing space for most vegetables and are particularly useful where soil conditions are poor. Raised beds are effectively large, bottomless containers filled with soil. The walls can be made from wood, plastic, old bricks or salvaged railway sleepers, and can be made as high or low as desired. Soil conditions can be improved much more easily in this confined environment, compared with the time, effort and expense needed to alter a large, flat space of land. The height allows the vegetable roots to sit above water–logged, clay, heavy or compacted soil, and the conditions in each bed can be varied to support a wider range of vegetables.

▲ You'll be amazed how many new plants you can produce even in a small area.

▼ Fresh herbs are a must for all kitchen gardens, and add interest to well-worn recipes.

An allotment

IF YOU live in the UK and have no growing space, consider requesting an allotment if you have really caught the gardening bug. The Allotment Act of 1887 obliged local authorities to provide the public with land for private food production as required. Originally, this served to compensate

▼ Since they are so large, allotments are often a social community in their own right, so in securing a plot you may find yourself growing friendships as well as veg!

workers for the loss of gardens and green space that resulted from the building of new houses. Today the situation is similar, as many inner city residents simply do not have a garden at all. If you think that an allotment is for you, it is best to sign up as soon as possible. Since demand is high, you may be in for a long wait – check with your local authority for an estimate. Once you have been allocated a plot, you can expect to pay £30 to 100 per year. However, prices vary dramatically in different parts of the country. If your plot is productive you can easily generate enough fresh

▲ **An allotment plot can keep you and your family self-sufficient in veg throughout the course of the year.**

produce to feed a family of four, which will greatly reduce your shopping bill. If the prospect of a large plot is daunting, consider sharing the work (and produce) with neighbours, friends or colleagues. This arrangement will ensure that you have someone to tend to your plants if you are away.

Aside from vegetables, many local authorities will allow plot holders to keep a small number of chickens, provided that they are well looked after and securely contained. Some allotments also allow beekeeping. It is well worth checking with your council to see exactly what is permitted, whether your plans involve livestock, bees or simply a new shed.

◀ **Although hard work, taking on a new plot is a great way to get fit.**

When deciding to take on a new plot there are a number of factors to consider:

How much time will I have each day/week to tend to the plants?

During the summer months, it may be necessary to water your vegetables every day. For this reason, apply for an allotment as close to home as possible. If you can, share duties with a fellow allotmenteer or family member.

Do I have time to maintain my plot?

Many people begin with good intentions, only to let their allotment go to waste. Weeds from untended beds will find their way onto adjacent plots, making extra work for your neighbours. If you take on an allotment only to find that it isn't for you, be sure to give up your plot so that others on the waiting list can benefit.

How will I secure my belongings?

Unfortunately, allotments can be targeted by vandals and thieves, so only leave items that you can afford to lose. This may seem pessimistic, but

▼ **A good-quality tool kit is an investment, but make sure it is stored away, out of the reach of thieves.**

▲ **During the summer your plot will require daily watering, so share the labour with another plot-holder.**

it is better to be prepared than to lose a treasured or expensive item. Most sites allow plot holders to build a shed, which means that tools can be left on site. However, these are not totally foolproof, and are unlikely to deter the more determined criminals. If the worst does happen, always report any thefts (no matter how trivial) to the police, as this may prompt the local authority to improve security.

Varieties for beginners and impatient gardeners

Runner beans

As well as being simple to grow, runner bean plants produce a very large crop. This intrepid legume will scramble up a trellis, covering it with small red flowers. When the pods have formed, harvest them immediately. The more the plant is picked, the more productive it will be.

▲ Salad leaves are amongst the easiest crops to grow, and can be ready to eat in as little as ten weeks.

▶ Courgettes and marrows can get very large and are fun for children to grow.

Mixed salad

During the summer months, sow a pinch of mixed salad seeds every few weeks to ensure a constant supply. Salad leaves also make a rapid yet compact filler in spaces left by other harvested crops.

Rocket

Sown in the same way as mixed salad, rocket is an effortless plant to grow. When home grown, its hot and peppery flavour is a world away from the limp supermarket variety.

Courgettes

Great fun to grow, courgette plants are amazingly productive. They need plenty of space, but will reward you with sweet and succulent fruit throughout the summer months.

Rainwater harvesting

EVEN A modest-sized garden is very thirsty, especially during the summer months. Tap water is often heavily treated with chemicals and is a costly resource, both financially and environmentally. It is therefore a sensible idea to collect rainwater for use on both vegetable and ornamental beds. Any horizontal surface will make a useful collector, but the roofs of sheds and greenhouses are by far the best, as they tend to stay clean and have a relatively large surface area. The water will stream down the surface into the guttering, and can then be directed into a water butt where it can be stored until needed.

Choosing a water butt

THERE ARE many different types of water butt available on the market, from plain plastic containers, beehive-shaped butts to replica barrels. As a rule of thumb, always choose the largest container possible, as you will inevitably exhaust your supply. Plastic is easier to clean than other materials, but the style you go for is, ultimately, a personal choice.

◀ **A good-quality watering can will last you for years.**

▼ **A liberal sprinkling of water on the surface of the soil will evaporate quickly, so aim to soak the roots of the plant.**

◀ **Water butts can be rigged to catch water from the shed, house or conservatory roof.**

If it proves unsightly, a water butt can be disguised by clever planting. It is important, however, to prune the area regularly to ensure easy access to the tap.

Installing a down-pipe connector kit

The easiest and most economical way to install a water butt is to buy a connector kit. The water butt should be placed as near to an existing down-pipe as possible (on a greenhouse, shed or house). Most kits require you to make a small hole in the pipe that allows a rainwater diverter to be fitted. This then joins the butt to the down

▼ **A downpipe connector kit is quick and easy to install and only costs a few pounds to buy.**

▲ A hosepipe that draws from a water butt (even if supplied by a pump) is exempt from hosepipe bans and restrictions.

pipe. Once the butt is full the water will have nowhere to go, so will simply flow down the down-pipe as usual.

Size and situation

When filled to the top even a small butt can prove impossible to move, so choose your site carefully – before the rain begins.

If space is no object, consider buying a large water butt. These are now available with huge capacities of 1000l (220gals) or more. These big tanks can be expensive, but they do save you the effort of extra plumbing and tend to look rather neater than a line of smaller butts. Be aware that a large volume of water can be very heavy (1000l/220gals weighs 1t) so the tank needs to be situated on solid ground.

If space is limited, it is still possible to harvest a surprising amount of rainwater in a small container. It is now possible to buy slimline water butts that can be installed in particularly small, awkward places. If heavy rain is forecast then you can also leave your watering can open outside, along with a few buckets – you'll be surprised how just much can be collected from even a moderate downpour.

Using a stand

Most models are fitted with a tap that allows the collected water to be dispensed easily. If the tap is too close to the ground, however, you will not be able to fit the can underneath. This necessitates tilting the can and holding it under the tap until part full. A stand (or a couple of bricks) will raise the butt higher, allowing the can to be comfortably fitted underneath without the need to hold it in place.

Increasing the supply

A s YOUR vegetable plot grows, so too will your water requirements. An easy solution is to add extra water butts, each fed from the overflow of the last. This enables more water to be caught during periods of rainfall. To join them together the best option is to buy a simple linking kit, available from most garden centres. The butts should be situated next to each other, ideally all at the same level, or slowly stepping down from one butt to the next. If any butt is higher than the previous one, it won't fill up to its maximum capacity.

Using a pump and hose

If your plot is situated a long way from your water source, or you have a large area to cover, it is well worth considering a pump. When submersed in the water butt, the pump will provide sufficient pressure to operate a hose with a spray attachment. This can save trekking back and forth with the watering can.

▲ Water butts are available in an array of colours, styles and shapes. Choose one to suit your garden.

▼ In a large garden it may be worth installing a permanent system of hoses.

Shopping and Lifestyle

Every time we put something into our shopping basket we are making an important choice, both environmentally and ethically. The concept of 'food miles' (see page 96) has become common currency over the last few years, and describes the vast distances that our fruit, vegetables and other consumables have to travel before they reach our plate. Animal testing, fair trade and suitability for recycling are also factors to consider when choosing products.

There are a number of simple steps we can take to minimize the impact our lifestyle has upon the environment. Far from being just a 'worthy' exercise, hunting for second-hand gems at a boot fair can be great fun, as can swapping clothes with friends or making your own cleaning products. Adopting a greener, more sustainable lifestyle is as much about creativity as common sense – you may well find that adopting a 'make do and mend' attitude can quickly become addictive!

Health and beauty

WHILE MANY products claim to contain 'natural' ingredients, these often make up only a fraction of the finished product. Choosing toiletries often involves an ethical balancing act – one product may have ethically sourced ingredients, but may also use preservatives that have triggered health concerns. Similarly, organic does not necessarily mean animal or cruelty free.

Animal testing

AN EU–WIDE ban on animal testing was agreed in 2003; however, it won't come into effect until 2009 or 2013. A complete ban on the sale of new animal-tested products will not become official before 2013, and may well take longer. For this reason, it is still necessary to check products carefully.

To avoid products tested on animals, look for the leaping bunny symbol in the UK. This scheme is managed by the British Union for the Abolition of Vivisection (BUAV), and ensures retailers adhere to strict standards. To use the logo, the company must have agreed to an annual, independent audit of their supply chain to ensure all products are cruelty free. In addition, they must have a specified cut–off date from which all of their ingredients and products no longer involve animal testing. At present the

▼ **Until the full EU ban on animal-tested products comes into force, choose your cosmetics carefully.**

▲ **Despite the sustainability issues related to its manufacture, palm oil is still used in most soap.**

leaping bunny logo is the only way to ensure freedom from cruelty. Products that are labelled as 'free from animal testing' or use other rabbit logos or symbols may still use ingredients that are tested on animals. Similarly, companies that claim to 'invest in cruelty–free alternatives' may continue to use products tested on animals.

Ethics

MANY OF the ingredients used in toiletries are unsustainable. Palm oil, for instance, is widely used in soap, shampoo and several other cosmetics. Unfortunately, palm oil plantations encroach upon the natural habitat of many endangered species, including the Sumatran orang–utan. The conversion of the Indonesian and Malaysian rainforest into commercial growing areas has prompted some manufacturers to invest in alternatives to palm oil or to support sustainable agriculture. The palm oil industry is also connected with the forcible occupation of land previously inhabited by indigenous peoples. Look for toiletries manufacturers, such as Lush in the UK, that use a palm–free soap base.

▶ **Looking good and remaining a responsible consumer can be something of a balancing act.**

Animal ingredients

If you are avoiding animal products, look for the Vegan or Vegetarian Society symbols in the UK. However, since many companies don't invest in certification, many animal–free products are easy to overlook. The only solution is to check the ingredients carefully. It is also important to note that while the leaping bunny label guarantees a product free from animal testing, it still may contain animal–derived ingredients.

Health

Parabens are used to preserve products, and because they contain oestrogen they have been linked to hormonal disturbance in women.

There is a great deal of controversy surrounding parabens and breast cancer, although the link as yet remains unproven.

Phthalates are widely used in cosmetic products, despite the EU ruling that they should be regarded as causing foetal damage and fertility problems. They are licensed for use in cosmetics in extremely weak dilutions. However, since an individual may use a number of phthalate–containing products, the concentrations we are exposed to may prove higher than expected.

Sodium Lauryl Sulphate (SLS) is a detergent used to generate foam in bath and haircare products. It has been shown to linger in the body, and to cause skin irritation. SLS is in fact used in laboratory experiments as a skin irritant. Whilst some individuals are more sensitive to it than others, it can cause redness and swelling after prolonged use.

◀ **Natural bath products, such as scented salts, can be made at home with a minimum of ingredients.**

Sustainable, ethical and healthy alternatives

THE BUAV produces a pocket-sized consumer guide listing all the UK companies approved under the Humane Cosmetics Standard and the Humane Household Products Standard. For sustainability concerns, the Green Guide books are a useful resource, covering everything from ethical household products to green weddings. On the internet, the Ethical Consumer Organization provides a comprehensive directory of companies that have met their criteria for sustainable, responsible manufacture.

▼ **Where possible, it is best to opt for natural products with a minimum of packaging.**

Packaging

ASIDE FROM their content, the packaging of shaving foams, soap, shampoos and deodorants presents an environmental problem. Many cosmetics are wrapped in excessive layers of non-biodegradable plastic that is destined for landfill sites. If possible, avoid excessively packaged products. Some ethically minded retailers produce fresh cosmetics, which use a minimum of packaging. Others use materials suitable for recycling (check the label to be sure). And look out for the CFC-free symbol to avoid purchasing harmful aerosols.

Green cleaning

MANY OF us unknowingly possess an arsenal of poisons in the guise of kitchen, bathroom and general household cleaners. The toxins in these products find their way into our waterways, the food chain and cause damage to marine wildlife. A number of household cleaning products contain substances that take an exceptionally long time to degrade, leading to long–term pollution. Phosphates found in detergents causes excess algae growth, which affects freshwater habitats and their wildlife.

Aside from the environmental impact, concerns have been raised over the presence of volatile organic compounds (VOCs) in many commercial products. These compounds become air–borne and can cause a number of respiratory and general heath problems. Bleach, for example, has been identified as a source of VOCs and can cause eye and lung irritation. Long–term exposure to the compounds in household cleaners has also been linked to asthma and increased allergic sensitivity, particularly in children. Along with the environmental issues, these health concerns have prompted many companies to produce eco–friendly alternatives.

Cleaning in moderation

MANY OF us do not have much time for housework and many commercial products are simply quicker and more efficient than old–fashioned elbow grease. As with most problems, the solution lies in a compromise. Whether starting a big clean–up or day–to–day chores, the question to ask is, 'do I need to use bleach for this job?'. Perhaps surprisingly, the answer is often 'no'. Television advertising encourages us to use highly concentrated, powerful agents for even the most cursory cleaning tasks. Adding a potentially toxic stain–remover into every wash 'just in case' and using bleach–based sprays just to wipe down a worktop is overkill.

▼ **Many of us stock an arsenal of commercial cleaning products under our sink, some of which are highly toxic.**

Organic alternatives to chemical cleaners

Disinfectant

Try eucalyptus oil diluted 1:100 in water. Alternatively, boil chopped rosemary for 20 minutes, strain and pour into a spray bottle.

Furniture polish

Add the juice of one lemon to a small cup of vegetable (or olive) oil. Apply a thin layer before buffing to achieve a deep shine.

Lime-scale remover

Neat vinegar will remove hard water deposits as well as any commercial preparation. Apply with a cloth, but be sure to remove thoroughly. For stubborn deposits, apply vinegar–soaked paper towels and leave overnight.

Carpet freshener

Combine dried herbs with a cup of baking soda and whizz together in a food processor. This will allow the scent to infuse the powder. Then use in the same way as a commercial preparation –

▲ Lemon juice and vinegar are useful for cleaning, as they cut through grease and remove stains.

sprinkle over carpets, leave for ten minutes and vacuum up. Finely chopped fresh herbs can be used, but could stain light-coloured carpets.

De-greaser

Lemons and limes will disperse oil when rubbed directly onto saucepans or surfaces. You can use fruit that is past its best. For larger spills, dilute distilled vinegar.

Window cleaner

Vinegar or lemon will provide excellent shine. Dilute ¼ cup of white vinegar in a 1l (1¾pt) of water. Dry and buff with old newspaper.

Scouring cleanser

Use baking soda and a damp sponge. Salt can also be used to make a heavy–duty abrasive.

Bleach

Lemon juice is suitable for removing heavy-duty stains.

◀ Bicarbonate of soda has been used for centuries as a stain and odour-removing product.

Something in the air

THERE'S NO getting away from it, our sense of smell is inextricably linked to our sense of home. Savvy real estate agents know that the aroma of warm bread creates an appealing, homely atmosphere likely to encourage potential buyers. Similarly, commercials try to sell us a slice of the countryside or a mountain pine grove in the form of air freshening plug–ins. New timed–release sprays ensure that the spell isn't broken by less appealing household smells. As a result, the home fragrance industry is booming, and there are more toxins in our home than ever before. Many scented products contain potentially harmful VOCs. Although it is strenuously denied by the British Aerosol Manufacturer's Association, many studies have suggested a link between these compounds and minor ailments such as earache, headaches and mild depression. Even if we accept that the research is not entirely conclusive, we still have to ask whether we need to be spraying fragrances quite so often; some timed–release aerosols can be set to spray every few minutes.

Adopting a relatively scrupulous cleaning regime should prevent any really offensive odours, and opening the windows for an hour every day should prevent stuffiness. Nevertheless, it is a fact that all homes smell. The food we cook, the cleaning products we use and the paints used to decorate our homes all combine to create our unique signature scent. Unfortunately, we are led to believe that this aroma is embarrassing and inherently unpleasant, and so must be eradicated at all costs. Perhaps it would be better to use air fresheners only when we want to experience a particular smell, rather than simply to mask our own.

▼ **Fresh or dried, scented flowers are a much healthier choice than artificially perfumed aerosol sprays.**

For this purpose, there are many natural alternatives available that are not propelled by pressurized gas.

Odour eliminator

For mild pet and cooking smells, an odour eliminator can be created by mixing baking powder with a few drops of essential oil. Place the container somewhere discrete where it will absorb odour. It can also be sprinkled on carpets before vacuuming as an instant freshener.

Pot pourri

Having pot pourri in your home has gone out of fashion in recent years, but it can look really attractive – particularly if you dry your own lemons, oranges and herbs. When the fragrance fades, freshen it up with a few drops of essential oil.

Light bulb rings

These discrete gadgets fit over a standard bulb and release fragrance as they warm. They can be dotted with an essential oil of your choice.

Oil burners

There are many different varieties of burner available on the market; some extremely decorative. A small bowl of water and essential oil is suspended above a tea light, which heats the bowl to create scented steam. Many candles give off pollutants; try a soy rather than paraffin-based tea light.

Essential-oil vapourizers

These sophisticated gadgets use an extremely low-energy warmer to propel essential oils into the atmosphere. They are far milder than conventional aerosols.

▼ **Pot pourri looks great, smells divine and is cheap and fun to make.**

Houseplants

URING THE process of respiration, plants absorb carbon dioxide (CO_2) and release oxygen, making them ideal air purifiers. NASA recently compiled a list of the most efficient plants as part of a trial into air–filtering in space stations. As well as producing oxygen, a number of common houseplants were shown to eradicate pollutants such as benzene, formaldehyde and trichloroethylene. The presence of these substances in the home is a result of building materials and furnishings, as well as paints and varnishes used in decorating. When confined in the house, the levels of these toxins accumulate, leading some researchers to link them to the controversial 'sick–building syndrome'.

Aside from their air–cleansing qualities, plants are beneficial to health in other ways. Nowadays, people spend the majority of their time indoors without coming into contact with the natural world. A look around your living space will reveal plastics, paper, metals as opposed to living things. Houseplants, therefore, provide a daily link with nature and can be a source of interest in their own right.

Happily, some of the most effective air–purifying plants are extremely attractive. Most varieties suitable for indoor growing come

▼ Spider plants are easy to keep, and reproduce easily. The 'plantlets', shown here attached to the parent, could be re-potted to produce new plants.

▲ **Weeping fig thrives in bright, sunny conditions and acts as a superb air purifier.**

▶ **A flowering peace lily can provide an attractive focal point in a living room or bedroom.**

from topical or sub–tropical environments. This means that they are reasonably well adapted to warm conditions and lower light levels. Most are cultivated in the UK despite their exotic origins, meaning that they do not add air miles to your carbon footprint. Once you have a few healthy specimens it is likely that they will produce offshoots, which will then provide you with more new plants.

Easy houseplants for clean air

Spider plant (*Chlorophytum comosum*)

A common sight in homes everywhere, the spider plant is exceptionally efficient in removing nitrogen and carbon monoxide from the air. Since it is very tolerant of neglect and drought, the spider plant is an ideal choice for the beginner. A healthy plant will often produce plantlets that can be rooted in soil or water to produce a new plant.

Peace lily (*Spathiphyllum wallissi*)

This plant boasts dark, glossy leaves and superb white flowers. Research has shown it to be one of the best varieties for air filtering.

Weeping fig (*Ficus benjamina*)

With its attractive, flowing leaves and air–purifying qualities, weeping fig is an ideal plant for a bright spot in the home.

Rubber plant (*Ficus elastica Bostoniensis*)

Another cleansing plant, the large, dark leaves make a striking feature against a bare wall. However, this species should be avoided if you have inquisitive children or pets, since the sap can irritate the skin.

Boston fern (*Nephrolepis exaltata*)

The soft, lush foliage of the Boston fern is best suited to a shady, cool spot but is easier to grow than many other fern varieties.

Green parenting

SOMETIMES IT can seem as if the requirements of a new baby are endless. When starting out, the list can seem very long: pram, cot, toys, clothes, blankets, nappies, changing mats and high chairs. All these suddenly become expensive yet essential items. Although small in stature, the infant or young child invariably becomes a large consumer of goods! There are, however, ways to entertain, clothe and feed children to reduce both their financial and environmental impact.

The essentials

IT IS easy to get carried away when planning for a new baby. Advertising tell us that babies need an incredible array of equipment. Whilst there are a number of useful items available on the market, many are not essential. Other parents will often be able to give you advice as to what is really necessary and what they found to be a waste of money.

Nappies

Although convenient, disposable nappies present a huge environmental problem. Most end up in landfills, where they can take thousands of years to degrade. Given the number of discarded nappies produced by one child, the environmental impact is far–reaching.

Reusable nappies have come a long way from the traditional fold–and–pin squares. It is now possible to buy washable versions in any array of colours and fastening styles. If you can't face the thought of washing them yourself, many local authorities offer a nappy laundering service for a small fee, so it is worth checking what facilities are available in your area.

▶ **Nearly three billion disposable nappies are sent to landfill each year in the UK. Reusable designs, if washed sensibly, are a better option.**

Food

While the adage 'breast is best' is undoubtedly right, some mothers are unable to provide breast milk. There are a number of organic formulas on the market that can act as a substitute should breast feeding not be possible.

▲ **Giving toys to charity is an great way to boost your green credentials and contribute to a deserving cause.**

As your child starts weaning, there are a number of organic baby foods that are available. It may, however, be more cost–effective and eco-friendly to make your own. Small amounts of puréed vegetables can help to ease the transition from milk to solids.

Toys

Environmental concerns, coupled with a number of health scares, have led many parents to buy toys made from natural materials. Plastics are slow to degrade, and present a long–term problem if they are not recycled. A number of mass–produced toys from China were also identified as containing dangerous levels of lead. A number of companies now offer wooden toys that are finished with baby–safe varnishes.

Wooden toys are a natural choice but be sure to opt for sustainable wood – those made of hardwood may compromise the tropical habitats in which they are grown.

Transport

It is estimated that up to half of all children travel to school by car, even when the journey is less than a couple of miles. As well as contributing to urban congestion and pollution, taking the car may exacerbate the growing problem of childhood obesity, as today's youngsters lead increasingly sedentary lives. A morning walk can also provide a valuable opportunity for conversation without the distractions of driving, television or the internet.

If the distance you need to go makes driving the only option, how about seeing if you can 'buddy up' with other parents and take it in turns to drop off the children?

clothing and textiles

SYNTHETIC FABRICS are a relatively recent development. Nylon was first created during the mid–1930s, and did not appear on the high street until the 1940s; polyester made its debut in the early 1950s. Today, these man–made substances have eclipsed the use of naturally derived fibre in the production of clothes and household textiles. Sadly, many synthetic fabrics are created from petrochemicals. As such, they are non–biodegradable, and a great deal of energy is used in their manufacture.

Surprisingly, it isn't just man–made fibres that are unsustainable – cotton is extremely costly in terms of its environmental impact. It is estimated that more than 10 per cent of the world's pesticides (and almost 25 per cent of the world's insecticides) are used in cotton production. This makes it the most chemically dependent crop on the planet. As well as endangering the health of agricultural workers, many pesticides cause irrevocable damage to the local ecosystem. When one species is eliminated, the population of its prey booms. As a result, pesticides can actually cause a pest outbreak.

There, are, however a number of sustainable options for clothing, soft furnishings and other household textiles.

▼ Since many of our fabrics are produced by the worlds' poorest nations, it wise to check that the workers involved have received a fare wage.

▲ Cotton is one of the most pesticide-intensive crops, so choose organic for clothes and furnishings.

▲ Bamboo needs less water than the cotton plant, so it is a more sustainable option for long-term agriculture.

Moral fibre

GREENER FABRIC choices are increasingly available to the consumer. Many chain stores now stock garments made from organic cotton, although there tends to be a small selection to choose from. Independent retailers are often the best bet for ethically sourced textiles, and many such items are available online.

Organic cotton

Grown without pesticides, cotton is far less damaging to the environment and the workers who process it. Organic cotton is usually free from artificial dye and bleach.

Linen

Derived from flax, linen is a durable fabric used for beddings, soft furnishings and clothing. Flax requires far less water and pesticides than the cotton plant.

Bamboo

The bamboo plant is naturally resilient to most pests, making it an ideal candidate for organic production. Its growth is rapid and unimpeded by both poor soil conditions and mild drought. For this reason it can be grown on sharply sloping ground where other crops fail to thrive. It also has a higher yield, and dramatically lower water requirements than cotton.

Hemp

Just like bamboo, hemp is an exceptionally undemanding crop with high yields per metre. Hemp fell out of favour during the 1930s due to its association with marijuana, although industrial hemp has no narcotic effect. In recent years it has undergone something of a renaissance, and is widely used by independent retailers to produce eco–clothing.

Buying recycled goods

EVEN THE most eco-friendly fibres increase our carbon footprint to some degree. It is unrealistic to suggest that people shouldn't buy any new clothes at all, but the sheer amount we buy is undoubtedly an issue. Throwaway fashion is a waste of resources, but is encouraged by many retailers. Charity shops are an excellent alternative, providing a range of clothes for the limited budget and the eco–minded shopper. Many vintage items also pre–date the excessive reliance upon man–made fibres. As such, it is possible (with a little rummaging about) to find stylish, sturdy and unique pieces at very affordable prices.

Charity shops usually retail a range of other goods too, from furniture and books to children's toys and decorative items. Kid's buggies, garden and indoor furniture can be found in the small ads in your local newspaper or at a nearby shop. It is really worth looking for these items in such places, as they can be very costly bought new.

▶ **Learning how to repair and alter your own clothes can save you a fortune in the long term.**

▼ **With a little know-how, charity shop finds can be updated or modernized to suit your tastes.**

Make do and mend

GARMENTS THAT have gone out of style can be renovated with minimal expense and effort. The skills of repairing and mending have almost disappeared from our modern lives, but are extremely useful when maintaining a wardrobe. Changing buttons, altering a hemline or adding a new trim can totally change the appearance of an outfit or bring it up to date. Our parents and grandparents generally learned more about sewing than ourselves, especially if they were schooled before the advent of bulk–buy, cheap fashion. If you've never picked up a needle before, you may find their advice useful! If help isn't at hand, books on needlecraft

▲ **A clothes-swap can be a great way to update your wardrobe, as well as an excuse for a party!**

can usually be purchased second-hand from charity shops. After mastering the basics, you can experiment with more challenging, creative projects – such as using old fabric to make new clothes. It is much cheaper than buying a 'retro'-style garment on the high street!

Clothing swaps

IF, LIKE many of us, you simply can't shake the 'must buy a new outfit' bug, swapping can provide a great alternative. Invite friends to bring their clean but unwanted clothes to your house, where they can be tried-on and exchanged. One person's trash is another's treasure! Swapping parties work best when organized on a larger scale – inviting work colleagues and their friends will increase the pool of clothes that are available. However, it pays to be courteous; always stipulate what is and what is not suitable. If you are only interested in a designer or plus-sized swap, for instance, it is polite to let your guests know before the event.

Hand-me-downs

SINCE CHILDREN grow so quickly, only foolish parents scoff at hand-me-downs. Far from being someone's grubby rejects, baby clothes are often scarcely used before the child has grown out of them, making them ideal to pass on to others.

▲ **Car boot sales and secondhand stores can be a wonderful source of bargain furniture.**

New parents are frequently inundated with newborn–sized clothes, gifted by enthusiastic relatives. If your family and friends can't resist buying another ten bunny romper suits, ask them to buy outfits sized 6 to 18 months, otherwise you'll have a drawer full of unworn but too-small clothes just a month or two after the baby arrives.

Furniture

WHETHER YOU are setting up home or simply revamping your living space, new furniture can prove expensive. For this reason, many people turn to flat–packed furniture as an affordable solution. Unfortunately, these usually have a short life as they are not sufficiently robust to withstand everyday wear and tear. It is often cheaper to buy older, second–hand items that have been built to last. Many charity shops sell furniture, and will offer kerbside delivery for a small fee. Alternatively, items sold at local auction rooms are often surprisingly affordable. It is usually possible to purchase sturdy, solid wood items for £30 to £40, which would cost hundreds of pounds new. If you are looking for a more polished look, sanding and re-painting (or varnishing) will freshen up an old chair or table, as well as allowing you to customize the item to suit your décor.

▲ The ubiquitous plastic bag; a feature of our streets, trees and waterways.

▼ A clever way to recycle plastic is to create a textile from it, such as the example shown here.

Carrier bags

THE ENVIRONMENTAL impact of plastic carrier bags has been highlighted in the last few years. These bags are often flimsy, and are intended for the single trip from supermarket to home. Since most are not biodegradable, they are a permanent problem destined for landfill or our waterways. There are, however, many green alternatives available. Hemp, canvas and linen shoppers are easy to obtain, and can now be purchased at most supermarket checkouts. These bags are sturdy, and can be re-used. If you tend to carry a lot of shopping, purchase a fold-away version which can be stored in a pocket or handbag. As these can be compacted, it is usually possible to carry a few round at a time. Alternatively, you could invest in a shopping trolley, which can last for years. Even with the best intentions, there will always be occasions when you'll forget your eco-bag and have to take the flimsy, plastic option. If this is the case, try to find other uses for it at home before it is thrown away.

Finance

Eco-renovation/renewable grants

W HETHER YOU are seeking finance for a green-build or are looking to undertake an eco-renovation on an existing property, it is well worth investigating grants available for your project. In the UK, there are a number of schemes to assist home-owners in 'greening' their home. Home Information Packs, for instance, are distributed to new buyers and are now obliged to include an Energy Performance Certificate (EPC), which makes it far easier for the new owner to apply for funding. The average home-owner is entitled to £1 to £300 towards the cost of cavity-wall insulation as part of the governments' push to reduce energy-consumption. The EPC gives homes a rating from A to G, in a similar way to household appliances, A being the most efficient down to G being the poorest. Should you choose to generate your own solar heat, you are entitled to a grant in the region of £400 towards the price of the panels. Policies are likely to change as eco-issues become increasingly well recognized, so it is always a good idea to check with your local authority to see what is available.

▼ Detailed designs will assist you in obtaining funding for an ecologically sound building.

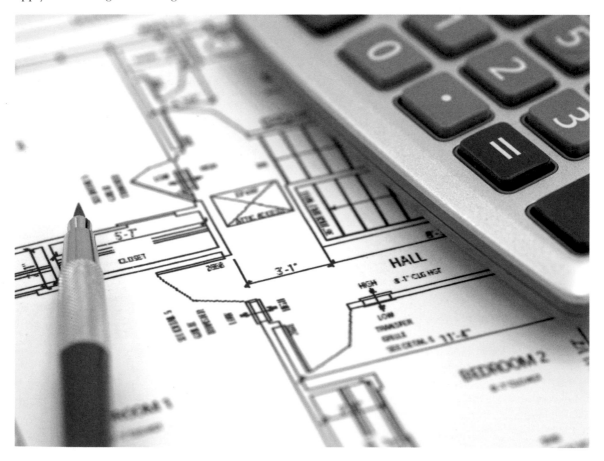

▲ **When you come to buy a new house, the Home Information Pack will now include an Energy Performance Certificate.**

Mortgages for your green build

IF YOU are attempting a sustainable self-build project, you may be eligible to apply for a 'green' mortgage. Acceptance onto such a scheme confers many benefits – firstly, you may qualify for a lower rate of interest to fund projects that reduce the environmental impact of your home, whether this be a loan for improvements on an existing dwelling, or a long-term reduced rate for a new build. Secondly, some lenders will also pledge donations to an environmental charity on behalf of the borrower, or may be involved in the promotion of sustainable building.

Make sure you check carefully the 'green' credentials of your mortgage – some offer little more than the offer to plant a tree each year, and do not require you actually to have a green build in the first place. Unfortunately, 'green' is often used as more of a marketing label, so be sure to ask plenty of questions as to how the scheme will work.

Ethical investments and banking

WHILE YOU might not have enough money to buy shares, it is important to realize that you are an investor simply through holding a bank account or having a mortgage. For this reason, it is wise to find out a little more about your bank before you become a customer.

Socially responsible investing (SRI) focuses less upon blacklisting sectors with dubious moral practices and more on supporting companies within a certain sector who are genuinely showing improvement. The financial investments are given in order to act as an industry-wide incentive for other companies to follow suit An ethical fund-management company will generally avoid investing money in ventures that are costly to the environment, human rights or animal welfare. For this reason, such companies will typically avoid buying shares in any business believed to be involved in the arms trade, animal exploitation or using child labour.

▼ **Using a bank automatically makes you an investor. This raises an important question: what are you investing in?**

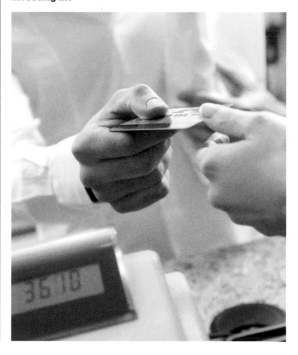

Transport and travel

IN THE UK road transport accounts for more than a third of all carbon emissions and is therefore a key area to focus on if you are looking for a greener lifestyle. The first obvious step you can take is on foot – walking is healthier, cleaner and often quicker if travelling in an inner–city area. It is estimated that only half of all children walk to school, even when the average drive can actually take longer than walking. Since many of us have office–based jobs, the morning walk to work can often be the only opportunity for an extended brisk walk.

Cycling

WHERE DISTANCE makes walking impractical, cycling is the next best option in terms of energy–consumption. An average cycle to work uses about as much energy as a car does just to power its headlights, and you get fit too! Many local authorities have cycle lanes, which

▼ **If the distance is under three miles, consider walking or cycling rather than getting stuck in traffic.**

▲ **Cycling in many cities has been made far easier and more pleasant with the introduction of cycle lanes.**

helps to reduce the danger from other passing traffic. Remember that as a cyclist you are far more vulnerable than other road travellers, and therefore need to focus on making yourself visible. Always wear reflective clothing and maintain your bicycle lights.

Public transport

IF YOU are unable to cycle, public transport is the next best option in terms of carbon emissions. If you have hitherto been a committed driver you may find it rather freeing to read a book, listen to music or plan tomorrow's jobs on the way home from work. If travelling by bus, many cities now have a designated bus lane, which means less time spent sitting in traffic. If you intend to start using the train, look into buying a season ticket to reduce costs.

▶ **Travelling by public transport can be a far more sociable experience than by car, and is often cheaper.**

▲ **As technology improves, electric cars are becoming a more feasible option for the general public.**

Car sharing

IF YOU work in an area that is not served by public transport, you may have no other option but to use your car. If this is the case, consider a car share. Perhaps you and a colleague could take it in turns to drive to work, thus saving on both petrol costs and carbon emissions. Often your local authority will be able to provide details of schemes in your area. Alternatively, pin a notice up at work – there may well be other people living sufficiently near you to make a share worthwhile.

Electric cars

WHILE THEY remain somewhat expensive, electric cars are an extremely clean way to travel in terms of carbon emissions. Since they use a battery and electric motor, there are zero carbon emissions if the car is charged with renewable energy. Even if the energy used is initially sourced from power stations using fossil fuel, an electric car will still consume far less energy than the internal combustion engine of a regular vehicle. Many local authorities offer a number of incentives to encourage electric-car ownership, such as free, designated parking in otherwise expensive and congested inner-city areas.

Eco-tourism

SINCE MANY of us fly to our annual holiday destination, the yearly trip abroad is extremely costly to the environment. There are measures you can take to reduce the impact of your trip, such as carbon offsetting (see pages 170–1) but ultimately, the most sustainable option is to take a vacation within your own country. As well as supporting local economies, taking a domestic holiday may save you a great deal of money. Of course, for many of us, the trip abroad is our yearly highlight, making it very hard to pass up. If you do decide to go abroad, why not opt for an entirely different experience? Many tour operators now offer activity breaks to exotic but deprived areas of the globe. Here, you can assist with building projects and schemes to improve the local infrastructure. Far from being just hard work, this type of holiday gives you a real taste of another culture and an experience you are unlikely to forget.

▼ Scenes such as the one below show why domestic holidays need not be considered as second best.

▲ While travel to exotic locations is now cheap and easy, our carbon-hungry holidays are taken at the risk of destroying many of these natural wonders.

Carbon offsetting

Whenever you travel by air, use your car or simply heat your home, you create CO_2 emissions as a result. The idea behind carbon offsetting is to compensate for the emissions produced by making savings elsewhere. The first step is to calculate the amount of carbon produced, then buy credits from an offsetting scheme, in tandem with taking practical steps to reduce emissions. While the idea has been used in industrial circles for some years, carbon offsetting for individual consumers is only now catching up. The idea is much the same, but on a smaller scale; use a carbon 'calculator' to discover how much harmful CO_2 your lifestyle makes you responsible for, then invest enough money in a suitable scheme in order to pay for the damage. By donating money to be invested in green technologies and environmental projects, or 'retiring' government carbon credits allocated to big businesses, you are theoretically making good the harm you are doing.

Offsets can be made in a number of ways, one of which is by buying–up carbon 'credits' through a carbon emission reduction (CER) scheme. In simple terms, the EU and UN issue companies with a limited quota of credits. Heavy polluters must trade in their own quota against the carbon dioxide they emit and buy more credits from elsewhere, while clean companies can sell their credits to the polluters for cash, and develop more rapidly as a result. By buying and holding onto some of these credits (with your money), carbon–offset schemes drive up the price and force industry to adopt cleaner technologies and practices.

On a smaller scale are the verified emission reduction (VER) schemes, which are less well regulated and involve the investment of funds in clean technologies, sustainable power generation and energy waste reduction (such as low–energy lighting). These have been criticized for their lack of accountability, but some environmentalists say they are a vital way to inject money at the grass-roots level, and that they fund smaller projects that the CER schemes would overlook.

Choosing a scheme

If carbon offsetting seems straightforward, the reality is anything but. For a start the dozens of schemes now competing for your attention all use different calculations, meaning the same 'lifestyle' will produce varying results with each different offset provider. Furthermore, the schemes charge wildly different amounts per tonne of CO_2, and invest your money in confusingly diverse ways – not all of them independently scrutinized. There is no watchdog, accreditation schemes are still in their early stages, and there are widespread concerns over the way some companies process their offsets. So, until the industry is better regulated, the best advice is to do your research before committing to a particular scheme. There are some basic questions you should be asking before making a choice of scheme:

Where are the funds invested?

Does it matter to you if the funds go to solar-energy schemes in Africa – or would you prefer to see wind turbines in Wales? You might object to your money being spent on hydroelectric power if that means a new dam gets built.

▶ **Carbon offsetting can help you to enjoy your holiday in good conscience.**

Do you feel the cost is fair?

With such a range of prices for apparently similar data, it is difficult to choose where to direct your money. Try out a few different carbon calculators (including those that don't sell offsets) so you get an idea what price seems right.

What is the scheme linked to?

Some offset schemes are run as non–profit organizations or even charities, but others have been set up by power companies who's record is far from green.

Is reforestation involved?

One type of VER scheme is tree planting. This 'soaks up' CO_2 in the atmosphere but has received criticism lately for being too slow to take effect. Many scientists are now pointing out that trees won't soak up CO_2 until many years in the future (when it could be too late) and don't hold onto it for long, releasing it when they rot or are burned.

Does the scheme cater for you?

If, generally, you are environmentally conscious, will you care if you are overpaying for an 'average' footprint? Conversely, if you are wasteful, is it fair that you get away lightly? Look for a scheme that tailors its results to you.

About the authors

LAURA COOK is a freelance journalist and a regular contributor to a wide range of magazines, including gardening, health, 'green lifestyle' and craft titles. She has a long–standing interest in natural cosmetics and perfumery and has first–hand experience of gardening in tight spaces. She lives in Norwich, England, and enjoys spending time in her small, but productive garden, hoping her cats won't dig all her plants.

PAUL WAGLAND is an RHS–qualified gardener as well as an experienced writer and designer, specializing in DIY and horticulture. He is the former editor of two popular magazines (*Pond & Gardening* and *Grow Your Own*) and divides most of his free time between his own garden and three allotments in suburban Essex, England.

Suppliers

Ruby Red
Organic bath products with recyclable packaging.
+44 (0)7526 526 909
www.rubyredcosmetics.co.uk
International orders welcome.

Biggreensmile.com
Gifts and energy-saving gadgets.
+44 (0)845 230 2365
International orders welcome.

UK juicers
Sells a range of sprouters.
+44 (0)1904 757 070
www.ukjuicers.com
International orders welcome.

Thompson& Morgan
Vegetable seed and plants.
+44 (0)844 2485 383
www.thompson-morgan.com
International orders welcome.

My Greener Home
Energy meters and eco-appliances.
+44 (0)208 133 9002
www.mygreenerhome.co.uk
International orders welcome.

Screwfix
DIY fixtures and fittings.
+44 (0)500 414 141
www.screwfix.com

Ethicalsuperstore.com
Large range of green, ethical and energy-efficient products.
+44 (0)800 999 2134
www.ethicalsuperstore.com
International orders welcome.

Ecofreak
Energy-saving gadgets for the home.
+44 (0)1664 430 126
www.ecofreak.co.uk

Wigglywigglers
Supplier of wormeries and Bokashi composting systems.
+44 (0)1981 500 391
www.wigglywigglers.co.uk
International orders welcome.

Link-a-bord
Supplier of raised garden bed kits.
+44 (0)773 590 566
www.linkabord.co.uk/home.page

Bella Pierre
Mineral cosmetics.
+44 (0)800 023 4190
www.bellapierre.com
International orders welcome.

Ecover
Range of green household cleaners.
www.ecover.com
International orders welcome.

Yorkshire Ecological Solutions
Reed bed specialist.
+44 (0)113 252 4786
www.yes-reedbeds.co.uk

The Organic Gardening Catalogue
+44 (0)845 130 1304
www.organiccatalog.com

Useful information

The Energy Saving Trust
+44 (0)800 512 012
www.energysavingtrust.org.uk

Recycle Now
Useful information on local facilities and subsidised compost bins.
+44 (0)845 331 3131
www.recyclenow.com

Waterwise
Advice on saving water in the home.
+44 (0)207 344 1882
www.waterwise.org

British Union for the Abolition of Vivisection (BUAV)
+44 (0)207 700 4888
www.buav.org/home

Green Guides
Publishes handbooks on green holidays, shopping and weddings.
www.greenguide.co.uk

The Fairtrade Foundation
www.fairtrade.org.uk

Association of Charity Shops
www.charityshops.org.uk

Garden Organic
+44 (0)24 7630 3517
www.gardenorganic.org.uk

Conversions

1 gallon = 1.20 US gallons
1 tonne = 0.98 tons
1 pint = 1.20 US pints

Index

To place an order, or to request a catalogue, contact:
GMC Publications
Castle Place, 166 High Street, Lewes, East Sussex, BN7 1XU
United Kingdom
Tel: 01273 488005 Fax: 01273 402866
Website: www.gmcbooks.com
Orders by credit card are accepted